E. Franklin Dukes
Marina A. Piscolish
John B. Stephens
Foreword by Mark Gerzon

REACHING for ~~COMMON~~ *Higher* GROUND

Creating Purpose-driven, Principled & Powerful Groups

For more information about this book and its authors,
go to www.reachingforhigherground.com.

To become part of our virtual community,
go to www.highergroundswell.com.

Copyright © 2008 Dukes, Piscolish & Stephens
All rights reserved.
ISBN: 1-4392-1487-5.

To order additional copies, please visit either of our websites:
www.reachingforhigherground.com or www.highergroundswell.com

You can also contact
BookSurge Publishing
www.booksurge.com
1-866-308-6235
orders@booksurge.com

Second edition

"Anyone who works with people - and that means all of us - should read this book. For educators, *Reaching for Higher Ground* offers crucial lessons to support consensus, community building, and lasting change within classrooms, in school decision-making bodies, and in the policy making by state and local school boards. This book could move us beyond the dance of the dichotomies that so often sidetracks meaningful reforms to a higher ground that focuses on the needs of children and the right to learn."

**- Linda Darling-Hammond,
author of *The Right to Learn***

"Have you worked with a group that just wasn't working? Where unspoken rules kept the group from making progress? This book helps break through old uncomfortable ways of relating in organizations and goups, committees and families."

**- Sally Herndon Malek,
North Carolina Department of Health and Human Services**

"Thoughtful reflections and practical tools dot the landscape of this well-organized, wise, and refreshing book....for anyone who plans, conducts or participates in any kind of meeting where time is precious and outcomes matter to those involved."

**- Laura Chasin,
Director, Public Conversations Project
Watertown, Massachusetts**

*To Lenore Hankins Dukes, who in learning
to make music with her father inspired the tune
that guided us in writing this book. And to each other,
for the chance to sing in three-part harmony.*

Contents

Foreword — xi
    Mark Gerzon

Preface — xv

Acknowledgments — xxi

1. Reaching for Higher Ground — 1
2. Unspoken Expectations and Rules of Engagement — 17
3. Common Practice with Ground Rules: How They Fail Us and We Fail Them — 39
4. Beyond Common Ground Rules: Reaching for *Higher* Ground — 59
5. Creating Shared Expectations: The Six Keys to Success — 81
6. Putting Ground Rules to Work: Keeping the Group on the Path — 103
7. Too Big? Unbalanced? Quiet? Seething? The Art of Working with Less-Than-Perfect Groups — 131
8. Reaching for Higher Ground in Action: A Hospital Department Management Team at Work — 155
9. Beyond Boundaries: Bringing Higher Ground to Whole Communities — 191
10. Conclusion and Inspiration — 217

Appendix A: Typical Ground Rules 237

Appendix B: RHG Covenant of the "Wannabe Better"
    School District's Education Management Team 239

Appendix C: Negotiating Team RHG Pre-Negotiation
    Preparation Meeting Documentation 243

Appendix D: Bestdarned Community Group Tools
    for Reaching Higher Ground 247

References 249

Index 251

About the Authors 257

Foreword

Just as each of us experiences rites of passages in our lives—from childhood to adolescence, and then into adulthood and maturity—so do fields of knowledge.

Reaching for Higher Ground marks such a rite of passage for mediation and conflict resolution. It heralds a new, exciting stage in the development of this crucial field. Whether we are an expert practitioner in mediation or a concerned participant in family, community, or workplace conflict, this book makes us both wiser and more effective.

In the early years of this field, the word *compromise* was commonly used, as in "After lengthy negotiations, a compromise was reached." To achieve a compromise was certainly a better alternative than costly litigation, hostility, or even violence. But the word signified no major shift, no new awareness, no deeper change in the relationship between the antagonists. It meant that the adversaries had "split the difference."

Then the phrase *common ground* took center stage, as in "After the riots, blacks and whites searched for common ground." It, too, signified a step forward for this field. The phrase suggested that, beyond mere compromise, some kind of more fundamental change in position was required. Instead of standing on separate, polarized ground, stakeholders in complex conflicts could seek and sometimes find shared ground. By taking a step toward each other, they could find the place where *us* and *them* became *we*.

In this volume, the three coauthors, who are themselves highly skilled practitioners with a wealth of practical experience, challenge the field to take yet another step in its development. They focus on reaching for *higher ground*. The implications of this term, as it is brilliantly developed in the following pages, are far-reaching. Higher ground challenges all participants in a conflict, including the "neutral" professional third party, to open themselves to another level of awareness. It asks everyone not simply to take a step toward each other but to take a step upward toward a higher, and therefore unknown and mysterious, level of engagement.

Unavoidably, higher ground raises the stakes—for the practitioner, for the adversaries, and for the community or organization of which they are a part. As the extensive case studies in this book illustrate, higher ground does not belong to anyone. It is a province beyond laws, beyond regulations, beyond contracts, and beyond professional technique. It is a dimension in which words such as *spirit, mystery,* and *grace* inevitably arise.

To their credit, E. Franklin Dukes, Marina Piscolish, and John Stephens explore this higher ground with both competence and humility. They show why the upward spiraling path to higher ground begins with ordinary "ground rules." But in one of this book's most original contributions to the field, the authors show how to use ground rules so that they do not simply lead to compromise or common ground but actually open the participants' minds and hearts (and sometimes even souls) to higher possible outcomes.

In settings ranging from Chelsea, Massachusetts, to Catron County, New Mexico, and in policy conflicts as varied as tobacco farming and abortion rights, Dukes, Piscolish, and Stephens explain clearly how ground rules and expert facilitation can provide leverage for raising the level of conflict and, in the process, transforming it.

Although some conflicts that confront us can be approached adequately through compromise and common ground, an increasing number cannot. I can think of no book about conflict resolution that offers more guidance on how to handle conflicts of these kinds than the one you are holding in your hands.

If you respond to this book as I did, you will wish that you had read it years ago. I know it would have helped me immensely on many occasions, particularly in my work as head facilitator of bipartisan retreats for the U.S. House of Representatives. But as in our personal evolution, so it is in the evolution of this field of knowledge: we cannot apply what we know now to what happened in the past. Thanks to the work of these three colleagues, though, we have the opportunity to apply it now and in the future.

I intend to seize this opportunity—and this book—with gratitude and enthusiasm, and I encourage you to do the same.

April 2000   MARK GERZON
                                                  Boulder, Colorado

Preface

In 2000, we invited readers on a journey with the initial publication of this book. Now, we re-issue that invitation. We have even more enthusiasm grounded in broad and compelling evidence that it is a journey well worth taking. *Reaching for Higher Ground* is being republished because the message of building intentional community to enhance conflict prevention and group capacity found an enthusiastic audience – and the audience continues to grow. The methodology for creating an intentional and principled community has proven effective, adaptable and responsive to a wide variety of contexts and conflicts. So once again we invite you to join us on this journey. It is a journey whose final destination is unknowable, whose path may be strewn with unforeseen obstacles, and whose itinerary cannot be determined beforehand. In spite of this – or perhaps because of this – it is also an invitation to adventure, creativity and inspiration. This journey is the journey through conflict to *higher ground*.

Higher ground is nearly always within reach, but from where we typically stand in our families, schools, workplaces, and communities, the view is often obstructed by insensitivity, fear, ignorance, oppression, and prejudice, as well as more ordinary inefficiencies and unproductive habits of heart and mind. The Higher Ground we speak of in this book is a place where principled behavior is expected and rewarded. It is a refuge where challenging but essential conversations may be held in safety. Because it is a journey that happens in community with others, it is a place where you will create newly enlarged perspectives and achieve unexpected outcomes and more meaningful accomplishments. And because it is *all* of this, it is also a continuing challenge.

In groups of every kind, the unfulfilled promises and conspicuous problems of standard approaches to group facilitation and conflict resolution have prompted us to explore other ways of helping groups achieve a greater degree of integrity, creativity, effectiveness, and humanity. Leaders need ways to help group members engage one another in principled and authentic ways, while encouraging discussion of important matters even when – *especially* when – they surface conflict and strong, uncomfortable emotions. With increasing diversity a matter of both practical and moral imperative, we also need to help communities of people define for themselves the principles by which they operate, allowing for context- and culture-sensitive practices. Negotiating ways of working that do not unfairly privilege some over others by attending to the cultural norms, routines and group habits is an opportunity present in any group gathered around any task, at any time.

Here you will find sound guidance for developing proactive, shared norms for how groups can address their differences with integrity, creativity and care: these norms are covenants, protocols, and inspired ground rules. While we suggest specific tools, we also encourage you to be creative in applying our ideas. Like a jazz quartet improvising on a common theme, this experience can be fresh, inventive and spontaneous. While reaching higher ground can be a magical experience, it need not be a mystery. This book explains how.

Our Audience and Our Intentions

These ideas could have been expressed in many forms: as theory, as academic scholarship, even as philosophical treatise. But our interest is in serving the audiences that operate in the realm of action, including those who lead organizations (managers, administrators, and coordinators), those who serve communities and families (elected officials, clergy, social workers, therapists, and civic leaders) and the many practitioners of dispute resolution (mediators, facilitators, teachers and trainers). Finally, we believe that this book can also serve individuals and families no matter what your role. This means we limit the use of jargon and we emphasize concrete examples, tools, and techniques. The book is designed to be practical.

It is worth noting that since the first publication certain social trends have evolved, making this work even more significant. Many of the groups, communities and families we work with embrace the power of working from positive intention – from a spirit-infused approach that transcends any one particular faith in its recognition of the power of relationship. Science is beginning to document what teachers and mystics have long intuited: there is real power in our connections – our connections to deeper meaning, to each other, and to the divine, however those may be defined. *Reaching for Higher Ground* is a way of giving voice to what has been previously unspoken and untapped in group work.

Finding a way to reach out to one another from a place of morality and ethics, deeply held beliefs, and para-rational ways of knowing and perceiving can be deeply rewarding. This *higher ground* approach makes it possible to talk and work in a manner that is rooted in what matters most to the people involved, even if they use different language to describe it or attribute its source to disparate causes. This approach is particularly well suited to our times – a time of increasing complexity and diversity. Contemporary conflicts invoke fundamental challenges to identity rather than quirks of personality and conflict resolution necessarily places more value on holistic approaches and outcomes.

The Power of Language

Too often, the language we share for discussing the matters before us limits our expression of thoughts, and indeed the thoughts themselves. We are stuck with terms inadequate to what we need to accomplish.

Ground rules is the only term with broad currency for discussing a group's expectations regarding individual and group disposition and behavior. Yet we know that "ground rules" fails to capture our intentions, our interests, or our best experiences in working with groups. The common meaning of this term – rules imposed upon a group – represents the very problem that we want to overcome. We need different language – language that distinguishes itself from common practice and that captures our desire to help groups address a wide range of issues regarding their relationships and the processes by which they will work. We need a language that addresses these matters in a way that invites much needed attention to matters of spirit, culture, justice and power dynamics.

We began to supplant discussion of ground rules with a term intended to represent high aspirations and principled behavior. We found *shared expectations* an improvement on *ground rules*, but still insufficient. Even better is the term *covenant*. We like *covenant* because of the implication of shared, even sacred promises rather than rules. It allows for a vision, guiding values as well as practical agreements, and plans for continuous use. Finally, we prefer it because it is briefer than "shared expectations for higher ground"!

So here is the product of our shared interest: a book on how to help groups move beyond common ground to something more inspired, more challenging, but also more sustaining - *higher ground*. Our tool for accomplishing this goal is the development of shared expectations or covenants.

We do realize that we are attempting to reappropriate terminology, and that is tricky business for sure. Most people we work with embrace this shift in intent and language. However, our choice of terms is challenging for a few who have seen the term *higher ground* used in moralistic power plays against people and groups aspiring to recognition, rights, and respect. A small number of others express their impression of *covenant* as an artifact of religious doctrine and dogma or of restrictions on access to housing or community. It is our intent to offer these terms - *higher ground* and *covenant* - as practical concepts that nonetheless retain their spiritual quality, with "spiritual" meaning "that which nourishes the human spirit."

This is a challenging topic within the dispute resolution field. Some take issue with our choice of terms. A few take issue with our "nonneutral" values and intentions. The overwhelming majority of responses have been positive, even inspiring, as we hear from colleagues and others who have helped their groups and communities reach unimagined heights.

We have been greatly encouraged by this response to the first printing of this book. We hear "Yes - this is something we need and something we, too, seek." *Higher ground* has proved to be a rich metaphor. Values, principles, inspired behavior and spirit-supported work are no longer being left to families and churches alone.

This response to the first printing of the book is a signal to us that we are talking about something important. Others are using the concepts within this book to enhance their own work, and are moving into adventurous realms of their own. Because of that, we have embarked on the next exciting step of this journey: a virtual community to link those of us who are finding ways of building community out of conflict. This virtual community will be another way to share knowledge and inspiration and to build support for what can be challenging work. We are looking forward to the expanding conversation. We invite you to read on, and then speak up! We would love to know what you think and how these ideas work when placed in your skilled and caring hands.

Please read on and then log on to **Highergroundswell.com** and share your aspirations, experiences and ideas as well. We invite you once again to join us on this shared journey.

September 2008

E. FRANKLIN DUKES
Charlottesville, Virginia

MARINA A. PISCOLISH
Kailua, Hawaii

JOHN B. STEPHENS
Durham, North Carolina

Acknowledgments

A few personal thanks are in order to those whom we love. For the lifelong invitation to a place of enlarged perspective, truth telling and truth seeking, we thank our spouses, Linda, Paul, and Renee, for making our respective homes places of continuous love and learning about higher ground.

Beyond those few with whom we live, there is a wide array of colleagues, mentors, challengers, and co-laborers who deserve our gratitude. Our challenge is to acknowledge our debts appropriately in this limited space.

We offer thanks to several people who responded with enthusiastic critiques to our initial book proposal: Tom Fee, Michael Lang, Jim Stutzman, Paul Smith, and Laura Chasin.

As we were developing the book, Melinda Smith, Rafael Montalvo, and Carl Moore offered valuable perspectives on the higher-ground metaphor. Laura Chasin, Sally Malek, and Peter Adler provided support and encouragement and expended personal effort to assist us.

As we neared completion, Leah Wing's own work and our shared conversations strengthened our treatment of social justice—a dimension essential for reaching higher ground amid prejudice and structural oppression. Mark Gerzon offered his unguarded enthusiasm for this project at just the right time. Mike Smith, Tom Thornburg, Laurie Mesibov, Steve Clarke, and Frayda Bluestein offered timely guidance.

Special thanks go to Ron Neumann, Glenn Sigurdson, Chris Carlson, Lewis Michaelson, Mary Jacksteit, Melinda Smith, Susan

Podziba, Michael Chun, Charlene Hoe, and David Eyre for their contributions to Chapter Nine, as we sought examples of large-scale efforts consistent with reaching for higher ground.

We thank the many group participants—teachers, school administrators, pastors, farmers, health advocates, environmental activists, and extraordinary citizens—who are noted in examples of our work. We have learned much about higher ground from you. Similarly, we are grateful to participants in our 1998 and 1999 workshops at the Society of Professionals in Dispute Resolution conferences that gave us a chance to think out loud and refine our ideas.

Extra special thanks go to Leslie Berriman, our initial contact with Jossey-Bass Publishers, for her enthusiasm, encouragement, professionalism, and close attention to our work at its critical early stages. Thanks also go to our editors, Alan Rinzler and Amy Scott, for their hard work and insightful critiques. Finally, we are grateful for the production and marketing folks with whom we've worked at Jossey Bass—you've helped us to "get it right" and then "get it out there" so that people everywhere can reach for higher ground.

Chapter One

Reaching for Higher Ground

Forty-five minutes into the meeting, Janelle is getting nervous. There are two more important agenda items to work through with only thirty minutes left. For the past half-hour the group has been hashing over a proposal and there is still no consensus. Two of the group's members have seemingly squared off on this issue and no one is budging. Stalemate!

Then Rafael, a group member who is the facilitator for this meeting, calls a time-out. "It feels to me like we're digging ourselves a hole here. Does anyone else feel that way?" he asks. With a look of relief, nearly all of the group's members concur with his assessment. Rafael continues, "How do you want to handle this?"

Tanika enthusiastically offers, "Why don't we take just a minute and revisit our ground rules? This is just the kind of thing we built them for. They have never failed us yet." Rafael holds out his open hand, palm up, to the group, asking for reaction "OK, but let's keep it to ten minutes if we can," says Janelle.

Rafael moves into action as he passes out copies of a survey instrument that contains ten items. Each item corresponds to a different ground rule, or promise, that this group's members made to one another several months ago when they first came together and decided how they would work as a group. The survey items are as follows:

1. We are sharing information openly.
2. We are using objective information as a basis for discussion.
3. We are explicitly acknowledging the concerns of those with the most diverse viewpoints.

4. We are breaking larger problems into their smaller parts.
5. We are sharing responsibility for keeping the discussion on track.
6. We are working to find solutions that integrate the important needs of everyone.
7. We are preparing adequately before meetings so that we work efficiently in meetings.
8. We are communicating with others outside of these meetings in ways that support our work during meetings.
9. We are taking time to learn from our experiences.
10. We are making room and making time for risk taking, honesty, and missteps.

Each of the eleven people in the group goes to work on the survey, circling the most appropriate response on a scale ranging from 1 (strongly disagree) to 5 (strongly agree). Below each of the ten items is a space for "Examples/Specifics." As people complete their surveys they place them face down on the table in front of Rafael. Some people wander off to the restroom, some to the water fountain, and others to the coffeepot to freshen their cups.

Rafael quickly reviews the surveys and writes the ten items on a flip chart, placing hash marks for each response. A picture begins to form of the group's perception of its performance. Shortly everyone returns to the table and watches Rafael complete his summary of the survey data. After placing the last hash mark, he steps back as if to get a better perspective on it. "Well, what do you see here?" he asks.

Sammy pipes up, "Looks like we're getting lost, eh?" Tanika asks, "Well, what pulled us off track? What's at the root of the problem we're having right now?" Rafael follows with "Exactly, Tanika! That's the question. Any theories?" There is a long moment of silence. Then Corey reluctantly explains that he knows he is not handling himself very well in this conversation but he doesn't really feel like some of the group's members are listening to him because their minds were already made up when they came into the meeting.

Janelle can't pass up this opportunity. She looks at Corey and says, "I'm sorry you don't think we're open to addressing your concerns, but we had a long discussion on this proposal at our last meeting and put all the relevant information out on the table—the budget limitations, the schedule, the federal guidelines we have to stay within. We came in here to make a decision today and now there are these new concerns that you've raised, but I'm not sure where they're coming from. You say 'others' have these concerns. Who? How do you know? I need more objective information about this before I'm willing to change course. That is one of our agreements, right?" Corey nods acknowledgment to Janelle. Others express agreement with her point.

Corey confesses that a group of their community partners have been meeting with him on the side to discuss concerns they have about the agency. He explains that they have been unwilling to come to the full group or to the agency director because they don't think their issues will get a fair hearing. Indignant, Alex blurts out, "You're kidding me? You're meeting with partners without our knowing? What happened to 'sharing information openly' and 'communicating outside the group in a way that supports work inside the group'? I don't think going behind our backs with our partners is keeping with those two ground rules." Corey, head lowered, responds with "I know, I know! I've felt really caught in the middle on this one and I've been struggling to figure out how and when to bring it up. I guess I was trying to do that today by taking the position I did against the proposal in its current form." Rafael encourages Corey, "Say more."

Corey explains with whom he has been meeting, when it started, and what the partners seem to want. It turns out that the partners have some doubt about the agency's commitment to hiring service providers from the local communities in which they serve. They perceive that the agency director is responsible for failing to make good on a promise that was made more than a year ago. They think it shows a pattern of discrimination that favors white "outsiders" and "university graduates" over African American community folks who are qualified because of their experience. Some even have community college degrees. Corey admits he isn't sure what he believes about the accusation of discrimination, yet he knows it is a sensitive subject inside the agency. He thinks that perhaps he could help to address it by questioning the proposal at hand, because this proposal made no commitment to hire someone from the community.

Light is beginning to be shed on the last forty-minute debate on the proposal. Tanika summarizes, "So there is a perception that we are discriminating in our hiring practices and reneging on a promise to do otherwise, made over a year ago. It also seems that we have an image problem with some of our partners, to the point that they don't feel they can talk to us openly. More immediately, we've got a proposal that needs to be finalized in the next three days so we can process the 'request for hire.' And last but not least, we need to solve these various problems in a way that allows us to uphold our ground rules to one another inside this group, because when we don't stand together on those agreements, things get weird. How did I do?"

Rafael says, "Whew!" and the group applauds her and feigns bowing gestures in her direction. Corey says, "Nicely done, Tanika. Now what?"

After a few minutes of highly focused discussion, the group decides to delegate its final two agenda items to subcommittees, to be brought back to the larger group after some fact-finding. Liaisons are assigned to work with the subgroups. The group decides to extend the current meeting by twenty minutes so that they will have a half-hour to revisit the current proposal in light of the concerns Corey raised. Corey agrees to approach the concerned partners and invite them to have a conversation with the full group, of which the director is a member, sometime in the next month. Rafael offers to pull the files on the past year of new hires to gather more information on the issue to inform the discussion.

As the meeting is closing, Rafael begins the group's regular reflection on what they have learned from the day's meeting experience. Corey goes first, saying, "I needed to be reminded of how supportive you all can be when I trust you enough to share all my information. I'm sorry I forgot that. I took a load off in here today. Thank you." Janelle follows with her own reflection, saying, "I need to remember that when my stomach gets into a knot, others are probably feeling the same way. It was good that Rafael stopped us when he did. I need to remember that when someone isn't doing it for us, we need to step up and do it for ourselves. Thanks, Rafael!" Lucy, who had been quiet most of the meeting, says, "We may have to take a look at the distance between the values we espouse and the actions we take. I think I see what the community partners are saying. It's time to get more clear with ourselves about our priorities and the things we value most." This kind of sharing continues for a few minutes. Then, as they always do, they stand, each person extends one arm forward, and they pile their hands one on top of another. On the count of three, while breaking apart their hands they shout their team chant, "Stand together or fall apart. When we're good we're a work of art!" Smiling and laughing, they pass through the meeting room door and return to work refreshed, recharged, and recommitted to their tasks and one another.

"Frank! John! Wake up! We fell asleep during the lunch break. I just had the best dream," says Marina. "That is too weird. Me too!" says Frank. "You guys are scaring me now," says John. "I too had a great dream. It was about a really good group." Enthusiastically, Marina and Frank both shout, "That's right!" John cautions, "This is all fascinating, but the group is about to start meeting again. I hope we're ready for them because this group is really a mess! They were barely talking to one another before we broke for lunch. People ran off in different directions to eat with their cliques. I overheard some of those conversations. Nasty! It's gonna be chilly in there. I hope we have a plan."

Still looking a bit groggy from the nap, Frank doesn't seem to be responding to the concerns. Marina, puzzled, looks at Frank and says, "Why are you smiling? Do we have a plan?" Speaking softly, Frank looks at Marina and John with a glint of inspiration in his eyes and says, "I'm not sure we have a plan for this particular moment . . . but we have a dream, right?"

Frank, Marina, and John's dream is shared by many citizens, public officials, group leaders, and facilitators. Our dream is of families, groups, and communities that work—that build on one another's strengths to create a whole greater than the sum of its parts, and that do so in a caring and supportive atmosphere where all share responsibility for principled behavior. Dream on, you say? Well, not so fast, we say! We believe that there are things that can be done to turn this dream into reality.

People who participate in community groups, serve on committees, sit on advisory boards, or work at being a team in their family or at work may have a dream that is a bit different from ours or from a facilitator's. Most people dream that group work will be effortless. When it comes to people dealing with one another on the sticky stuff, on the interpersonal relationships and process side of group work, and on the prejudices that permeate our relationships, they would rather not have to deal with it at all. The dream is one in which no one has to talk openly about how the group is doing or what the problem seems to be or how anyone is feeling at a given moment. These people don't want to struggle with how to do the work or what to do next. To those dreamers, we say, "Dream on!"

The Power of Shared Expectations

All too often in families, in organizations, and in communities, when well-intentioned people find themselves struggling with difficult and contentious issues, there is a simple but powerful explanation: they haven't created the shared expectations—the ground rules—for working out their differences. And even when they do work out their differences, they often do so in ways that leave them frustrated, alienated from one another, resentful, and in dread of their next confrontation.

It doesn't have to be this way. There are ways for families, organizations, and communities to address conflict that are productive and affirming of one another's dignity. This book focuses on one important but often overlooked element for groups to get things done: the development and application of *shared expectations of behavior*—what is variously termed *covenants, community commitments,* or *ground rules*.

Developing and applying shared expectations about how to approach the task and how to treat one another in the process can enhance respectful problem solving and conflict resolution efforts. The tools and strategies we offer for developing and applying covenants, commitments, and ground rules can make any collaborative undertaking more successful. Success, as we define it, means not only reaching an agreement that resolves a recognized problem, but also solving it in a manner that strengthens relationships and imparts dignity and respect to everyone. This book teaches that it is possible to grow in community, through conflict, if you are willing to engage in problem solving in a manner that seeks not simply *common ground*, but *higher ground*.

Reaching for Higher Ground

Common ground is where my self-interest overlaps with your self-interest. Common ground is important. In some cases it may be sufficient. However, in many conflicts more is at stake than the presenting issue. Most difficult conflicts also involve struggles for such intangible elements as individual and communal identity, recognition, security, and status. In such conflicts, people need to move beyond finding where their predefined self-interests happen to coincide, and they need to acknowledge, tap into, and enhance these other concerns and longings.

Thus we have chosen the metaphor *higher ground*. The richness of the metaphor is explored throughout the book. Two of the metaphor's most important dimensions are *principled ground* and *new ground*. Principled ground springs from deep commitment to civil behavior that both demonstrates and invites respect, trust, recognition, and mutuality. To rise higher you must go deeper, accessing core values, attitudes, and intentions to create productive ways of listening, thinking, and speaking. New ground comes from the creation of what is yet to be imagined. Together, the new and principled ground of engagement leads to sustainable relationships—relationships that are not maintained by coercion or by reliance on the enforcement of rules.

The intentional pursuit of higher ground as people work through their problems is an idea and practice that can revitalize families, churches, workplaces, and communities. This work is nothing less than a little-practiced brand of democracy—public democracy—in which participation arises out of an ethic of care and responsibility, not only for one's self but also for others—for family members, colleagues, parishioners and citizens—as cobuilders and cobeneficiaries of the public or collective good.

The Trouble with Groups

No two groups are exactly alike. They vary in terms of expertise and skill. Some have no history as a group while others have long histories of less-than-productive habits. Many people experience group work as a place where much energy is expended yet little outcome is achieved. Too often, simply surviving a group experience becomes the primary objective. People watch the clock tick down the minutes, doodle on their papers, discreetly catch up on other work, pass notes, or engage in sidebar conversations. Many people keep a running commentary in their mind about what he said and she said, about what they should have done and would like to do (most of which, of course, seldom gets expressed out loud and some of which might well be illegal—or at least impractical!). They think about what else they could be doing—indeed, need to be doing. Often people keep one eye on the social and organizational politics being played out, which is the unexpressed but all too obvious subtext to the whole drama before them.

Some people choose leading roles in meetings, writing the script as they go, building tension along with the plot. Conversely, some people choose to play bit parts in the meeting. They await their starring role in the parking lot meeting that will occur as they head to their cars or in the staff lounge, the next day, or on the phone with someone who will hear their version of the events with rapt attention.

Too few people step up to play the diplomat or the mediator, the process guide, the planning assistant, or the critical friend. When groups are lucky enough to have one or more people play such constructive roles, others often grow dependent on them to keep things moving in the right direction. Groups are productive when these responsible group members are present. When they are gone, their groups flounder. Over time, group members lower their expectations for good group experiences. They grow more despairing about the inevitability of wasted time and futile effort. They become self-protective, avoiding group work when they can. They grow cynical.

This is a bleak picture befitting many group experiences. But not all group experiences are that grim. Some groups try to be efficient and effective. They may use a facilitator or a number of elements of effective meeting management, such as pre-meeting distribution of an agenda, the recording of meeting accomplishments, and even the sharing of important group roles, such as facilitator, timekeeper, and recorder. But sometimes even groups that to an outsider look like models of effectiveness find it hard to have sensitive conversations, to discuss the undiscussables, or to overcome the tendency to defer to the person in charge to manage the conflicts. In such groups, people walk away frustrated by the less than satisfying payoff from the effort being expended. Over time, histories of failure can build, grudges can be sustained, and honest conversations can be harder than ever to achieve.

Some people are lucky enough to have one group in their lives—be it one's immediate family, a social club, a task force, a church committee, or a work group—in which things just click. Such a group is both satisfying and highly effective at what it is charged to do. Participants are often uncertain about what accounts for the magic of it all: It's the mix of personalities. It's the shared commitment to the task. It's the food served at every meeting. Often participants have limited insight into why the group works, but everyone knows when it works and that it works: It feels good to be part of it. It feels like something in which it is worth investing their time and effort. It asks things of participants and gives them things in return—things of value, such as good decisions, thoughtful dialogue, a sense of connectedness, and a sense of power that comes from being valued, together, and effective. Sometimes it is even fun!

When people are lucky enough to have such experiences in their lives, they can never look at the other, less satisfying group experiences in quite the same way. It's almost as though the good experiences spoil them, making them less tolerant of—and more frustrated with—the six or seven other groups in their lives of which they are sentenced to be part. They despair even more knowing how good it can be.

Group Work: A Growing Trend

The quality of experiences in groups is a significant matter. More and more often people are expected to accomplish important work through group activities and decisions. Collaboration is a growing trend in public life through the proliferation of community boards, public hearings, community task forces, and so forth. Such work is also a by-product of process-intensive improvement strategies such as strategic planning, quality improvement, and shared governance. These strategies are turning up in workplaces, churches, professional organizations, and civic life. Add to this the growing awareness of the need for individuals to attend to their personal lives and responsibilities by communicating and working effectively with others. They arrange for sharing custody of children, they plan with siblings for the care of elderly or ill parents, they negotiate with others on the condominium committee, and they struggle to find ways of communicating with their teenagers, ex-spouses, and partners.

Never before have people been expected to get such important work done through groups of people, many times with near strangers.

The idea of *stakeholders*, now a household term, means that diverse groups are routinely called on to sit at the same table, to participate and bring forth varied and sometimes divisive views. Traditional notions of power and authority grow increasingly antiquated. This makes group process even more complex. And while good leadership is ever more essential, it is even more elusive.

These are the times in which we live. Expectations for collaboration are growing, along with its complexity and its importance for accomplishing the things people care about. Teams, partnerships, work groups, and other collaborative processes are where the important conversations are happening and the important decisions are being made. So what choice do people have? To hope for the best? To expect the worst? To stay away from difficult groups?

A Common Need and a Shared View

In one of the most popular and influential works for practitioners in the conflict resolution field, *Getting Disputes Resolved* (Ury, Brett, and Goldberg, 1988), the authors suggest that there are basically three ways of dealing with disputes: determining who has more power, determining who is right, and moving beyond rigid positions to reconciling the underlying interests, or needs, of the disputing parties.

The last of these ways, interest-based bargaining, has become enormously popular as an approach to dispute resolution. It took the dispute resolution field by storm and is now being applied in the workplace and other settings. The idea that people in conflict with one another can, through careful communication and creative problem solving, find ways in which their own interests can be satisfied without denying the needs of others has been an inspiration to many individuals and groups. People are discovering how to move beyond intimidation, coercion, and litigation to get their needs met. But even with these improvements in the way people solve problems, it is clear that the absence of aggression is not enough, nor is the presence of fairness. The quest for relatedness—connecting with others in ways that affirm both oneself and the other—is emerging as the next frontier in dispute resolution (Bush and Folger, 1994; Dukes, 1996; Ury, 1999).

We are searching for practical ways for humans to transcend self-interest, seeking not just common *ground* but also the common *good*, and aspiring to something better, something unknown and unknowable outside of community. So we add to the triad of power, rights, and interests a fourth approach to dispute resolution: *relatedness* (Dukes, 1996).

Necessity is indeed the mother of invention. Anomie, the absence of guiding moral values or norms of expected behavior, is alive in the world, in the United States, in its communities, and even in its families. The pressure to address this problem is increased by the recognition of growing multicultural, global connections—many peoples, many cultures, and many ways of being. The rules of decency, manners, and protocol are rapidly being revised. What is right and wrong? What is expected? How do others want to be treated? Notions of what is "normal" or "civil" increasingly are recognized as relative to given contexts, settings, and groups. Few people recognize that groups need to define the terms on which members care to relate to one another. But it is not only a promising idea, it is also a necessity.

The development of shared expectations about ways of anticipating and resolving conflict is typically reduced to the development of ground rules for how a group will work. These ground rules rarely bring about relatedness, much less the constructive resolution of conflict. They are becoming a regular part of practice for many facilitators and group leaders in all sectors. Yet based on our experiences in groups as participants as well as our experiences in groups as mediators and facilitators, common approaches to ground rules are insufficient.

As people are exposed to the typical uses of ground rules, they are growing jaded and cynical about the value of such rules. In some settings, ground rules have become a joke. In our experience, no effective alternative to ordinary approaches to ground rules has yet emerged. So, ground rules remain the first line of defense against unproductive or even destructive group experiences, but they are a weak defense. Many people are looking for something more. Individually, and collectively, they know that something more is possible.

We are motivated by a conviction that people are capable of more than they typically offer in group settings. "Where much is expected from an individual, he may rise to the level of events and make the dream come true" (Hubbard, 1927). If only we could find a way to help groups stretch and reach for something beyond the ordinary, the power of human potential and aspirations could be tapped as a resource. Pulitzer Prize–winning columnist William Raspberry (1999) offered his own theory of this phenomenon. He asserted that people desire to be with those whose ethics are higher than theirs; they are convinced that their own ethics would rise to the higher standard. Our own experiences confirm this. So how do groups tap into this dynamic? How can facilitators increase the chances of this happening?

❖ *Snapshot.* One of the most challenging and rewarding tasks of Frank's career has been his work as mediator and facilitator of discussions among tobacco farming and public health interests, work that began in 1994 and continues as this book goes to press. Tobacco farmers and their communities faced steadily declining production quotas and prices in the 1990s. That decline translated into real hardship for tens of thousands of farmers and many hundreds of farm communities. In the meantime, while the harms of tobacco use were gaining public attention in other parts of the United States, many public health advocates in tobacco-producing states felt that they were unable to gain comparable attention and improvements to public health.

In 1994, a small group of public health advocates began a process of contact, dialogue, and mutual education with tobacco-producing interests. Many people thought that irreconcilable differences between the two groups left nothing to talk about, and high stakes and continuing controversy surrounded both tobacco production and antismoking efforts. Participants on both sides were criticized just for meeting with "the other side," much less for continuing to meet on a regular basis. Not surprisingly, the effort began with caution and suspicion, and progress was slow and uneven. What was surprising to many observers (and for many participants, too, for that matter) is that enough dialogue, learning, and discovery of new common—and higher—ground occurred to offer serious and substantial contributions to thinking about the long-term future of tobacco-growing communities.

As late as spring 1997, many public health and farm leaders dismissed the dialogue between tobacco growers and public health advocates by saying, "There is no common ground." They were correct in the sense that common ground among deeply divided parties is not to be found just by looking; like farmland, common ground needs the hard work of cultivation. That they were incorrect in another sense was demonstrated on March 18, 1998, when a press conference featuring three tobacco farming leaders and four public health leaders announced the creation of the Core Principles Statement Between the Public Health Community and the Tobacco Producers Community. These core principles included not only general statements about the need for healthy farm families, but specific agreements as well, including support from public health advocates for a continued tobacco program of price supports and quotas, on the one hand, and support from farm leadership for FDA regulation of manufactured tobacco products on the other hand. More than seventy organizations and many prominent individuals endorsed these core principles.

A subsequent significant outcome of the effort was legislation in tobacco farming states sponsored jointly by tobacco farm groups and public health groups that directed money toward both tobacco farming communities and tobacco control efforts. These former adversaries are collaborating on other issues—such as harm reduction strategies for tobacco products and biotechnological uses of tobacco leaf—as they seek ways to sustain rural communities in tobacco-producing regions while promoting public health goals.

◆◆ *Reflection.* How did this happen? Much hard work and willingness to take risks was required of both public health advocates and tobacco farmers, and a not insignificant contribution came from the emphasis on creating a norm of principled dialogue and behavior—the development of shared expectations for higher ground—that marked the many private meetings, public hearings, and other mediated forums required to reach that point.

Two examples of the impact of the emphasis on higher ground are noteworthy. At a conference on the future of healthy tobacco farming communities in a rural Virginia town in late 1999, first a tobacco farm leader, then a public health advocate, and finally a tobacco district legislator all asserted the importance of not only common ground but also *higher ground*—the ground of principled, creative, relation-affirming dialogue. That affirmation followed by a few months one of several roundtable meetings of some public health advocates, tobacco farm leaders, extension agents, university researchers, and community development officials. A newcomer to the dialogue had made a series of claims that aroused anger. As facilitator, Frank wondered how to address this issue. But no intervention was necessary—both tobacco farm and public health long-time participants in the dialogue addressed the newcomer's claims by evoking the norm of the group that had been established over the years.

As both farmers and public health advocates asserted the history of principled behavior, high-quality information, open dialogue, and problem-solving orientation that had come to characterize the interactions of this group, Frank could only wish that he could share this moment with the world. Those farm and public health leaders had achieved what had been only barely imaginable a few years before. They had begun engaging with one another when there were no predictable benefits, no guaranteed outcomes, not even assurances that others would participate in discussions, and they had moved from this beginning to develop relationships in which good faith, commitment, hard work, and mutual respect were both expected and rewarded.

If this group of former antagonists—people who do have continuing differences—could make this transformation, cannot your group—your family, your workplace, and your community—do so, too?

What You Will Learn

This book is a collection of ideas and examples about helping a group tap into its collective higher aspirations. To accomplish this, we identify some of the limitations of relying exclusively on common ground rules for behavior. We show the ways that common dos and don'ts fail to reflect the values that individuals, families, groups, and communities wish to enact with one another. We lay out ways to engage one another productively to create together explicit, effective, value-based, shared expectations for behavior—covenants, community commitments, and ground rules—that will allow you to confront conflict productively.

At a time when the fields of dispute resolution, leadership, and group facilitation are struggling to address criticism that their predominant approaches are too Western, white, and male, this book offers a highly elicitive and diversity-honoring approach to group process. The process should reflect the unique needs of the group and its members. We suggest many ways to enact your own shared expectations, to reinforce their use, and to confront people productively when they act outside these agreements. Finally, we provide tools for assessing group behavior relative to these shared expectations and ideas for how to help a group use that knowledge to strengthen itself.

Enjoy the journey!

Chapter Two

Unspoken Expectations and Rules of Engagement

Everybody can point to examples of unproductive and even deadly conflict. Everyone knows of—and many people live in—communities whose race, class, economic, cultural, and religious differences produce an unsightly battlefield of antagonism and division instead of a radiant mosaic of innovation and appreciation!

Sometimes the ways in which conflicts are fought reflect unexpected behavior. But conflict behavior more typically follows predictable, even highly ritualized patterns of behavior. When difference is ugly, or even merely unproductive, these patterns of behavior too often reflect *unspoken* rules of engagement—expectations that have never truly been agreed to or consciously considered but that are honored in practice every bit as much as a set of written rules.

These unspoken rules can be helpful, such as when there is an implicit understanding that work is to be shared evenly or that everyone should be given an opportunity to speak. Frequently, however, such unspoken rules are unproductive and even harmful, especially when mixed with conflict.

In addition, too often members of a family, small group, organization, or community bring to the group *competing* understandings of how conflict should be handled. In these circumstances, these unspoken and unshared rules vie for dominance—and again too often, the least productive and most destructive expectations win.

Think of our society's most contentious issues. How many of us have had good experiences working through controversies that involve race, gender, sexual orientation, and other "hot" topics?

These are precisely the matters that most need carefully crafted, direct discussion. Yet in most settings people don't have any idea how to talk about these issues without evoking embarrassment, recrimination, or turbulent, fuming silence. Hence, important questions such as "Did discrimination cause this African American applicant to be passed over for promotion?" rarely get asked in group settings. Or if they do get asked, they draw responses such as "We're not going to talk about *that,* are we?" or "Oh, my God, here we go again!"

In this chapter we examine the consequences of such unspoken rules of engagement—the norms and expectations for conflict behavior that groups may never discuss and, in many cases, do not even realize they are following. In the first section, we identify seven such common rules that produce neither common nor higher ground. The second section explores what happens when competing understandings of conflict vie for dominance. In the third and final section we offer three real-life scenarios from family, work group, and community settings that demonstrate how these unspoken rules can lead to hurtful conflict.

Unspoken Rules of Engagement

Most groups operate without explicit agreements about how members will prevent and address conflicts. This is true whether the group is of short-term or long-term duration. Family members may care deeply about one another and interact intimately with one another for decades. Yet few families, if any, have spent a single hour or have had even one conversation discussing how they wish to address differences, much less how they might foster higher ground out of those differences. How many workplaces have such guidelines? Does your community have leadership that consistently seeks higher ground?

There are many reasons why so many people avoid preparing for conflict. One reason is that they just assume that goodwill and common sense will carry them through. Most groups have a general sense that "we can work out problems as we go" by following the general standards of reasonable people. So, for example, if I take notes in a meeting this time, naturally someone else will share the burden by doing it next time. If I let others have their say, of course they will do the same for me.

Sometimes, when the stars are all aligned properly, such implicit expectations work. However, when problems arise, the blame is often personalized: some individual or individuals are refusing to follow the leader, or they lack the common sense that everyone else seems to have. Relying on these implicit expectations is a little like building a house without creating a firm foundation—the ground can shift and cause disasters after the house is built.

A second reason that people fail to prepare for conflict is, paradoxically, just the opposite of the first reason. Rather than believing that goodwill or good sense will carry them through, people believe that conflict's by-products—ill will and troublesome behavior—are inevitable. "My experience with Mary is that she always blows up if anybody challenges her," or "The environmentalists always oppose everything we try to do," or "Those parents just want to get in the newspaper." If nasty conflict is inevitable, then why do people fool themselves into thinking they can avoid the unavoidable? For one who believes in this logic, ground rules would be only an exercise in futility.

What are these unspoken ground rules? We have observed seven such rules occurring in groups that don't directly confront the need for shared expectations.

UNSPOKEN RULE 1: *If dissent isn't spoken, it must not exist.*

This rule must be engraved somewhere in the (unwritten but very popular!) guide for unsuccessful group leadership, because far too many groups operate on this principle. How many times have you seen groups in which the leadership races through an agenda without any apparent opposition, only to have problems emerge later? Or even worse, in which the question, "Anybody opposed?" actually means, "I'm ready to move on and no one had better slow us down!"

The conflict that emerges later invariably has broadened to include the motivations of those who raise differences: "They should have said something earlier!" In fact, it is a good bet that conflict that is hidden or suppressed will surface later. Yet the art of surfacing different opinions is little respected and rarely practiced. For if one surfaces conflicts, one must deal with them—and that's a violation of Unspoken Rule 2.

UNSPOKEN RULE 2: *Conflict is bad, and conflict or even difference is therefore to be avoided.*

Trainings in conflict resolution and consensus building often begin with an exercise designed to ferret out the source of individuals' attitudes toward conflict. Invariably people recall messages they received from their parents while they were growing up. With few exceptions, people identify "Conflict is bad and the best strategy for dealing with it is to avoid it" as a powerful, lingering message. As adults, people are continually bombarded with sayings that, however well intentioned, reinforce that message; for instance, "If you don't have anything nice to say, don't say anything at all," "There's no point in saying anything—you'll only make matters worse," "Just learn to keep your mouth shut and you'll be better off," or "Go along to get along."

People offer both *personal* and *structural* justifications for avoiding conflict. On the personal level, many individuals believe that conflict is bad because it produces strong emotions and they get upset or afraid when they face strong feelings. Who wants to deal with a coworker who may yell or cry or be resentful if one can avoid those unpleasantries by avoiding the conflict?

Some groups avoid conflict because certain members use confrontation to intimidate those who fear conflict. Other groups may avoid conflict because of what is at stake: the more that one risks, the more likely it is that difference will be seen as a threat.

One illustration of this rule appears in families, groups, and communities whose shared understanding is that conflict represents a form of moral deficiency. Groups that aspire to some type of noble purpose—social justice groups, for instance, or religious communities—are particularly vulnerable to this problem. Their reasoning goes something like this: (1) we are gathered to do good; (2) people who do good don't have the problems that others do, such as competition for resources, turf issues, status concerns, and the need for individual exaltation (that is, pride); (3) if we do have conflict it must mean we are not doing good; (4) therefore we don't have (or can't publicly admit) problems and conflicts. This problem is endemic not just in churches but also in schools, social service agencies, and even the dispute resolution community itself.

Of course, when you combine an ordinary conflict with the guilt of broken aspirations, you reach Unspoken Rule 3.

UNSPOKEN RULE 3: *Anyone whose views differ from mine must be deficient or misguided.*

Few people have experience in settings where different views are encouraged and celebrated. Judith Innes (1999) has found that one of the characteristics of successful collaboration among diverse interests is the freedom to challenge assumptions. Yet far too often the unspoken rule is that disagreement and difference are indicators of personal deficiencies.

Elgin (1997) suggests that in order to truly understand others, one must assume that others have a legitimate basis for their views and attempt to ascertain what that basis is. Unspoken Rule 3 invokes the converse: one misunderstands what others mean because one disagrees with what they are saying. One then tries to imagine what's wrong with the individual who said it. Individuals who practice this behavior claim that their opponents' motives are suspect, that their opponents are unreliable, that they knowingly spread misinformation, that they engage in behavior that a decent person would never do, and so forth.

If opponents are deficient or misguided, how do you deal with them? The logical consequence of Unspoken Rule 3 is Unspoken Rule 4.

UNSPOKEN RULE 4: *Because your opponents are deficient or misguided, it is all right—even necessary—to ignore their needs and demonize and dehumanize them.*

Everyone has seen the public arena fouled by the discourse of personal attack. Labels substitute for dialogue—witness the conservative-liberal debate as it is spoken in terms of greed versus big spending or godless versus bigot or welfare versus wealthy. Everyone knows the language; it is spoken on radio and television, and it is used in newspaper editorials, campaign advertisements, and letters to the editor.

Although intense political partisanship is widely decried, stereotypes abound of what constitutes liberal and conservative views and weaknesses. All too quickly someone's different view is labeled as wrongheaded or bizarre. It is just a short step from discounting that person's general intelligence to withholding respect for all of the person's views.

We see this happening on a smaller scale in workplaces, community groups, and some families. People see quirky or bothersome behavior and quickly highlight that perception as how they define a coworker or neighbor. "Here comes long-winded George; flee before the breeze knocks you over" or "She is just so picky; everything has to be just right all the time!" Granted, there are many personality traits or foibles that can be irritating. However, labeling and stereotyping allows one to put the blanket judgment of "deficiency" or "not like us" on people, and it plants the seeds of shunning or even cruelty.

Individuals justify such behavior in familiar ways: "Everybody does it" or "They had it coming to them." The 1980s saw a variation on this theme that still has conflict analysts puzzled: many computerized communication forums (such as e-mail listservs and Internet chatrooms) are devastated by particularly egregious criticism and attack. It is not yet known whether this phenomenon is a product of the relative anonymity of electronic mail, the distance that precludes a physical response, the absence of verbal or visual cues that might ameliorate what looks harsh in print, or some combination of these and other factors. Many electronic forums are finding ways of developing ground rules in an effort to eliminate such attacks (see Chapter Three for discussion and examples of such ground rules).

Everyone knows circumstances—many people have been victims—in which such attacks are reported indirectly. Particularly in extended families and in family-like settings such as the workplace, this common approach to conflict is expressed in another common rule—Unspoken Rule 5.

UNSPOKEN RULE 5: *Tell everyone I know about what's wrong with my opponent.*

Do you like feeling righteous? Do you want to ensure the continued growth of your conflict? Would you like to see the development of sharply divided cliques? Then follow Rule 5 closely!

Most people sense that speaking badly of others behind their backs is unproductive, and often is wrong. Yet the temptation to do so is so strong! Not only do you get to vent without risk of confrontation—at least for the short-term—but talking about how many faults your opponents have also allows you to maintain Unspoken Rule 6.

UNSPOKEN RULE 6: *Because we don't know them, we're not responsible for the impact our behavior has on them.*

As mediators, the authors have had the experience of hearing disputants describe their opponents. Many times their descriptions of one another are exactly alike: the opponents are strange, their behavior is erratic or unpredictable, and their motivations are suspect, if not illegitimate. Because each opponent views the other as not like them, they both also see the other's concerns, feelings, needs, and values as clearly less important than their own.

The corollary to this rule is, *We are better off not knowing our presumed opponents, because if we do learn about them and understand their needs and concerns, we might have to confront our responsibility to them as we realize how our behavior affects those needs and concerns.*

Finally, perhaps the most familiar of all these unspoken rules (and you may well have others unique to your own experience) is Unspoken Rule 7.

UNSPOKEN RULE 7: *Conflict is a win-lose battle, so you had better win before you lose.*

Most people have heard about, and believe that they seek, win-win solutions to conflict. But when faced with a conflict in which they have a lot at stake, few people are able to keep faith with their intentions. For every message they remember that evokes a positive response to difference (such as "Blessed are the peacemakers," or "Treat others as you would be treated"), they can recall four or five other messages that reinforce their instinct to protect their concerns (such as "All is fair in love and war," "The ends justify the means," "Hit first before they hit you," "Winning isn't everything; it's the only thing," or "Keep your powder dry").

For some individuals facing the possibility of intense conflict, this rule drives them out of the game. They withdraw from any effort to address differences or they give in just to avoid trouble. For others, this rule brings out their adversarial nature and they enter the conflict like gangbusters—at least until they end up on the losing side.

When Unspoken Rules Clash

When family, community, or organization members hold competing understandings of how conflict should be handled, these unspoken and unshared rules vie for dominance. In the previous section we discussed the consequences of unproductive and unspoken but nonetheless shared expectations. Such situations produce an unfortunate but consistent and even predictable pattern of behavior among participants.

In reality, unspoken expectations are just as likely to be competing as shared. This creates a whole other set of challenges as individuals experience other participants as breaking the rules even though those rules were never spoken or agreed upon. This moment of realization—that we are not operating from the same rules—can contribute to feelings of fear and even despair for participants. It moves an individual from the relative comfort of knowing what to expect from others to the uneasy position of realizing that there are no rules. Familiar, implicit, and contradictory ground rules include the following:

- "Talking about problems only makes matters worse" versus "We'll never solve this unless we talk it out."
- "Freely expressing strong emotions (such as crying, yelling, or cursing) is healthy and inevitable" versus "I won't participate if you can't control your emotions."
- "Participation should be voluntary" versus "Everybody must speak their mind."
- "My discussion with you is confidential" versus "What you say I can share with others."
- "I come to the table with the goal of *claiming* what is mine by right" versus "I come to the table to *create* what will work best for all of us" (Kritek, 1996).
- "I need to get to know you before I can talk about our real differences" versus "I want to lay my cards on the table right away."

Some of these clashes result from different preferences for how conflict should be handled, and often those preferences are based on our earliest experiences of conflict during formative years and experiences. Kenneth W. Thomas and R. H. Kilmann (Thomas, 1990) have identified five styles or preferences for addressing conflict: *avoidance, accommodation, compromise, competition,* and *collaboration* (see Figure 2.1). Most individuals have a favored style, although

Figure 2.1. Five Conflict-Handling Modes

The Thomas-Kilmann Conflict Mode Instrument is designed to assess an individual's behavior in conflict situations. Conflict situations are those in which the concerns of two people appear to be incompatible. In such situations, a person's behavior can be described along two basic dimensions: (1) *assertiveness*, the extent to which the individual attempts to satisfy his or her own concerns; and (2) *cooperativeness*, the extent to which the individual attempts to satisfy the other person's concerns. These two dimensions of behavior can be used to define the five specific methods of dealing with conflicts.

Source: Adapted from Thomas, 1990. Used by permission.

some individuals are able to draw from a range of styles better than others, and the preference may vary depending on the context as well.

The problem is not that any particular style is bad: each of these styles may be appropriate or inappropriate depending on the circumstances. As in highway traffic, where speed differential rather than outright speed is the greater predictor of accidents, it is the clash of styles that can make conflict between individuals so difficult to address.

Implicit and unshared expectations about the way things should be done can be the source of endless struggle and conflict in a group. Depending on their experiences and preferences, individuals may hold a myriad of beliefs about appropriate behavior in group settings. They have opinions about how the meeting agenda should be created, when it should be shared, and who should be responsible for it. They hold beliefs about who should be allowed to participate in the process. Ideas vary about what constitutes common courtesy in how long each person speaks in a group discussion. Participants have decided views about whether they should have to prepare for certain kinds of meetings (such as staff meetings) or just show up at the allotted time. They hold views about what types of behavior should and should not be tolerated or what topics are off-limits.

In varying contexts and settings, individuals might respond differently to the issues just raised. They believe and act as though the "right" answer is self-evident. Chances are that each person holds that opinion about each other person's very different views on these matters. It is this type of presumption and egocentrism that produces a variety of responses and behaviors in group settings that bring members into conflict with one another. When implicit and unshared expectations about group behavior in general clash and produce conflict in the group, then implicit and unshared expectations about how to handle conflict itself come into play. Procedural conflict born of substantive conflict is a messy situation. Unfortunately, workgroups, families, and communities all too often find themselves in just this situation.

Consequences of Unspoken Rules of Engagement

Leo Tolstoy observed that all happy families are alike, but unhappy families find their own particular way of being unhappy. While we agree that each dispute has unique elements, we argue that the patterns of dysfunction around unspoken rules of engagement are quite predictable. Furthermore, they extend beyond the family to communities, the workplace, and other group settings. Let's look at three examples: a family at war, a workplace at war, and a community at war.

Family at War

This section takes issue with Tolstoy's view by offering a description that will be familiar to many a family whose members are unable to address their conflicts in ways that allow free expression of one another's views, ensure mutual understanding, and affirm one another's dignity. Such problems are shared even by families whose members do love and care for one another.

❖ *Snapshot.* Marina knows of a delightful man, a deeply religious and devout family man, who shared his sad story of family division that came about as a result of clashing expectations about how to solve a problem. This gentleman—we'll call him James—was the eldest of four siblings. Just after their mother's death, James asked the siblings to come together to discuss her will and how best to handle the affairs of her estate. James's youngest and favorite sibling arrived at the meeting with his wife, intent on having her participate in the decision making. James expressed his belief that this was a "family matter" and took a stand against the right of his sister-in-law to participate, because none of the other in-laws were present.

Prior strained relations between the sister-in-law and James contributed to their opposing positions on this matter and to the strong emotions that were evoked by the conflict. The youngest brother defended his wife's right to be there. The brothers squared off. James, as the eldest and as the executor of the will, held his ground. His younger brother and his brother's wife left before the meeting began. Thirteen years later, though they live in the same small town in the midst of a large circle of family and shared lifelong friends, they still do not speak.

As James shared this story with Marina, his sadness and regret were evident. Still questioning who was right in the matter, he had no question about the costs and consequences of their failure to agree on the rules for that meeting so long ago.

◆ **Reflection.** James had several options for minimizing the clash between himself and his brother and sister-in-law. Their mother was elderly and sick for a period of time. The need to resolve matters of the will could have been anticipated. Getting agreement while their mother was still alive about who would and would not participate in the conversation might have made a big difference.

With that opportunity missed, James could have expressed his wishes to his brother prior to calling the meeting. He could have expressed in private his concerns and desires and enlisted his brother's help to resolve the matter in a way that would have kept the family strong. James could have discussed this issue with his other siblings to determine if the sister-in-law's participation was a concern to others and to decide how best to broach the subject with the youngest brother and his wife. Had any of these ideas been tried and failed, they could have always talked about it after the fact, and continued working for a resolution.

The point of each of these possible conversations is to clarify the implicit expectations that are operating and the reason for those expectations. Then, as differences in expectations are made evident, the challenge becomes one of building a shared commitment to keeping matters in perspective, and caring for the relationships while the differences in expectation are resolved.

Marina wonders if James's sister-in-law feared that certain of her own expectations regarding the process would not be met without her involvement. Perhaps she believed that James held too much sway in the group and that his siblings were not likely to challenge him, even if they disagreed with him. Her own husband, being the youngest, might have had a history of deferring to his siblings, especially his oldest brother. The sister-in-law might also have been objecting to being left out as merely a matter of principle.

Perhaps the sister-in-law was afraid that the group would not uphold her expectation that their decisions should be fair to all. Such concerns would be sufficient to cause someone to push an unpopular position. If her husband shared her concerns, he may well have wanted her in the conversation to say the things he felt but that he and his sister might be reluctant to say.

Had some shared expectations been laid out beforehand, everyone's wishes could have been made explicit, fear could have been alleviated, and conflict might have been avoided. But as is so often the case in family situations, explicit attention to group process is unfamiliar and seems unnecessary—that is, until it's too late.

Workplace at War

It has been said that no one likes change except a wet baby. Yet it is commonplace that organizations report a need for ambitious reform, or pressures for improved performance, or at least recognition that individuals and departments will have to work together more effectively to bring about needed changes.

In comes the consultant-trainer, who is charged with motivating the staff to support the latest reform plan. Participation in the sessions is passive. Occasionally, hostile comments are made about the consultant, the value of the activity, the organization's leadership, or the reform agenda. Seldom are such comments dealt with openly and constructively. Some members of the group dominate the discussion while most say nothing at all. People sit in well-formed cliques and everybody watches the clock, anxiously waiting for the process to be over. The leadership move in and out of the meetings as their schedules permit. No one—including the consultant—believes anything will change as a result of these sessions.

This is not an uncommon scene, whether the venue is a public or a private organization. Even those who are struggling to adhere to the tenets of "new age" management suffer disappointment about the politics and interpersonal dysfunction that often characterize life in organizations, impeding their efforts at improvement.

❖❖ *Snapshot.* An ad hoc committee of faculty members at a university was directed to come up with a recommendation regarding the implementation of a planned reorganization. After several stressful meetings led by the committee chair, it was suggested that a neutral facilitator might be able to bring the group to a consensus. A colleague of Marina's was asked to step into this role two days before the committee was to meet again. With little time to prepare, the facilitator met with the chair to get clarity about the task and the history of the group's efforts. Just as the facilitator was about to clarify her understanding of the task and her role with respect to the chair, he informed her that he had other obligations and would have to end their meeting before hearing the information she wanted to share. He assured her it was a small group and things would be fine.

It was apparent from the start that this would not be an easy meeting for the facilitator. The chair began the meeting and proceeded to lay out the agenda, making no reference to the facilitator or her role. He didn't introduce her to the group or invite her to participate in any way. After a few minutes of observing the group's dynamics, the facilitator awkwardly injected herself into the meeting, seeking to clarify her understanding of the task and her role. The group responded well to her effort and seemed grateful for the clarification because they had all agreed such a person was necessary.

As the facilitator began to bring to the surface multiple views on the issue at hand, the chair grew visibly uncomfortable with the direction of the conversation. He commandeered the leadership of the meeting away from the facilitator several times before the facilitator decided to hang back and see what developed.

As the time for the meeting's end drew near, the facilitator tried once again to step into the discussion for the purpose of clarifying where each member stood with respect to the proposal put forward by the chair. Her purpose in doing this was to assist the group in seeing where various members stood on the proposal so that concerns could be recognized and addressed. Now visibly agitated with the facilitator, the chair abruptly called the meeting to an end.

That same afternoon a memo was distributed to the university administration and was copied to all committee members. The memo was a recommendation from the committee to the administration regarding the reorganization. It had been drafted by the chair without the consent of the committee. A cover memo said, "As chair I am responsible for bringing the group's work to its conclusion on schedule. Our inability to reach agreement in the committee left me no choice but to put forward my best recommendation on our behalf."

The facilitator was angry and embarrassed. The committee was livid. The chair was reported to have said that the facilitator was "no help whatsoever."

❖ *Reflection.* It was clear that the members of the group had many implicit and unshared expectations operating simultaneously: expectations about the chair's role, members' roles, and the facilitator's role were an obvious source of confusion and conflict; expectations about the decision-making process were not addressed; expectations about the time line for the group's work were not shared; and expectations about conflict and how it should be handled also shaped the experience. All parties, operating from personal assumptions about the rightness of their views, acted in ways consistent with their assumptions. The result was a dissatisfying and unproductive experience. The committee not only failed to agree on a recommendation, but also damaged relationships in the process. In the end, everyone involved had one more reason to say "Committee work stinks!"

Community at War

Whether you live in a small neighborhood or a large city, you know communities in which members are polarized over every issue, where public forums are dominated by the loudest and most aggressive citizens and public officials, and where trust or a sense of common purpose is scattered and elusive.

The public hearing, a basic tool of democratic governance, is intended to mitigate conflict by allowing citizens to voice freely and publicly their concerns, interests, and values. Unfortunately, at public hearings about any sort of controversy, there is typically more speaking—even yelling or demanding—than *hearing* and true *listening*. The formal settings for public hearings, with elected officials on a raised dais, often intimidate the ordinary citizen. Perhaps even more significant, often when an issue reaches a public hearing it is too late in the process to consider significant changes. This creates more frustration and anger in citizens, who feel excluded from the process, which in turn prompts greater demands and less compromise. Typical ground rules focus on formal, procedural matters but do not encourage informal and multiple forums in which citizens may be involved in neighborhood and city affairs.

❖ *Snapshot.* A growing school district near Frank's home was making plans to open a new middle school (grades 6–8). Opening this school required shifting the feeder patterns from several elementary schools. Many parents, concerned about whether and how their children would be affected, took an intense interest in the redistricting process.

One elementary school in particular, whose children previously had all moved upon graduation to a single middle school, faced significant changes. Two proposals for how the school should be redistricted quickly surfaced. One proposal (Proposal A) had the majority of the graduating fifth graders attending the same middle school (let's call it "SameOld Middle School") as those preceding them attended, while a significant minority would attend another existing middle school ("OtherOne Middle School"). The other proposal (Proposal B) suggested that either of these two middle schools (SameOld or OtherOne) would be satisfactory but all students ought to go to the same middle school. Neither proposal involved sending any children to the newly built middle school, which was much further away than the other two middle schools.

In the eyes of some, but not all, parents, OtherOne Middle School was considered a less attractive school than SameOld. SameOld drew a significant portion of its students from the most affluent part of the area and was almost entirely white; OtherOne had a more diverse population.

The school board, which was responsible for any redistricting decisions, put out a map prepared by the transportation division showing how possible redistricting options would affect transportation patterns and costs. The least costly option was Proposal A, by which graduating fifth graders would attend different middle schools depending on where they lived. Some parents interpreted this map as a final statement of how the redistricting would occur.

At this point, the school community rapidly became polarized. Parents whose children would continue to attend SameOld Middle School pronounced themselves satisfied with Proposal A. Some parents whose children would attend OtherOne were extremely upset. Among those parents, some merely wanted the new boundary line adjusted so that their own children would join the majority at SameOld. Others favored Proposal B, which might mean that all graduating students would go to OtherOne. Parents lobbied the school board members, the elementary school principal, and each other. Dispute behavior included rumors of individual political influence and accusations of racism among parents who did not want their children going to OtherOne. A public hearing on the redistricting proposal held a month before the decision was to be made degraded into a shouting match and personal insults.

The school board ultimately supported a version of Proposal A that sent some students from the elementary school to SameOld Middle School and other students to OtherOne Middle School. Some disillusioned parents dropped out of the public school system, some withdrew their involvement as volunteers in their children's schools, and a few others no longer spoke with former friends. The parent-teacher organization brought Frank in for two well-attended meetings to allow parents to reflect on what had happened and to think of ways to rebuild the school community.

❖ *Reflection.* From the point of view of the school administration, they did everything possible to make the redistricting as fair as possible for both students and parents. They announced the prospective redistricting early (at least six months before the final decision was to be made), they tried to use objective criteria (such as transportation costs) as much as possible, they held lengthy public hearings, and individual school board members as well as staff undoubtedly spent considerable time answering many telephone calls from concerned parents.

However, the perspective of many parents was quite different. Some had not known about the redistricting plans because they hadn't heard the announcements. Others were not aware of when the final decision would be made and how their children might actually be affected until specific options were announced. This uncertainty heightened defensiveness and exacerbated existing tensions.

Many parents objected to the absence of clear criteria for redistricting. The objective criteria that were used—in particular, transportation costs—were considered by many parents to be much less important than more significant values such as keeping friends and school communities together.

When there are no clear criteria for important decisions, it is easy for suspicion to develop about the motivations of individual parents and officials. Many parents believed that other parents wielded private influence over some school board members. This suspicion was not helped by the inevitable contradictory information and rumors passed among parents who had spoken to different board members, and of course rumor and uncertainty serve only to heighten the anxiety of parents about the future of their children.

The concern over where their children would be sent to middle school was matched by parents' uncertainty about how the decision would be made.

Finally, the public hearing format produced acrimony and conflict but little hearing, and even less understanding. Many parents expected a public forum for learning about the issues and discussing their concerns; the public hearing gave them neither. The intimidation of spotlights, podiums, microphones, and the formal setting kept many parents from speaking at all. Furthermore, the format allowed for no discussion, no response, no rebuttal, no opportunity for clarification, and no dialogue.

Life goes on after the redistricting. Many parents are quite happy with their children's schools, as are the children, who often adjust to change more easily than adults. But the effects of the redistricting lingered in many ways—in children transferred to private schools, in parents so hurt by the acrimony that they no longer volunteered at school, and in lingering public perception of inequity in how decisions get made. The pain probably continued among some of the school board members and staff who were most involved.

Public involvement that both educates and seeks input takes a good deal of time and costs money and human resources in order to be done right. But how much time and how many resources are spent in picking up the pieces after controversies of this sort? An up-front investment may be less expensive in the long run.

Few public decisions affecting many people will avoid controversy and conflict entirely; some stakeholders will undoubtedly be unhappy with whatever decisions are ultimately made. But a process that readily provides information, that allows for real participation, that has the time and resources necessary to do a good job, and that produces decisions made on the basis of equitable criteria known before those decisions are made will help bring a community together rather than drive it apart.

The problems to be resolved in each of the three scenarios are substantive, complex, and important. The causes of the problems are varied and represent an accumulation of personal and group history. The solutions appropriate to each situation will be unique to those involved. Nonetheless, the three scenarios share one critical element—an absence of explicit and shared expectations for constructive engagement—expectations that would motivate individuals to take personal responsibility for contributing to the problem's definition, to its thoughtful analysis, and to its resolution.

Without hope there is despair. Without trust there is fear. The "slippery seven" problems of unstated or assumed approaches to dealing with conflict are significant barriers. Covenants, commitments, and ground rules, developed through dialogue among participants, can provide powerful ways of overcoming fear and hopelessness. More and more groups do adopt explicit ground rules in order to try to do their work better. Sometimes these ground rules work well enough. Unfortunately, common ground rules often do not really represent shared expectations for constructive behavior. They seldom address the issues that need addressing and they are too often used as weapons of coercion rather than as tools of construction. We explore in Chapter Three why this is the case.

Chapter Three

Common Practice with Ground Rules
How They Fail Us and We Fail Them

"I know we've run out of time but I have something important to bring up. It should take only ten more minutes."

"We are close to consensus, so I think we can move on."

"If you want to keep working here, you'd better not ever disagree with me in front of the board again!"

These statements are often the beginnings of frustration, resignation, or outright conflict as people work in committees, teams, coalitions, and other kinds of groups. Many groups try to prevent these problems by adopting ground rules to govern their work. Specific admonitions such as "Don't interrupt" or general aspirations such as "Treat each other with respect" are common ways of stating the rules of the game for committees, community groups, work groups, and even families.

So isn't this a good thing? Aren't these basic guidelines needed to keep things on track? As drivers share the road, they may not like one another's choice in cars, but as long as everyone stops when the light is red, passes safely on the left, and takes turns in merging traffic, they'll be OK. Right?

Well, not exactly. In this chapter we examine how many kinds of ground rules fall short of what is needed for the health and productivity of people working in groups. Common practice with ground rules may be helpful in guiding people toward common ground, and common ground may be a welcomed achievement. However, reaching for common ground is not the same as reaching for *higher* ground.

Although we think that many kinds of ground rules can bring value to a group, we can also demonstrate many shortcomings of common ground rules and the ways in which they are used.

When we use the term *ground rules,* we mean the following:

- Shared guidelines for how people work in groups
- Specific standards for procedures and routine action—for example, how topics are brought up and discussed or who makes a binding decision
- A range of focus and detail, varying from general aspirations, hopes, or goals to more specific, easily observed behaviors (for example, *Don't interrupt*)
- Guidelines that can be modified without a change of law or administrative procedure

What we *don't* mean by ground rules is

- Extensive bylaws or a constitution. Ground rules are not the same as identifying the lines of authority or the structure of a large organization.
- Laws set by an external authority.

Common ground rules, when they are clear, accepted, and honored, can be quite valuable. We are not calling for people to give up any particular rules, such as "Don't interrupt" or "Treat each other with respect." However, we see three major problems with common ground rule practices:

- Common ground rules are routinely introduced as necessary inconveniences that need to be covered before getting into "the real business." This attitude undermines their effectiveness.
- Once they are introduced, common ground rules are typically used only to point out someone's deviance from a rule. This

often creates fragility and polarization rather than strength and community.
- Common ground rules seldom help groups improve, learn, and recognize the linkage between process and the substance of the group's work. This often leaves groups floundering and group members wondering why they wasted their time on rules that aren't working.

In this chapter we examine these three problems—how ground rules are commonly introduced, how they are misused, and what they fail to do.

How Ground Rules Are Introduced

The first problem with ordinary ground rules arises in how they are introduced to a group. Typically, a list of ground rules is brought to the group by its chair or leader, or they are given to a committee or work group by the boss, who may or may not be a member of the group. Most people think this approach is acceptable or even expected, because the leader is in the right position to offer direction, or at least to get things started.

We've identified four problems with this approach:

1. The ground rules are offered in a directive rather than an elicitive manner.
2. They are formal, limited, and prohibitive, describing what you *cannot* do rather than affirming what you *should* do.
3. They are offered in ways that make clear that they are less valuable than really doing the work.
4. There is little opportunity to illustrate, understand, or revise the rules.

Now let's take a look at each of these problems in turn.

Directive Rather Than Elicitive

Ground rules are too often introduced in a highly directive manner. While a token indication of openness to revision may be offered, that openness is usually accompanied by implicit or explicit messages about not wasting time trying to modify a list of ground rules.

We hear some readers asking, "Isn't it up to the leader to set the tone, lay down the law, and be responsible for the working of the group?" We reply that committee chairs or bosses may indeed be expected to define the task for the group, to set deadlines, and to make other expectations clear. However, many needs that groups have cannot be met by orders from a superior.

When ground rules are imposed on a group and there is little or no discussion to clarify the purpose of the rules, people will have varying levels of buy-in. What may strike one person as reasonable guidelines for working together can be seen by a compatriot as something to tolerate merely because obedience is the path of least resistance.

Most groups operate without a clear understanding that changes to the proposed ground rules are welcome. Although it takes a brave person to initiate a discussion about whether or not ground rules are being violated, it is even riskier to voice concern that the rules themselves may be the problem. It's hard to buy in to ground rules if you don't think it is your place to put forward ideas for how to change the rules of the game.

As you will see in Chapter Five, ground rules have meaning to a group to the extent that everyone had a hand in creating, endorsing, and deciding how and when they should be applied and enforced.

Formal, Limited, and Prohibitive

While ground rules may set some good parameters for the work of a group, they are often limited, formal, and prohibitive. Do the following rules sound familiar?

- Don't interrupt!
- Begin and end on time!
- Stay on the topic!
- Be brief in making comments!
- Let everyone have a say!

Everyone needs clear directions. However, for groups doing important work over any extended period, this kind of approach to ground rules is inadequate. It stresses problems to avoid rather than opportunities to build strong, positive working relationships.

For example, unless people are skilled at asking how an apparently unrelated idea or suggestion relates to the topic at hand, applying the rule "Stay on the topic!" can stifle creativity and prohibit making important connections between topics.

❖❖   *Snapshot.*

Agenda topic: How the family car is used

Participants: Fritz, the father; Sophie, the mother; Karen, their sixteen-year-old daughter

Sophie: OK, we set this time for the family powwow. Fifteen minutes to lay out concerns and ideas, fifteen minutes to try to reach a solution. Remember our rules: don't interrupt, stay on time, stay on the topic, be brief in making comments— I suggest a one-minute rule, and let everyone have their say. Are we ready to begin?

Fritz: Ready.

Karen: I guess so.

Sophie: Karen, why don't you go first.

Karen: I need to have the car more for lots of reasons. First, I need to get more experience driving. I hate it when you try to correct me—I get so nervous. I work better with Aunt Eileen coaching me on my driving. OK, next, I need to get to my work at Steak and Shake on Tuesday, Thursday, and

Saturday nights. I know you want to drop me off and pick me up, but it doesn't let me stop by at Freida's or Joy's or Shelley's house on the way home to compare homework. Also, I don't know when I'll get out on Tuesday and Thursday nights, so I can't rely on someone else to give me a ride—

Fritz: [interrupting] Karen, you know that Tuesday night is my bowling night!

Sophie: Fritz, honey, we agreed—no interruptions.

Fritz: Ok, sorry.

Karen: Well, that's all for now, I guess.

Sophie: Fritz, OK, your turn.

Fritz: Well, Tuesday is my bowling night. I've tried getting a ride with one of my teammates, but that hasn't worked. And John sometimes has three or four beers and I don't like to ride back with him. So I have tried to get to bowling without taking the car, but I do need it. Thursday is also the best night for me to tinker on the car, or for us to clean it and be sure it has our beach or camping gear in it for the weekend, but I think we can work something else out.

Sophie: OK, my turn. We do have a problem on Thursday night. It is the best night for me to pick up Eileen and for us to visit mom at the rest home. Mom really likes the consistency of every Thursday for us to visit, and then for you two to visit every other Sunday, as best you can.

Karen: I've been *trying* to get there on Sundays but I've been out of town with field hockey for the last three Saturdays! I need Sunday to do homework and have a little time with friends! Give me a break!

Fritz: One topic at a time, Karen. We're dealing with the car, not visiting grandmom.

Karen: But if Dad has the car on Tuesday and you have it on Thursday, then I can't work at Steak and Shake! You tell me to earn money for some clothes or a CD player or to save up for a summer trip with Joy to their cabin on the lake, but then I can't get to my job. See, I just don't get treated like an adult! I try to work for what I want just like you say, and I can't get to my job!

Sophie: Karen, Karen. We are still talking about how we want to use the car. I know your job is important. Let's see what we can work out. Are there any other things we need to talk about for how each of us wants to use the car?

❖ *Reflection.* While Karen's lament may strike parents of teenagers as all too familiar, the conversation raised other issues that need to be addressed. These include Karen's range of commitments, such as visiting her grandmother, sports, and work, and her judgment about the degree of support she receives from her parents versus being able to earn her own money and gain some independence. Of course this discussion could lead into a much more far-ranging dialogue about, for example, Fritz's options for bowling on another night or using some other form of transportation, Sophie's schedule for visiting her mother, and Karen's work schedule or the option of finding a new job. Even in this short example, the rule "one topic at a time" can be constraining rather than useful.

Distraction from the Real Work

The third problem with the way ground rules are usually brought to a group is that they are presented as a step preliminary to really doing work. Too often the attitude of leaders and group members alike is, "Let's get this stuff settled and get down to substantive matters."

The hard distinction between the "how" and the "what" of family, workplace, volunteer board, and neighborhood group activities diminishes the value of intertwining task-oriented behavior with ground rules that maintain and strengthen relationships. So much of what truly counts in groups rests on qualitative factors such as trust, familiarity, appreciation, creativity, humor, and reflection.

Unfortunately, the usual approach is to lay out the ground rules—and move on. We believe that most sets of ongoing relationships—families, neighborhoods, and voluntary associations as well as the workplace—need more than the "no biting, no kicking, break when the ref says so" kinds of rules. The procedural dimension of "how we will work together"—particularly how we will work together when our views differ—needs to be more integrated with the substance of a task or decision.

At first glance, the question of guidelines, such as who speaks when, may pale in comparison to a group's vision of the outcome they seek, such as a neighborhood group agreeing on a petition to close a suspected crackhouse, a cross-departmental group recommending a merit pay policy, or a family determining a fair division of responsibility in order to care for an ailing elder. Process is often undervalued and then undermined by the way ground rules are typically introduced. As a result, their potential effectiveness is undercut.

Some organizations use team-building activities in an attempt to strengthen the process and relationship dimensions of groups. Ropes courses, innovative ways to make introductions (for example, giving your name and favorite vacation spot), or other ways of learning about group members' backgrounds, skills, and personalities are common tools.

Even here, the approach to team building seldom contributes to substantive improvements in relationships or team functioning. Viewing team building as separate and unrelated to the development of shared aspirations and expectations is a continuing weakness in the ways many nonprofit and for-profit organizations support their staff, volunteers, and board members.

Little Opportunity to Illustrate, Understand, or Revise

Common practice in how ground rules are given—whoops, we mean "proposed"—by the leader or boss leaves uncertainty as to how questions or criticisms of the rules will be handled. Confusion or uncertainty on this point can lead to indifference or even resistance to the ground rules. Those who probe for clarification or suggest additional or different rules may feel that they are going way out on a limb. Does one risk being labeled a "troublemaker" and challenge the rules, or just tolerate the process? There may be some irony in that moment in which one realizes it is risky business to challenge the guidelines being adopted—guidelines intended, in part, to help people feel safe.

❖❖   *Snapshot.* The assistant director of human resources of a large company has created a short-term task force of twelve people to make recommendations for changes in personnel policies that will be more "family friendly." The members of the task force represent different parts of the company and have been told to expect monthly meetings for the next three to four months. The first meeting is for people to meet one another, hear a brief history of how the family-friendly initiative got started, and get clear on the goals and next steps for the task force's work. Fay, the assistant director of human resources, opens the meeting.

>   *Fay:* I'm Fay Ramirez and I'm glad you are here. You have in front of you an agenda and some other documents that we'll review in a minute. Before I ask you to introduce yourself, I'd like to mention some ground rules that I think make committee work productive. What I propose comes from a popular book called *Getting to Yes* (Fisher and Ury, 1991). It calls for separating people from the problem, focusing on interests, not just on a person's positions or demands, seeking objective standards that can be used to fairly measure different potential solutions, and creating options for mutual gain. Are these ground rules acceptable?
>   *George:* I don't know what you mean by "separating people from the problem." I've heard a lot of resentment in my customer service department about certain employees taking a lot of

time for children or elderly parents. How can you separate what they do—the people—from the problem they create for their coworkers?

Fay: What is meant by "separating people from the problem" is that we don't want to get into name-calling or criticism of individuals. Our goal is look at the policies and trade-offs that make sense for us to be a productive organization and family friendly at the same time.

George: [looks confused but remains silent and slowly nods his head]

Fay: Are we ready for introductions? Good, how about—

Tammy: [interrupting] Fay, I don't want to be a stick in the mud but can you tell me what you mean by "seeking objective standards to measure potential solutions"?

Fay: Tammy, thanks for asking—that's a good question. I'm sure other folks may be unsure about what this rule means. OK, what this ground rule means is that we need to look for a fair measuring stick for whatever we do. Let's say we consider a proposal for part-days off for the purpose of a parent meeting with a teacher or an employee taking an older parent to a doctor's appointment. We would need to figure out the potential effects of the policy and see if we can balance out the lost productivity in other ways.

Tammy: Thanks, Fay, that helps some, but I still don't know where "objective standard" comes in.

Fay: Well, the objective standard will be to look at our company's history on time off and perhaps the history of other companies our size to figure out the cost of such a policy.

Tammy: Just one more thing. Like George, I hear some grumbling about the current policies and how they affect workers who don't have kids or ill parents who live far away. Are these people's views too subjective to be part of an objective-standard ground rule?

Fay: [getting a little impatient] Tammy, like I said to George, we don't want to get into name-calling or individual complaints, but we want to look broadly at policies that can make sense for everyone. We will get to your and George's points about some people worrying about how long their coworkers currently get off for family needs. You know, I think these guidelines will get clearer as we get into the heart of our work, so let's just move forward with some introductions.

◆❖ *Reflection.* Fay has a list of ground rules that make sense to her. But without explanation or illustration of what they are trying to accomplish, confusion reigns. As Tammy's and George's questions imply, taking a minute or two to give an example of how to use the ground rules would help the group.

Unfortunately, Fay was eager to move on—to get down to the "real business"—and was not ready for a real discussion. Many of us have seen ground rules work for one group but not thought about why. It is far easier to see when ground rules are working correctly than to explain the ground rules adequately from the start.

How Ground Rules Are Used

Once the ground rules are introduced, they have to be used. Our experience is that another set of problems arises in the typical uses of common ground rules:

1. The ground rules are not applied consistently.
2. Deviations are handled in a heavy-handed manner.
3. There is no recognition of tensions between certain rules.
4. There is no agreed-upon process for revising the rules.

Inconsistent Application of Ground Rules

It is common practice to apply ground rules unevenly. The ground rules may not be referenced at the beginning of each meeting, and they tend to be forgotten. Certain rules may be obvious: beginning and ending on time is an easy one to remember and evaluate. It may take practice to make other ground rules work well. "Focus on interests, not positions"—a very useful ground rule—is not always easy to honor if someone is ignoring it as he or she argues a particular point.

The chair or group leader, who is often deeply involved in the substance of the group's discussion, may selectively notice instances of people straying from the rules. Not surprisingly, leaders, bosses, and chairs seldom acknowledge their own divergence from the ground rules. Thus the dim memory of the initial consideration of the rules, combined with their inconsistent application, discredits how useful ground rules can be.

Violations of the Ground Rules

Straying from the ground rules is often seen as a personal failure. Attitudes about and approaches to violations can vary widely, from a gentle reminder to a sharp reproach. The ways in which ground rules are commonly used do not promote learning and improvement of the group as a whole.

❖ *Snapshot.* We return to the task force on family-friendly personnel policies.

At the third meeting, members are reporting on research that they agreed to conduct after the second meeting. At the beginning of the second meeting, some additional ground rules were added, including "Come to meetings prepared."

> *Fay:* David, you are up next.
> *David:* I did a lot of research on flextime policies and family needs and demands. Brigit and I were splitting the work and we had a miscommunication about who was preparing the report. I thought she was and she thought I was. We just found out about the mix-up a couple of minutes before our meeting, due to the e-mail problems we all experienced earlier this week.

Fay: I'm sorry there was a miscommunication, David, but how can we move forward without your report? Why didn't you call Brigit?

David: I did call, and left her a message, and she called back and I was on the phone. Anyway, to save you the whole story, we did try to get things straight by phone but were unable to.

Fay: I appreciate your effort to try to get the report done, but this failure to be ready for a meeting does hold us up and is inconsistent with one of the ground rules we adopted at the last meeting. I guess we will just move ahead as best we can.

❖ *Reflection.* Granted, Fay may seem a little unsympathetic with what seems to be reasonable efforts by David and Brigit to handle the communication problems and come prepared for the meeting, but isn't her tone familiar? Not living up to an expectation, or particular rule, presumes personal failure.

A more productive discussion would be on the rule about being prepared in relation to shared responsibility. David and Brigit should have described their experience and compared it with other people who were working in subgroups on particular topics. Finally, the idea of rescheduling the meeting because of the e-mail problems could have been raised.

No Recognition of Tensions Between Competing Rules

All too often, people who are exposed to ground rules and see them work well do not notice the tension between individual rules. The ground rules may have worked because the tensions did not come up. More likely, someone else—perhaps a skilled group leader or a facilitator or mediator—helped guide the group through the competing needs embodied by the rules in such a way as to avoid or minimize the tensions. The tensions were not fully appreciated because they were managed smoothly. Without such skilled leadership, such tensions and contradictions in the rules are harder to mask.

One popular decision-making rule is to reach consensus. Rarely is consensus defined. Does consensus mean 100 percent agreement with every detail of a solution or agreement? Does it mean, "Well, I can live with it"? How is it different from a series of compromises that yields a package that people grudgingly support? Is there an explicit way to determine how some kind of decision will be made when consensus cannot be reached? The implicit tension here is between completing a task within a specified period and taking the time needed to seek understanding and be creative in crafting an agreement that satisfies everyone.

In the task force on family-friendly personnel policies, Fay presented the ground rule "Separate the people from the problem." Her colleagues indicated that some people *are* the problem. How some employees used time for family matters created some grumbling from coworkers.

Although the ground rule "separate the people from the problem" tries to elicit productive discussion of issues without pointing the finger at personalities, it may cover up the fact that some issues are intimately connected to individuals' problematic behaviors. Merely saying "separate the people from the problem" does not raise and explore some of the tensions over how issues seem to be tied to particular people.

A final example of hidden tensions among well-meaning ground rules comes from one effort to civilize computer network online groups. The ability to communicate using e-mail and chat rooms raises new questions about appropriate ground rules, or "computer manners." How can you tell if someone is kidding when you only know what he or she thinks through words on a computer screen? Internet chat rooms, or Web forums, have raised the question of what kind of "netiquette" is needed, without unduly restricting the freedom and breadth of discussion many people enjoy on the Internet.

One group involved in a distance education program established the following ground rules:

1. Complete honesty *at all times*.
2. Thoughtful and genuine feedback.
3. Professional and considerate interaction.
4. Ethically aware behavior.
5. No side dishes please. We prefer that everyone discuss their issues concerning this seminar on-line so if we encounter a difficult issue we can attempt to work it through on the [Web] board.
6. Be up front about your own agenda and please post it to the board (Strickland, 1998).

Rules 1 and 3 could certainly come into conflict, because some people interpret "considerate interaction" as clashing with "complete honesty *at all times*." Also, "ethically aware behavior" may not sit comfortably with posting information about one's own agenda (that is, needs or goals). Because these rules came from a stable on-line group rather than from the changing arrangements in chat rooms or listservs, the group may have worked through these gray areas or tensions. However, our general observation is real: rarely are basic tensions in a set of rules identified and discussed at the beginning of a group's work.

No Agreed-Upon Process for Revising the Rules

A final difficulty in how most ground rules are commonly applied is that there is no explicit way to assess and revise them after they are adopted. If someone other than the chair asks for additional rules or expectations, or questions the usefulness of a rule, he or she may risk alienation from other group members or censure from a leader.

Requesting midcourse changes in ground rules when the group leader has made no invitation to do so is especially risky business. For example, suggesting partway into a group experience that a new rule might be needed, such as "No one should dominate the discussion," is a delicate, if not politically costly, maneuver for a group member. Chances are that the felt need for a change is the result of some unproductive behavior that can be attributed to some group member. Even if you don't name the individuals, naming the behavior is a tip-off to discontent and can put a group on edge.

❖❖   *Snapshot.* The family-friendly task force members are now in their third meeting.

> *Fay:* Jody, you have the next report: current uses of flextime and anticipated changes due to employees' child and elder care needs.
>
> *Jody:* Fay, you know we're still having those e-mail problems, so my survey to employees was bounced back twice. I managed to do only an informal focus group to try to get some sense of the demand.
>
> *Fay:* I'm sorry there were those difficulties. What do you have?
>
> *Jody:* [pauses] Before I tell you what little I have, I have to say how frustrated I am with the short time between meetings and how much we are asked to do. I know one of our ground rules is "come to meetings prepared" and it makes sense at first glance. But can't we look at some kind of adjustment when things beyond our control frustrate our efforts?
>
> *David:* If we are raising issues to discuss about the ground rules, I'd like to have some discussion on "begin and end meetings on time." I know that in this meeting while we were waiting for two people to join us—they had a good reason for the delay: their emergency meeting with the executive director—we had some really good informal catch-up and discussion. I don't want to lose that quality of conversation for the remaining meetings we have.
>
> *Fay:* Well, I don't want to stand in the way of improving how we work, but I don't see a lot of time in today's agenda to review the rules or deal with problems that undercut people being prepared for our meetings. Hmmmm.

◆◆ *Reflection.* In this case, certain individuals recognized the need for ways of evaluating and revising their expectations of how the group does business. Without building in the time to do so—or the expectation that such a focus on process matters—the evaluation is disruptive and a cause of resentment. Had the group included a periodic opportunity to reflect and revise the ground rules, such disruption and resentment might have been avoided.

What Ordinary Ground Rules Don't Do

Despite the weaknesses we have shown, many groups do benefit from the common practice of ground rules. Groups that adopt ground rules do so because they expect them to fulfill the need for predictability and clear guidance. However, groups have needs greater than those at the functional level, and ordinary ground rules and how they are used do not meet those needs.

Common Rules Are Culture Bound

Most common ground rules in use today have evolved from a Western tradition that emphasizes efficiency and individuality. These are not necessarily unimportant values. However, in today's workplaces, communities, and even families, diverse cultural and racial representation are not uncommon. Such diversity requires additional considerations. For instance, mediators commonly use the ground rule "speak only for yourself" without a second thought. Conflict resolution trainers emphasize the need to teach people to use "I-statements," as in "When you don't show up at our agreed-upon time, I get angry because I work hard to be on time." Yet some cultures would view I-statements as inappropriate, ego-centered statements that violate a cultural norm of giving greater weight to the community's views than to any individual's perspective.

A further problem with common rules of this sort is that they may ignore the realities of racial, cultural, and gender differences and in so doing reinforce hierarchy and domination along racial or cultural lines. An elicitive and inductive approach to creating shared expectations may prevent this problem. However, it may well be necessary for a group leader or facilitator to offer special attention to the dynamics of race, culture, and gender in order to allow groups to confront their differences directly and in a positive way. There is a strong habit of silence on such potentially sensitive and controversial matters, especially in mixed groups. That silence will not likely be broken without an explicit invitation to do so.

Rules Overlook Assets and Opportunities

By their nature, rules connote standards and strictures to prevent disorder, unfairness, or harm. They have a negative cast: their goal is to avoid pitfalls or deficiencies in people or groups. Many ground rules are prohibitive, telling people what not to do.

Ordinary ground rules direct people away from ways to be inspired or to seek the potential benefits of their interaction. As we describe later, there is a way to rethink ground rules as "shared expectations" and jointly created values and aspirations. While ordinary rules may be useful to some extent, they become more meaningful and valuable through a perspective that promotes reaching for higher ground.

Lack of Focus on Outcomes

Common ground rules do not raise our expectations or our aspirations regarding the good that can come from shared work and the experience of accomplishing the work together. Ground rules can be useful as a support for group work if they speak less of order and more of meaningful accomplishments and desired outcomes.

No Explicit Link to Underlying Principles and Goals

Rarely are the principles or goals behind ground rules clearly stated (Schwarz, 1994). Even less often is the nature of the group's membership and its history or experience with ground rules examined.

Without a firm understanding of the values underlying a particular set of ground rules, control can become constraint, brevity of rules can leave too much uncertainty, and following the rules can diminish creativity and hinder reaching good decisions.

Finally, we showed earlier that ground rules are usually given to a group rather than created by them. The directive nature of the introduction of ground rules is a significant defect. Similarly, because the attitude in presenting ground rules is one of moving quickly through some preliminaries, real understanding of the ground rules and the opportunity to probe, revise, and test the rules to ensure common understanding is absent. If there is a way to look efficiently at how people want to work together and to clarify some general aspirations and expectations, group members are more likely to have a common view about the usefulness of any particular ground rule, and about how all the rules work together.

In the previous chapter, we showed that often there are no jointly developed shared expectations—only the "slippery seven" assumed and unspoken rules for responding to conflict. In this chapter, we looked at how ordinary ground rules are introduced and commonly used. The shortcomings we have noted may be minimal in any particular setting, but given enough time they almost inevitably create problems for many kinds of groups, whether parent-teacher organizations, neighborhood associations, or interdepartmental teams in the workplace. So what is a better way to create and use ground rules?

The better way is to reach for higher ground. At the beginning of the book, we drew a picture of the difference between common ground and higher ground. In the next chapter we explore in some detail the meaning of higher ground. Then, in Chapter Five we examine specific steps for developing explicit, shared expectations for reaching higher ground in many kinds of groups. To round out the general picture of higher ground, Chapter Six offers tools for evaluating a group's functioning in relation to higher-ground ideals, and practical advice for helping group members uncover deeper values to guide their work.

Chapter Four

Beyond Common Ground Rules

Reaching for *Higher* Ground

So, if the usual ways that mediators, facilitators, and other group leaders approach ground rules have flaws, what can be done differently? What exactly does it mean to reach for higher ground?

In the previous chapter we highlighted much of what you have already experienced—all that can go wrong when you have not cocreated and honored shared expectations. In the Preface we introduced the several dimensions of higher ground: *principled* ground, *new* ground, a *refuge*, a *place of enlarged perspective, shared ground,* and a continuing *challenge*. In this chapter we begin our exploration of this new territory as we define *higher ground* and draw a picture of what we mean by reaching for higher ground (RHG). We offer an approach that moves what passes for shared expectations—common ground rules—from being used as a precursor to group work, swiftly addressed and quickly forgotten, to being an ongoing and essential part of accomplishing the work.

Reaching high sounds daunting and maybe unrealistic for *your* group or community, right? There's not enough time and there is little inclination to explore fundamental aspirations when a decision has to be reached *today*. Reaching *common* ground is hard enough in your family, workplace, or community and is more valuable than chasing some kind of elusive higher ground, right? Well, we don't think so!

Although it may be neither quick nor easy, RHG fulfills many groups' needs for purpose and direction better than deadlines, crises, and shifting politics. It is no accident when a family, group, or community works through its problems, challenges, or conflicts in a manner that nurtures authentically strengthened relationships and sustainable solutions to problems rather than through ritually polite behavior and uneasy and fragile truces. Such outcomes require vision, leadership, and skill. RHG offers group leaders the possibility of increasing a group's capacity to do its business and make decisions each and every time members sit down together. Continuously improving a group's process is one sure way to increase its productivity; but even more important, working this way is ultimately more effective, efficient, humane, enjoyable, and culture-enhancing.

We've introduced higher ground as a powerful metaphor for behavior that allows us to bring community out of conflict. It is a place where people treat each other as they themselves wish to be treated, and in doing so they come to new understandings about their shared work, their relationships, and their collective potential. It is a *destination* as well as an *outcome*. RHG means, then, developing the strategies, skills, and stamina for the journey, and exercising the leadership necessary to guide others to this unfamiliar, principled, and promising place. We spend the next several chapters offering the tools for you to do just that. But RHG first requires a vision of what is possible. Each of the elements of higher ground represents a requirement for building community in the midst of conflict. So let's take a look at the several dimensions of the metaphor and see what they mean in practice.

Principled Ground

Higher ground is first and foremost *principled* ground. RHG means seeking the high road, where truth telling and truth seeking are honored, where integrity is valued, and where trust is given because trust is earned.

Very often group work seems to require compromising your principles. Total honesty can get you into trouble. Concern for fairness may be a way of being taken to the cleaners by a wily opponent. Inclusion of diverse viewpoints just complicates things and bogs down the work.

Open discussion and pursuit of principles or ideals are not common in many public settings and sadly, for many people, they are not even common in our private lives. Professional and community contexts prove a particular challenge when work is carried out amid egos, politics, and the constant pressure to expedite matters. But the RHG approach makes discussion and practice of such matters practical and appropriate.

RHG means inviting people to create an environment in which principled behavior is demanded and, when agreed to by all, expected. This aspect of higher ground elevates the conversation about ground rules, moving it from a discussion of lowest-common-denominator rules of conduct for politeness and efficiency to a discussion of principled behavior for solid, meaningful relationships.

❖ *Snapshot.* From 1997 to 1998, a group of twenty-three leaders—bishops, professors, and lay leaders—in the United Methodist Church (UMC) struggled with whether there could be a way to maintain their denominational unity amid theological division. They were called together to try to help their denomination see some way forward after many contentious conventions at the regional and national level. The most prominent division was, and continues to be, over how to deal with homosexuality in the church setting.

These Methodists were called together to dialogue. But before they had even sat down, they developed core principles about how best to approach dialogue amid distrust, divergent values, and high stakes. The UMC agency sponsoring the dialogue was widely seen as aligned with the more liberal wing of the denomination. How could anything they sponsor be trusted by moderates and conservatives? The principled ground they used in setting up the dialogue was to convene five people—two conservatives, two liberals, and the agency director—to direct all aspects of the dialogue.

The planning group decided the dialogue's purpose, who participated, the materials distributed in advance, and how to deal with the press. John was the facilitator of this group. The first time he met the five-person planning group face to face was at the initial dialogue session. He saw how the principles of equality, fairness, and inclusion were essential both to how the dialogue was designed and to how the goal was envisioned. In this way, principles become core elements of both *how* they did things and what they sought.

❖ *Reflection.* How could a facilitator feel comfortable working with a group like this only through conference calls until the first dialogue session?

It is a big challenge. In this case, John had previous contacts that lessened this obstacle. First, two of the organizers, one conservative and one liberal, were interviewees for research he had conducted earlier on the homosexuality and standards of faith conflict in the UMC. He had interviewed them by phone after reading a book they had jointly edited. In the book, contributors from each side spoke to specific points of contention on homosexuality: biblical interpretation, how the UMC takes and enforces stands on social issues, pastoral care of homosexuals, and so on. In fact, the book was conceived as part of some informal dialogues among the two organizers and other leading pastors and theology school professors. Thus they had already made some clear moves to "reach across the aisle." Finally John was asked to attend the semi-annual board meeting of the UMC organizing agency in October 1998, where he met the executive director.

The eight million plus members of the UMC are far from common ground on homosexuality. However, the dialogue was hailed not only by the liberals and conservatives in the room but also by many others as a fresh step and as an effort imbued with inclusion and respect amid differences to see if there remained ways to keep the "United" in United Methodist Church.

New Ground

Higher ground also represents *new ground:* an opportunity to explore and discover that which is as yet unimagined. Too often, work on a team project, in a neighborhood group, or in a civic association asks us to accept less than we need and far less than we want. Multiply that outcome by the number of people involved and it is no wonder that group work is often feared as a necessary evil, an invitation to mediocrity, and a virtual guarantee of less than satisfying outcomes.

Too often the response to conflict is a quick compromise. Compromise can be useful, but a group falls short of its potential when compromise results from fear of conflict or a failure of imagination. Split the difference; give and take; threaten, promise and cajole—what is acceptable is often simply a matter of seeing the middle ground and figuring out the trade-offs needed to reach what is already seen.

RHG calls for openness to imagination, exploration, and discovery. The contours of higher ground can seldom be seen from where you start. The mountain is before you but you don't have an airplane from which to look down on it from above. You have many choices of how to ascend the mountain. The peak itself is often a surprise—in terms of both what you can see back at the base and what you can see from the crest. RHG techniques are creative, exploratory, and filled with the tension of discovery—the risk, the fear, and the excitement.

❖❖   *Snapshot.* Across the United States, mental health advocacy organizations and health service providers have been working for years to achieve what is called *parity of insurance benefits* between behavioral (or mental health) disorders and what are commonly thought of as physical illnesses. Such efforts have met with resistance from many members of the business community and the insurance industry, as well as public officials, all of whom are wary of adding additional costs on top of already burgeoning health care expenses.

A bill was introduced in one state legislature that would have mandated parity between mental and physical health for most group insurance benefits. Because the bill involved an insurance mandate, it was deferred for consideration and referred to a special advisory commission to make recommendations to the state legislature for the following legislative session. An Insurance Parity Task Force, representing all the key stakeholders, was appointed by the commission to examine the issues and see whether they could make a recommendation acceptable to all parties. Frank and a colleague co-mediated the task force. Membership included representatives from insurance companies, the business community, mental health advocacy organizations, and mental health service providers, as well as state legislators and agency representatives.

At the first meeting, Frank and his co-mediator offered a set of recommended protocols for the task force. The mediators emphasized the meaning of consensus, which in this case meant that each task force member needed to endorse any recommendations to the commission. Frank heard through more than one informal channel that some task force members found the first meeting's emphasis on ground rules and consensus overbearing and even patronizing. This assessment reflected in part different understandings among task force members about how the group would make decisions. The mediators' understanding had always been that a full consensus (agreement among all members) would be required to report any recommendations. Some task force members came into the process thinking that they would use majority rule for any recommendations.

For purposes of the task force, consensus was defined as having the following characteristics:

- Everyone can live with the final agreements without compromising issues of fundamental importance.
- Individual portions of the agreement may be less than ideal for some members, but the overall package is worthy of support.

- Individuals will work to support the full agreement and not just the parts they like best.

Reasons for using consensus included the following:

- Individual participants who might be skeptical of working with opponents or with people they don't know are reassured by having veto power over any decisions.
- Group members know that they need to attempt to satisfy the needs of all participants.
- Minority views that may have been summarily dismissed are given real consideration.
- A norm of responsibility for the group may be enhanced.
- As a practical matter, decisions with broad-based support are more likely to be implemented. In this instance, any one of the parties could have derailed recommendations made by the rest of the group.

A first prerequisite for reaching consensus is the commitment of group members to the process. The mediators periodically noted that a consensus-based decision process requires patience, listening, active participation, and a good bit of faith in the participants as well as in the process. It means coming to meetings prepared. It also means accepting and sharing responsibility for the process and the outcome.

As it turned out, the early emphasis on the ground rules and consensus made a vital contribution to the eventual agreement of the task force. Eight full meetings were held along with numerous telephone and in-person discussions among various parties and several smaller meetings of three task force subcommittees. The last meeting concluded with endorsement of eight "areas of agreement," three policy recommendations, and many pages of supporting reasoning.

The group's enthusiasm for these results was quickly dampened, however, when the single member who was absent from the previous meeting raised substantial objections to the language of one of the areas of agreement. Unfortunately, although not coincidentally, that language had been the subject of intense discussion at the previous meeting, and the compromise that had been reached had tested the patience of several members. The objecting member made clear his intention to withhold support from the report, and those representing different interests refused to consider any changes.

This objection and its repercussions reflected the importance of consensus as a ground rule. When questioned about whether a single member could destroy the consensus of the rest of the group, Frank was able to return to the ground rules, pointing out not only the violation of task force policy and the spirit of collaboration that such an action would entail, but also the likely impact on implementation that a key figure's active opposition would cause.

One group member then went directly to the objector, inviting this person to explain the objections and explore whether new language might be crafted that would satisfy everybody's interests. To everyone's surprise, and delight, the changes the objector wanted not only made clearer what had been somewhat ambiguous (in this case deliberately, because of continuing differences), but they also reflected a view that was preferred by the whole group to the original language. In this case, the task force members' agreement to seek consensus not only allowed but also demanded that they find new ground when impasse was threatened.

The task force was only too pleased to endorse the new language. The advisory commission, whose judgment on any legislation was given great weight by the state legislature, was also more than pleased to pass along these recommendations. Legislation was then passed easily.

◆◆ *Reflection.* It is typical for groups to resist and resent spending valuable time on what they think is unnecessary, and many people think that attention to ground rules is unnecessary. It is never too early to begin educating people about the need for attention to how members of a group will work together. This task force, however, was fully assembled before Frank and his co-mediator were brought in, which made it difficult to educate participants before the first meeting about the requirements of consensus processes. Frank did contact each task force member by telephone before the first meeting and realizes in retrospect that he could have better emphasized how important it was for task force members to develop their ground rules during those conversations.

Recent research (Innes, 1999) supports the need for participant development of group process and ground rules. Frank now brings that research to the attention of groups. Providing such justification, whether through research or other rationale, can help allay concerns that taking time to develop ground rules as a group is just a mediator's or facilitator's way of wasting time.

A New and Enlarged Perspective

Higher ground also offers a new and enlarged perspective—a new view not only of the whole picture but also of how each individual fits into that picture.

Can people truly see and agree on the big picture? What does that mean? At the core of any sound group experience is mutual and reciprocal education that contributes to a shared framing of the problem. All too often, when threatened by conflict we fall back on our positions and defend them against all attack, real or imagined. Yet it is precisely when conflict occurs that we most need to seek understanding of one another's needs, values, and concerns. This type of understanding is not necessarily comforting. The size of problems can be even bigger than realized, such as when you get on a hill and see the extent of a flood or fire. But without an understanding of what is really at stake, of the meaning people bring to an issue, and of a problem's impact on each member of the community, individuals and groups will not have the opportunity to bring forth their best ideas for tasks, options, needs, and potential solutions.

❖❖ **Snapshot.** Neighborhood activists were outraged when a state department of transportation proposed an enormous "fly-over" for an intersection of an interstate highway adjacent to a treasured city park. Business and other community leaders, however, argued that something needed to be done to alleviate growing congestion and safety concerns. An advisory group of citizens and technical support staff was formed as a result of the controversy to work in conjunction with the technical studies being conducted. Because the issues had generated significant conflict that lingered a full year after the initial fly-over proposal came to light, the advisory group engaged Frank and a co-mediator to lead the process. Considerable time was spent developing process protocols and ground rules for behavior. Yet what was not actually listed in these ground rules—the need and opportunity for learning—became the most important shared expectation of the group. Members commented repeatedly about the learning that occurred and about the new and enlarged perspective they developed. In the evaluation conducted after an agreement was reached and a final report was issued, comments about what participants valued the most included, "The open discussion that allowed us to understand each neighborhood's problems" and "Information and education." Indeed, eleven of thirteen members responding gave the highest ranking possible to the question, "Do you have a greater understanding of the issues?"

◆◆ **Reflection.** In this case, what was *not* listed in the ground rules—the need and opportunity for learning—is what became the most important shared expectation of the group. Was this an oversight in creating the ground rules? Should it have been stated up front?

Frank's answer is a strong "perhaps." Some advisory committee members came into the process with an understanding that they would be learning about transportation, land-use planning, and the concerns and needs of parties to the dispute. It may well have been useful to ask the whole group to include in its protocols and ground rules an explicit statement about the need for learning.

However, as is typical in disputes where positions have already been staked out and opposition has been identified, most participants entered into the process with a great deal of skepticism about its potential and convinced that their main task was to advocate for their views. It was only in the process of seeking information and exchanging views that members came to realize how much they *were* learning and how much they *needed* to learn, and how valuable it was to engage people with different views and experiences.

It was the *attitude* toward learning that changed and that needed to change. Adding a rule at the beginning of the process that had little support would not have helped change that attitude and might have provoked opposition. This perspective is common to all successful groups. Frank and his co-mediator led the group to formalize the recognition of the importance of learning and an enlarged view not through a change of ground rules but through periodic evaluation, both formal (within the group) and informal (in individual conversations among advisory committee members).

Think back to John's work with the Methodists on homosexuality. Although there are still continuing differences about the relationship between individuals' beliefs and their interaction with those who hold different views, the religious context presented an opportunity for everyone to reflect on an important question: No matter what we each believe on this particular matter, how would God want us to act toward one another?

Highlighting how one goes about advocating one's views on important theological matters put several values in the forefront and helped redefine the conflict, at least in part. One outcome was the realization that some members from both sides of the conflict—conservative and liberal—had the same view about the likely future of the conflict. These "incompatibilists" judged that all the discussion that was needed had already occurred. They concluded that the contending views were essentially incompatible and that one side would eventually have to leave the denomination. At the same time, the dialogue group also learned that other conservatives and liberals believed that the UMC had not reached the breaking point.

They looked to differences on other important issues—abortion, for example—where there was continuing significant contention over the denomination's policy, but members were not talking about leaving the church over that issue. Thus, the new and enlarged perspective showed that the compatibilist/incompatiblist difference is an important alignment related to homosexuality and the future of the UMC that does not reinforce liberal and conservative divisions.

A Refuge

Higher ground is a *refuge*—a safe haven from the incivility and outright nastiness that too often accompany conflict.

Imagine yourself being overwhelmed by a flood of unwanted emotions or unforeseen and insurmountable obstacles. Higher ground can be a refuge just as actual high ground is from a real flood. Sometimes such refuge may mean that an individual retreats from social demands for a time for much needed solitude and reflection. However, in the RHG perspective, refuge is a safe, even sacred space where people from different backgrounds know they will be heard and understood, where their needs and ideas will be respected, and where they can do the difficult work of reconciling differences. It is a place where neither flight nor fight is necessary, regardless of the unpopularity of your views or the number of your allies. The RHG approach builds in safety and freedom of expression for all participants.

At their best, churches often represent these ideas of welcoming, safety, and high purpose. Indeed, many buildings created for overtly spiritual purposes are called sanctuaries. These places resonate with many faiths' ideas of a higher power who offers a spiritual security that transcends material wants and deprivations.

We do not advocate seeking principled ground in the same way that religion often calls for adherence to certain doctrines and rituals. Indeed, these shared expectations that make up the journey and destination of higher ground must be created together to have their greatest import. Yet we recognize that as we paint a picture of principled behavior, the dimension of spirit and emotion must be part of the palette. This may seem out of place with the vision of the workplace or civic group as secular and compassionate but definitely not churchlike. We agree with those who express concern that workplace and community groups are too removed from engaging the passion, spirit, and emotional connection needed for RHG. Therefore, RHG, like pastoral counseling, seeks to create safety for venting, for recognizing humility and sometimes humiliation, and for expressing pain and anger. RHG means making the spaces we create for problem solving and conflict resolution more resonant with the spirit of every person in the group.

❖ *Snapshot.* In a school district that had long enjoyed an amicable labor-management relationship, a clash developed between the teachers' union and the school board and administration over a proposed plan for merit pay. It derailed contract negotiations and threatened to redefine what had long been a productive partnership. The group agreed to settle other parts of the contract and defer any decision on the merit pay proposal until a joint effort could be undertaken to study the proposal and make recommendations.

Marina was enlisted to facilitate a group of ten union representatives and ten representatives of the school board, community, and administration. Her first task was to help create safe conditions and a productive context for discussing the issue. The teachers expressed great trepidation about openly confronting board members and administrators for fear of reprisal in contract negotiations, work conditions, or matters of personnel evaluation.

The development of shared expectations for how the group members would treat one another and about the conditions necessary for a constructive effort had to be forged before the group could discuss clearly and honestly the motivations each side brought to the merit pay issue. Each side needed to understand the confusion, fear, anger, and resentment that had developed within and between the groups in response to the merit pay proposal and the events that followed. Helping each side develop empathy for the other seemed essential prior to discussion of the original proposal's merits and flaws.

A mutual understanding of the problem was reached and was the basis for seeing what solutions were possible. Eventually the negotiators co-created a new plan they believed in and could jointly advocate to teachers, parents, and their community. As is so often the case, the group's work was more than developing a plan they could all live with. Group members needed to understand the importance of engendering a commitment to shape their shared future and respecting the conditions that would prove necessary for successfully completing this work together.

❖ *Reflection.* We've talked about how the RHG approach seeks to create safety for expressing uncomfortable emotions, such as pain, humiliation, and anger. Yet many groups would not readily appreciate the need to make time and space for this type of sharing.

Marina's perception that group members needed to address their feelings of anger and resentment was not shared by everyone in the group. Early on, some of the group's most powerful members expressed frustration with the process, saying, "Is this really necessary? Wouldn't it be better if we just got on with the task?" This is not an uncommon reaction and it is often a delicate point in the group's formation. It is also a delicate moment in which credibility and trust of the facilitator is enhanced or diminished.

In our experience, resistance to a facilitator's efforts to examine and address the emotional environment or context in which a negotiation is to occur often comes from the most powerful or privileged members of a group. In such moments we try to remember that if we fail to interrupt an unbalanced power dynamic at that early point in a group process, we will probably not fully recover our credibility with the less powerful members of the group. If we seem unable to address the imbalance of power, we are probably seen as incapable of creating a safe place, a refuge in which to do the work.

In this case, Marina had to help the group members learn about one another's sense of safety while at the same time not forcing her interpretations on the group. She did this by asking each member to complete the following sentences: "My greatest fear about participating in this process is . . ." and "My greatest hope for this group is. . . ." This exercise created a space for exposing the concerns that Marina sensed existed but that had not been openly acknowledged.

The discussion that ensued from the question about their greatest fears made clear that not everyone had the same level of confidence in or comfort with this process and their participation in it. Some board members were surprised by the teachers' comments about fear of retribution from superiors and being seen as traitors by their fellow union members for sitting down to discuss the pay-for-performance issue. It was clear that the board members did not comprehend the extent to which trust between the two groups had been broken. Likewise, upon hearing the board members express seemingly genuine surprise at this reality, teachers began questioning the sinister motives that had been attributed to the district's leadership in proposing the plan.

The members' responses to the question about their greatest hope began to guide the group toward common ground, and even toward higher ground about how people wished to feel about each other and the entire process at its conclusion. It opened the eyes of the less patient members to the need for moving carefully into the work and for working in a way that sought to repair the damage done in the past, not merely to build a plan for the future.

With this information now on the table, Marina invited the group to consider the need for developing ground rules or a set of shared expectations about how best to create a safe and productive place to do their work. A thoughtful set of guidelines was developed and the group demonstrated a high level of commitment to them throughout the six-month process. Had Marina jumped right into the task of building ground rules without attending to the need for sanctuary and refuge, teacher participation would likely have been guarded, board members would have judged as wasteful the time spent developing shared expectations for constructive engagement, and few would have participated as authentically as they did.

Shared Ground

Higher ground must also represent *shared* ground.

We can fool ourselves into thinking that higher ground can be an exclusive place, that we can simply retreat into a comfortable setting with those who think and act and maybe even look like ourselves. Higher ground may be taken as a refuge from responsibility, or it may imply looking down on others from our position of superiority. Too often we think that our way is the only higher way.

The metaphor of higher ground reminds us that groups and communities of all sizes function best when members consider one another's needs. Our expectations for dealing with each other must be created together or we will find ourselves alone on the hill. We may also find others resentful of being left behind and motivated to pull the king off the hill rather than share the peak. There is a fundamental dynamic tension at play in group problem solving—how to move ahead, while leaving no one behind.

A *commons* used to be a place where community business was conducted and where all members of the community could see their obligations to one another represented in the space of shared ground. Similarly, the most effective groups and communities are those whose members take responsibility for their own commons, in whatever forms it might take.

Very often, participants in negotiations represent constituencies unable to be present for direct talks. In many instances, the fruits of the shared work must be shared with those constituencies.

The RHG approach requires that practical strategies be used to expand the commons, reaching out to those who might otherwise be left behind. Failure to extend the invitation to reach for higher ground to all who share a stake in the group's business is to risk isolation from the group and failure of the agreements so painstakingly built by the group's representatives.

If everyone is to reach higher ground, the representatives must serve as guides and scouts to those who will follow. If those not directly involved do not develop trust in the process, the negotiators will find themselves without the support necessary to maintain their footing on higher ground. The RHG approach requires that such problems be avoided by making those issues a conscious and deliberate part of the group's shared expectations.

❖ *Snapshot.* In the previous case that Marina just shared, one important challenge to creating a transformative environment in which people feel safe to take risks and shift perspectives when the dialogue warrants such shifts was met by an emphasis on trust building through protection of confidentiality. But the effort to build trust, while successful within the negotiating group, wreaked havoc on the negotiated merit pay proposal process described earlier.

The negotiating group was greatly concerned about the problems that might arise from information being shared with others outside the meetings. Information taken out of context, information miscommunicated, or incomplete proposals could sabotage the process and thwart the group's efforts to be open and honest and to take risks. Yet they concluded that information had to be shared with others outside the group to keep them informed of the group's progress and invested in the outcome of the negotiation. They decided it would be wise to limit ongoing information to sharing details about the agendas and impressions of the value and quality of the process. Discussion of actual proposals would be kept inside the group until something firm existed and was agreed upon by all members. The group dutifully recorded and reported the appropriate information throughout the process. They recognized the inherent difficulty of achieving broad-based support for a once-rejected and emotionally charged idea. As a result of the conclusions of their work, great effort went into the design of a process for jointly communicating the plan and engaging the larger constituencies in evaluating and refining the plan.

Much to the group's dismay the plan failed to achieve the majority vote from teachers that was needed for its adoption. In the end the proposal was narrowly rejected simply because it wasn't trusted by enough people who had been excluded from the discussion. Ironically, the privacy established to create safety and trust among the negotiators as they hashed out options and created a new proposal created mistrust in the product of their work. People expressed confusion and suspicion about how the teachers who were directly involved could have come so far from their position of opposing the original merit pay plan. The transformation that occurred for both sides was evident in the proposal but seemed too great a leap to have been made in so short a time. Somehow and in some way, those not present in the room needed to make the climb to higher ground for themselves.

◆ *Reflection.* Could the group have reduced the likelihood of the teachers' rejection of the proposed plan?

One obvious possibility for bringing others to higher ground was to share more information about the substance of negotiations with rank-and-file teachers as the group did its work. However, such sharing may not have been constructive. The group was too fragile and their work was too controversial to expose it to critique until the ideas were well-formed and tentative agreements had been reached.

In hindsight, the group might have been better served by altering the end game. The group spent considerable effort thinking about how to "sell" the completed plan to the union membership. They decided that a joint presentation made by all stakeholders represented in the facilitated negotiation of the plan was essential. They also decided that it would be best to do it in one large group presentation so that the message was consistent and there was less chance of miscommunication, misinformation, and unconstructive hearsay. The group decided to convene the entire teaching staff of the district in an auditorium for an hour-and-a-half presentation. No information was given to teachers prior to the large-group presentation. Question and answer (Q&A) sessions led by teachers were scheduled at individual schools as follow-ups to the large-group presentation. The formal vote to ratify or reject the plan would follow the completion of the school-based Q&A sessions.

In retrospect, it would have been best if the written plan had been distributed to all teachers prior to any formal presentation. Perhaps the Q&A sessions at individual schools should have preceded the large-group session, with common concerns and issues being captured for greater attention during the districtwide session. It might have felt like teachers in each individual school were being given more voice and consideration in the process. Their reactions to the plan may have been more open and forthcoming in safer, more familiar environs (that is, in their own schools), and any points that needed clarification and refinement could have been addressed before the large-group presentation.

The principles applied to the negotiating group should have been applied to the large group: Start small and go slowly until safety and a degree of trust are established. Create a place for venting so that ideas can be viewed without the burden of strong emotion. These techniques worked in the negotiated group. It might have worked to secure interest and acceptance of the process and its outcomes by the union membership.

A Challenge

Reaching higher ground is always a challenge. After all, it does take effort to move uphill.

A search for principled ground implies a search for justice and fairness. A refuge, an enlarged perspective, and shared ground all call for imperatives to recognize injustice. We know that there are individuals who seek unfair advantage, who exploit racial or class or gender differences, and who prefer to maintain disparities that favor themselves. Challenging such behavior can mean considerable turmoil before a new, fairer order is achieved.

Guiding a family, a work group, or a community to higher ground is not easy, particularly where the old ground is well known and comfortable or where people are trying to hold you back. When you climb into the unknown, it is scary; you can slip and fall.

A poster that Frank saw next to the copier in his church delightfully illustrates this dimension. It proclaims that we are too often Protestant in our views about conflict and too seldom Buddhist. That is, we think that the community we seek will bring an end to conflict. In fact, the community we seek will not be without conflict, but it will include the expectation that conflict is normal, that people can confront one another over their differences without violating some unspoken principle about "being nice," and that the hard work of reconciling differences can bring satisfaction and fulfillment.

As the last snapshot illustrated, RHG is challenging. Marina was surprised and enriched by the group's generally upbeat attitudes in light of the proposal's failure. In spite of the apparent waste of countless hours and great personal effort on each of their parts, they were not devastated. As explanation, one board member who early on had expressed great frustration with the time being invested in the process said, "I don't believe we have failed here at all. I now know, without a doubt, that *we* can solve any problem that comes our way, if we do it together. *Nothing* can change that!" His comment was met with enthusiasm by the group. Things had changed. The process had changed them and offered a fresh start for future challenges.

We have begun to explore the many dimensions of higher ground—principled behavior, a new and enlarged view, new ground, a refuge, shared ground, and a challenge. For professionals in the workplace, for neighbors and citizens in their communities, and for parents and children in the family, RHG means transforming the very idea of ground rules. RHG changes rule making from a necessary and brief first step in doing business into a living, continuing part of the relationships that make business, community, and family durable, productive, safe, and supportive.

RHG involves risks, not the least of which is failure. RHG can also take more time in the beginning. But it can save time as well and make a group's time together more productive, effective, and fulfilling. RHG can provide the immediate pay-off of achieving sustainable agreements. But RHG offers more than agreements; it also helps to build effective groups and cohesive and highly functioning teams. It provides an avenue for ongoing personal learning. It nurtures the development of each individual involved. RHG is, at its essence, about the mutual and inseparable nature of growth and accomplishment.

How can this approach be practical in the real world of time-limited and resource-limited settings? How can it be put into action given the habit-bound cultures of our workplaces, our professions, our communities, and our families? How, indeed, can your efforts stand high as a beacon for others to follow? We take up these important and practical matters in the next chapter.

Chapter Five

Creating Shared Expectations

The Six Keys to Success

So you've decided that your work group, team, or committee has not been handling its members' differences very well; or a couple you're counseling can't talk to their adolescent children about important issues without angry recriminations; or the town you manage is facing a contentious public issue and experience indicates that you are going to be dealing with angry citizens and frustrated public officials for a long time. What concrete steps can you take to begin to develop higher ground?

In this chapter we present both principles and specific steps for developing explicit, shared expectations for higher ground in all sorts of groups. As we discussed in the Preface, in their most complete form such shared expectations may be thought of as *covenants*. Again, we do not mean the type of covenant that restricts entry into the group on the basis of race or religion; rather, we mean covenant as a mutual promise, entered into deliberately and deeply, that describes a group's highest aspirations. A covenant for higher ground consists of two parts: a *vision* describing the values and desired outcomes that define the higher ground a group seeks, and the specific behavioral agreements, or ground rules, that are intended to enact those values and achieve those outcomes.

Many groups will find the creation of a covenant (or whatever they call their agreements) a valuable, enlightening, and even exhilarating experience. However, not all groups can go so far as to create a covenant. For some groups or in some settings a written covenant would be inappropriate or impossible. This does not mean that such groups cannot reach for higher ground. But the process of creating such expectations in these circumstances requires adaptation of the model we describe in this chapter. Here we focus our attention on full implementation of the reaching for higher ground (RHG) approach. In later chapters we offer suggestions on how best to modify this approach for those settings where the fullest expression of higher ground is impractical or impossible.

In this chapter we introduce the concept of a *toolbox* of techniques. You will find these tips in the "From the Toolbox" sections throughout the text.

The Path to Higher Ground: Six Elements for Creating a Group Covenant

Most experienced facilitators and group leaders agree that it is important to establish some basic agreements about how a group will address differences, whether such agreements are called ground rules, group promises, community commitments, protocols, or other forms of shared expectations. But few people have spent much time thinking about how best to create these shared expectations. Indeed, many groups are guilty of a one-size-fits-all approach to working with ground rules. They have their routines that fit nicely in their comfort zone. Most people have some ideas for ground rules that they've picked up either by watching how other people lead groups or through their own trial-and-error experiences. Sometimes an approach seems helpful and sometimes it doesn't. Either way, the attitude of a group leader or facilitator is often "Let's get the ground rules over with so we can get on with the real business of the group."

If you look at successful groups whose interactions are characterized by open and civil discourse, mutual respect, and commitment to enacting a shared vision—in short, by higher ground—you will find that they have taken a variety of paths to get to the same destination. Yet those paths, while winding their way through different terrain, require the same planning and preparation, the same clearing of brush, the same firm surface underfoot, the same guardrails, and the same coordination of effort to define and proceed toward a common goal.

We have identified the following six key elements that will allow you to create your own path to higher ground, whatever your group:

1. *Establish the need:* Seek understanding and agreement about the need for shared expectations for higher ground
2. *Educate and inspire:* Offer sufficient support, including time for reflection and discussion, illustrations of other covenants or ground rules, examples of how the other rules have been used and abused, and indications of commitment from group leadership to developing and honoring a covenant
3. *Begin by envisioning desired outcomes:* What are the outcomes that will define higher ground for your group? After envisioning them, develop the specific ground rules that will allow you to reach these outcomes.
4. *Promote full participation:* Work hard to give each group member a voice in developing the covenant.
5. *Be accountable:* Honor the agreements contained in the covenant.
6. *Evaluate and revise:* Evaluate, modify, and recommit as appropriate.

Element 1: Establish the Need

The first element in creating a group covenant is establishing the need for shared expectations for higher ground.

Successful groups begin by assessing what their needs are. Group size, the degree of trust among members, the degree of members' trust in the group leader or facilitator, power imbalances, time constraints, the public or private nature of the process, the diversity of group members, and the intended duration of the relationships all have impacts on group needs. For example, a group that is discussing issues in which there is little controversy, or in which members do not vary significantly by race or culture or in which the stakes are not particularly high, may require little more than a few basic agreements about how group members will relate to one another to be productive. Such guidelines may be provided by recognized leadership and willingly accepted with little or no discussion by group members.

Conversely, a group whose members represent diverse backgrounds and interests, or who are discussing issues of great significance or who will be working together over a long period, has very different needs. The motivations of a leader who attempts to impose guidelines may be questioned, participants may have divergent ways of dealing with their differences, or they may have very different understandings about what makes a group effective.

Building a group's interest in and commitment to creating shared expectations is critical. One practical strategy for reducing the likelihood of unproductive behavior and group dynamics is simply to help people recognize their interdependence. Articulating shared expectations and commitments as part of the group's process can link members to one another and to their shared task. Even if a group's history is bitter and tangled, the group can still be helped by acknowledging that the discomfort will go on unless together they make it stop. Mediators perform this function when they congratulate people for coming to the mediation; they recognize that such an action is a major step toward solving the problem and building a different future.

If you sense that participants are not adequately buying into the value of agreements for working together, don't suppress that perception. Indeed, you should anticipate that perception in groups where race, gender, power, or other characteristics that engender differences exist, and work to bring those concerns to the surface. Bring them into the conversation by asking, "What alternatives are there to working this out together?" Then engage in a process of exploring "if-then" relationships between actions and likely consequences. If group members are deeply divided into opposing camps, this process may be best done in same-constituency (small) groups where conversation can be less guarded. Such a group would serve as a caucus for various parties, allowing them to determine the reasons for their commitment to, or skepticism about, the process.

❖❖ *Snapshot.* Marina once participated in a group training session on consensus building that began with session leaders presenting and imposing a set of ground rules. Little effort was made to establish the need for such rules. Instead, the leaders presumed that such rules were important. They presented a set of rules and then talked about the consequences of failing to follow the rules. Their recommended consequence for rule breaking was expulsion from the training session. As you might expect, the group rebelled. Several individuals began questioning the need for the rules, the appropriateness of imposing the rules, and the harshness of the consequences. The session leaders stood firm in their conviction about the need for and appropriateness of the rules and their approach.

Within minutes, nearly a fourth of the participants had left the room. By lunch, only half of the original group remained. Upon returning from lunch, less than a quarter were present. Much of the afternoon was spent processing "What happened?!" for the benefit of the session leaders.

These leaders failed to recognize the nature of the group's task and the characteristics of the group. It was a one-day training session that drew an audience whose members had little or no prior or future relationship with one another and who were already somewhat skilled at group process. Because it was an education setting, the group did not anticipate high-stakes controversy or conflict in connection with the training.

The approach used by the session leaders was heavy-handed and insensitive to the context in which they were working. The leaders further failed the group by resisting the members' efforts to express and communicate their discomfort and needs. The group members showed their rejection of the facilitators and the ground rules by exiting the session.

Not all groups have the physical freedom to exit. However, even when people cannot physically leave a setting because it feels unsafe or unproductive, they can accomplish the same thing by mentally and emotionally disengaging. Establishing the need for shared expectations is essential.

FROM THE TOOLBOX

- Let people shine about their accomplishments. If you are working with a new group, as part of the introductions at the first meeting ask people to say their name, affiliation, and something they bring to the group that will be of help.
- Prior to the meeting, send a questionnaire that lists key considerations so that group members have time to think about what they might need.
- Devote time up front to the agenda to consider these needs.
- Conduct interviews with group members beforehand, by telephone if necessary, to draw out concerns that may not be expressed in the group setting.
- If the group is large, appoint a smaller working group that represents the diversity of the full group to initiate development of the covenant.
- When invoking the need for promises to one another as part of a larger covenant, consider using a term other than ground rules, such as shared expectations, community commitments, group protocols, working agreements, statements of intent, enduring understandings, and group promises.
- Once participants have agreed to create a covenant or shared expectations, congratulate them on their willingness to meet to discuss and work out the problem or address the issue at hand. Where tension is high, acknowledge that whatever their differences, there seems to be agreement that it would be better if matters could be worked out and resolved.

Element 2: Educate and Inspire

The second key element on the path to higher ground is to educate and inspire, including providing sufficient support for the effort, especially time for reflection and discussion. You may give illustrations of other groups' covenants or ground rules, along with examples of how they have been used and abused. A facilitator should watch for words or behaviors that indicate the group leaders' commitment to developing and honoring a covenant.

Once you have established the need for developing shared expectations and you confirm that you have people's interest in doing so, it is imperative that you offer sufficient information and support to ensure the group's success. Perhaps the single greatest failing of groups that use typical ground rules in the customary manner is lack of support from leaders for the effective development, implementation, and revision of the rules. Good groups do not develop by accident—or at least you cannot count on that happening very often!

Support can come in many forms. One form of support is committing the necessary agenda time for reflection and discussion of shared expectations. A group needs to know that developing its covenant is not something that wastes their time before they get down to their real business. Facilitators and group leaders often create an agenda that makes no mention of time dedicated to addressing matters of group process. In doing so, they implicitly communicate that giving attention to such matters is something other than important group work.

Another element of support that educates and inspires is practical information and educational material about what makes a group effective, about how effective groups use covenants, about criteria to consider when developing a covenant, and examples of other groups' covenants. Such information provokes thought, motivates participants, and inspires confidence in the group, the process, and the leader.

Articulating possible foci for shared expectations can expand a group's thinking and bring to their attention aspects of their functioning that may never have been explicitly addressed but should be. Offering examples of the areas in which shared expectations could be useful is a practical strategy for engaging the group's members in self-reflection about how well or poorly the examples offered speak to their own needs and experience.

Such reflection can serve to expand the group's thinking about shared expectations and elevate the conversation from the mundane and predictable to the elusive aspects of group functioning. It also can inspire the pursuit of more ambitious and meaningful commitments to one another. The education and inspiration step is also a way to introduce issues that might otherwise be difficult to raise in certain settings. Focusing on the tools the group can use to work effectively can jump-start a conversation, expand the group's focus, and enrich the quality of the discussion (see Appendix B). But beware: providing examples of other covenants or ground rules cannot replace the process of development, for it is this process that ensures that a covenant reflects the needs of the particular group.

A final support needed to educate and inspire is securing indications of commitment from the group's leadership. Every group has one or more leaders. They may be formally recognized, such as a chair or team leader. They may be informal, such as an opinion leader or a person with important resources to broker, such as money, political influence, or expertise. Active engagement in and visible support for the development of shared expectations for higher ground by the group's most powerful members is critical to the group's success at creating and keeping a covenant. The group's ability to commit to the covenant can only be as strong as the commitment of the most powerful people in the group. If those who hold sway in the group signal their resistance or reject the development of such agreements, the agreement is at best unlikely to be upheld by the group in the long run. At worst, it may well give less powerful members of the group a false sense of security, thus putting them potentially at harm.

❖❖   *Snapshot.* The organizers of the United Methodist Church (UMC) dialogues on theological tensions facilitated by John (see Chapter Four) created ground rules resonant with their faith, citing scriptural passages and language familiar and important to Christians. Additionally, they added this wonderful image: "these ground rules are meant to be a lifeline, not a noose." They explained that the purpose was not to constrain and lay traps in order to find "violators" but to help encourage people to be at their best.

◆◆   *Reflection.* Now that is all well and good when you are in an explicitly religious setting, where such attention to ground rules is more naturally welcomed, if not always accomplished. But would the process the UMC group used work in more secular settings?

Many aspects of the UMC's process for creating its ground rules can apply to workplace and community settings. While a company's mission statement or a community group's bylaws certainly do not have the same standing as Holy Scripture, there are similar touchstones that can help secular groups focus on why certain ground rules are useful. As we have suggested, if a group has a functional vision and takes time to be clear about its desired outcomes, there are ways of capturing how members want to work together that are similar to the UMC's "lifeline, not a noose" approach to their shared expectations. For example, some of the Guidelines for Civility in the United Methodist Church that could easily be adopted by other groups are as follows (General Commission on Christian Unity and Interreligious Concerns, 1998):

- Carefully represent the views of those with whom we are in disagreement.
- Be careful in defining terms, avoiding needless use of inflammatory words.
- Be open to change in your own position and patient with the process of change in the thinking and behavior of others.

FROM THE TOOLBOX

- Offer a set of provocative prompts; for example, offer the group some predefined categories to consider in developing their own shared expectations, such as accomplishments, use of time, decision making, participation, membership, tone, sharing information outside the group, and so on.
- Share examples of covenants from other groups. When possible, use examples that are from settings similar to that of your group.
- Invite comment from the group's leaders regarding the importance of the shared expectations. You may want to talk with them about this request prior to the meeting and secure their willingness to comment. Ask them what they might say so you can advise or coach as appropriate. This is also a good way to gauge their commitment.
- Bring in someone who has real authority in the eyes of group members to give the commitment weight—but only if they truly do have the commitment.

Element 3: Begin by Envisioning Desired Outcomes

The third major element of the path to higher ground is to envision the desired outcomes that will define higher ground for your group. Once you have done that, you can then develop the specific principles and behaviors in the form of commitments or ground rules that will allow you to reach those outcomes.

A group that does not know where it is going may get there fast—but then what? It is this element—the linking of a vision of what the group can be with behavioral ground rules—more than any of the other elements that prepares the path for higher ground. The group needs to make explicit what its values are and how it wishes to enact those values as people engage one another.

There is good news here. In our work with a wide variety of groups, communities, and conflicts, we have found that most people are capable of expressing and, more importantly, supporting high expectations for how they want to be treated and how they want to work together. This is true even in high-conflict settings.

Each ground rule ought to reflect an intention that supports one or more principles. For example, a typical ground rule for groups is that one person speaks at a time. This ground rule codifies in behavioral terms a way to satisfy more than one principle, such as "Groups function better when members understand one another," "People get frustrated when they are interrupted," and "People value the fairness of giving each person a chance to speak without interruption."

❖❖ *Snapshot.* Many people believe that conflict of any sort is bad. This lesson is reinforced in many ways—it is learned from schools, from churches, and in the family. Not coincidentally, our families, churches, and schools are hotbeds of unresolved and repressed conflict. Churches in particularly seem to attract the bitterest kinds of conflict. In part this has to do with what is often at stake—fundamental values—and with how those values are expressed in worship or in choice of minister, for instance. But the main reason that such conflict becomes so destructive is that many churchgoers believe that conflict should not occur among observant members of the same faith. When disputes do arise, they are unprepared to address them.

A number of churches have recognized the costs of not preparing for conflict and are working to create the kinds of shared expectations that allow conflict to be productive and affirming of the ideal of church community. A Unitarian-Universalist congregation in Springfield, Massachusetts, that went through a painful capital campaign in which members "weren't as nice to each other as we could be" developed a covenant about how members wished to relate to one another (Skinner, 1999, p. 13). The Mennonite Church has developed guidelines called *Agreeing and Disagreeing in Love: Commitments for Mennonites in Times of Disagreement* (General Conference of the Mennonite Church and Mennonite Church General Board, 1995). The Mennonite document includes such guidelines as "Accept conflict," "Be quick to listen," and "Be open to mediation."

FROM THE TOOLBOX

- Invite group members to describe their vision for an ideal workplace, family, or neighborhood group. What would such a group look like? What would it sound like? What would it feel like? Make the feelings tangible!
- Ask, "What would you like your parents (or children) to say about you that you would feel proud about?" This focus on the families of group participants both humanizes and elevates people's identity.
- Provide a sheet with appropriate prompts for participants to consider as they reflect on their values and desired outcomes. Encourage free discussion of their views with one another, and give adequate time for reflection (perhaps even allowing participants to take the sheet home with them). You may use an instrument along the lines of the one in Exhibit 5.1 to encourage reflection and to open up discussion about how the group has been operating and how members would prefer to operate in the future.

**Exhibit 5.1. Worksheet:
Aspirations, Guidelines, and Dos and Don'ts**

- When we operate at our worst, we [look like, feel, sound like]. . . .
- When I imagine how we would operate at our best, I [see, feel, hear]. . . .
- When I envision how we should best work together, my highest *aspirations* are. . . .
- To make these aspirations come alive, the *principles* and *practices* we must follow are. . . .
- To enact these principles, we agree to the following *duties* and *behaviors:*
- *Categories to consider*
  Participation
  Use of information
  Decision making
  Confidentiality
  Use of time
  Roles in group
  Other

- Have members describe what they don't want to happen or what they fear the most—the undesired outcomes. Gently probe their experience in other groups for what contributed to undesirable interactions or results.
- Have members individually and silently complete the phrase, "This group will be a roaring success if our product is. . . ." Then compare the results and compile the replies by general categories (such as particular outcomes, how outsiders view the group, how long the group takes to finish its work, or durability of the outcome).
- Play "Five Whys" to surface the deeper values and meanings of common ground rules. For each rule offered by someone, ask why that rule is important. The individual who suggested the item then reframes the rule by talking about the need or value that the rule promotes. Keep asking "Why?" until the root value of the idea has been expressed.
- Invite people to develop questions they would like other participants to ask about their behavior. Examples of such questions include, Does my behavior increase or decrease the trust others have in me? Does my behavior reflect my consideration of its impact on others' interests? Have I given evidence and argument to support my views and actions? Am I listening to hear new understandings from others? Do I fully understand what is actually being proposed or what is being done? Have I given serious consideration to these differing views?

Element 4: Promote Full Participation

The fourth element of the path to higher ground is to promote full participation. Facilitators or leaders should work to give each group member a voice in developing the covenant.

This principle seems obvious—people are more likely to support what they've helped to create. The more people support the covenant, the more productive they will be.

Yet there are many pressures that cause groups to violate this principle. There may not appear to be enough time to hear at length from each group member, there may be a natural desire to avoid hearing from a "troublemaker," or certain individuals may resist participating no matter how much you say you want to hear from them.

Inclusion is not always easy. But over and over again we see the disastrous results of leaving people out of decisions that affect their lives.

❖❖ *Snapshot.* Among a five-member board of county commissioners, one member in particular was considered difficult, easily angered, and offensive. Following a meeting in which he loudly confronted the chair of the board and the county manager—he even barked like a dog at them—the chair decided there needed to be a code of decorum for all commissioners. The chair directed the county attorney to do research and bring a recommendation to the board.

The "difficult member" objected to what he saw as another effort by the three-member majority to ignore his demands, not share information with him, and create a code to try to shut him up. Another council member joined him in opposition. The code was adopted three to two, but the two dissenters continued their criticism of the rules. In the end, the three-member majority decided it was not worth it and voted to rescind the code.

◆ *Reflection.* So what do you do when you have to deal with a particularly difficult individual? Aren't there some circumstances in which an individual is too stubborn, too selfish, or too destructive to work with?

There certainly are situations in which a person is mentally unbalanced or lacking control and thus unable to participate. Unfortunately, it is too easy to label a person "crazy" or "not with it." Much of the time, some underlying frustration or anger has built up due to being disrespected, hurt, or ignored. These slights, whether real or imagined, may produce what is then viewed as irrational or difficult behavior.

If it appears that certain individuals are being too stubborn or selfish, they may simply have learned to use delay or obstruction as their best tool for getting something they want from the group. That person's underlying needs or interests should be probed several times before writing the person off as just an obstructionist. Remember: perceived stubbornness could be a matter of protecting a principle—if the stubborn person were you!

Finally, you should ask if such persons need to be included and what the ramifications are of trying to, and succeeding in, excluding them. If they have the power to significantly delay or prevent the group from reaching its objectives, it's almost always better to wrestle with a difficult person within the same room than to have them throwing rocks from the outside and complaining about how the group is being unfair by excluding them.

FROM THE TOOLBOX

- If you meet with resistance among some group members, observe their behavior (withdrawal, fidgetiness, limited participation, and uncomfortable body language) and invite an explanation. When the reluctance relates to other people in the room, you may need to do this at a break or in caucus in order to bring the real issues to the surface.
- If you are concerned about unequal power or about quiet versus talkative members, use Post-it Notes to record ideas, then arrange them in an affinity diagram, where you group like items together.
- At various times, go around the room one person at a time and invite people to offer ideas orally. No comments are allowed until all ideas are shared.
- Offer a means to begin discussion of general topics. Write down one topic per sheet of paper and start the sheets with different people in the group. Have each person write one or two ideas or comments on their sheet of paper, and circulate the sheets in the same direction to the next person, who adds his or her thoughts. Repeat the process until everyone has a chance to comment on each topic sheet (Moore and Montalvo, 1996).

Element 5: Be Accountable

The fifth element of the path to higher ground is to be accountable to your promises to one another.

A covenant is worthless if it is put on the shelf. As a matter of fact, it is much worse than worthless. When a group spends its time and effort creating a product that is then ignored, every element of group functioning suffers. Not only is leadership delegitimized, but the message that is conveyed is that this group does not do what it says that it will do.

Two apparently contradictory sayings actually contain synergistic wisdom: "Rules are meant to be broken," and "Promises are meant to be kept." It doesn't take an expert in psychology to know the truth of both of these old adages. Rules imposed by outsiders, however reasonable, are more likely to be broken than are *promises* made after their impact on and value to others is considered. The trick, then, is to help people become aware of and conscientious about their promises to one another rather than their obligation to the rules. The former inspires effort and integrity, the latter invites challenge and rebellion.

One way of inspiring an attitude of promise rather than rules is to enroll group members as leaders. A colleague of ours turned reluctance into enthusiasm when she described this covenanting process as an opportunity for them to provide her (their boss) with directions about how they should be treated—and to be able to hold her accountable to her promises! Encourage group members to see themselves as joint leaders or cofacilitators of the group and its work. This can give group members who might otherwise feel disconnected from one another a way of seeing themselves as a true team—as people with a shared goal and shared responsibility. In some groups—those prepared for high trust—this strategy of inviting shared leadership can be experienced as team building. In other groups—those with a history of distrust or more skeptical participants—you will find that this approach promotes a sense of engagement in the event and a personal responsibility for civil, supportive behavior.

This element is so important and so often problematic that we devote the next chapter to ways of keeping the group on the path of accountability.

❖ *Snapshot.* Marina worked with a group that involved union workers, managers, and members of the board of directors to help them redraw lines of authority for decision making in connection with a planned reform to decentralize the organization. Anticipating the potential difficulty of getting everyone to speak honestly about the topic under discussion, serious group effort was put into developing ground rules to guide the group's work. Although some members participated more actively in generating and discussing the ground rules, process techniques were used to engage all members in the final decision to endorse and adopt the ground rules.

The discussions that followed seemed candid. As facilitator, Marina was pleased with the apparent comfort felt by union members to speak their minds respectfully but forthrightly. By all appearances, things were going as they should have. However, by the next evening group members began calling Marina, explaining that management was breaking the group's final ground rule, which stated, "No harm shall come to those who speak their mind." The group members reported that reprimands and veiled threats had been made to some of the most vocal participants. No one wanted others to know that they had called her. No one was willing to bring the issue up at the next meeting. Marina had unwittingly helped create a feeling of safety that was unfounded. Most participants had been taking their direction from the ground rules they had built together, and it seemed they were now sitting ducks. Trust had been broken and there was no obvious way out of the dilemma.

◆ *Reflection.* Sometimes you do the best you can and still come up short. Marina followed good practice in encouraging openness prior to developing ground rules. In retrospect, however, there are a few things she could have done to anticipate and prevent this problem.

The group numbered about twenty-five people and during the development of the ground rules some of them participated more than others. Marina recognized at the time that those with more power were less actively engaged than the union members were. However, in her experience it was not uncommon for those with the highest status in a group to participate the least in intentional group process. She knew that they needed to go on record as supporting the ground rules, but at the time she had few ideas about how to engage them fully in the process of development.

Marina could have been more observant for signs that the group and its task required something more than mere ground rules. They needed something fuller, deeper, and more inspiring, like a covenant, an articulation of a values-based vision and guiding principles on which ground rules should have been built. In terms of approach, she could have used individual or small-group processes for generating discussion of shared expectations, and then observed differences in responses by group role. She could have read more into the meeting behavior of some members, recognizing that they were not fully committed to their agreements. They didn't participate without prompting, even in the substantive discussion of redistributing authority. Sometimes they would leave the room during discussions or engage in side conversations. They were passive rather than hostile participants. She could have shared her observation of this passivity with the group and asked them what this behavior meant and if it needed to be addressed.

In truth, she was unsure of how hard she should push them for fear of pushing them away. But given the power differences among participants, she could have and should have been more careful to secure full participation and individual accountability to the shared expectations. She should have recognized that to secure even common ground at the conclusion of these negotiations, the group would have to reach for higher ground in its manner and approach.

> **FROM THE TOOLBOX**
>
> - *Ceremonialize the commitment.* Deputize everyone in the group, explaining that they are responsible for upholding the group's agreements by first monitoring their own performance and then being responsible for keeping the group on track, gently reminding one another of agreements as they are violated. This can be a lighthearted way of bringing home the message that everyone has a role in maintaining peace and justice in the group.
> - Continuing to play with this metaphor, you can talk about "friendly warnings," "citizen arrests," and a spirit of "community policing." You might even give people paper armbands or plastic sheriff's stars if it helps to make the point.
> - *Divide monitoring duties* by assigning particular responsibilities to different people, such as staying on time, generating many alternatives before evaluating, and so forth.
> - *Enlarge the covenant* on large sheets of paper (you can even laminate it) and post it prominently at all meetings.
> - *Just say what you see.* Offer an occasional comment regarding your observation of the group's performance in light of their agreements. Describe what you see in broken agreements or areas needing attention. Limit your comments to descriptions of what you see. Ask if they see it, too. Ask if the behavior or straying from the agreements concerns them, and what if anything should be done about it. Also be sure to encourage and recognize their efforts and successes, when evident.

Element 6: Evaluate and Revise

The sixth and final element of the path to higher ground is to evaluate, modify, and recommit to your covenant as appropriate.

In the next chapter we explore how groups have different levels of implementation of and commitment to their covenant. Certainly not all groups need to take the time and make the effort to revisit their commitments. But a group striving for higher ground must be able to learn from its experience and to use that learning to improve its functioning. The three steps to this learning and improvement process—evaluate, modify, and recommit—need not take up an inordinate amount of time.

- *Evaluate:* Determine the adequacy of the shared expectations.
- *Modify:* Suggest changes, additions and other improvements.
- *Recommit:* Ceremonialize consensus.

❖ **Snapshot.** A citizens' advisory group whose deliberations were mediated by Frank and a colleague had spent a good deal of time developing its protocols. The protocols dealt not only with behavioral ground rules but also with questions of representation and accountability, group membership, media contacts, the role of mediators, and other concerns. The development of these protocols unearthed and exacerbated cleavages that already existed among group members. Members expressed considerable frustration that the protocols took so long to develop, and relief when the protocols were finally completed.

◆ **Reflection.** This was a group that did not want to devote any extra time to revisiting their commitments to one another. Indeed, they were working with an external deadline. As citizen volunteers, they were not paid for their involvement in this task force. They had limited free time to digest substantial technical information and were expected to address the concerns and ideas of fellow group members. But Frank and his co-mediator knew how important it was to assess group process and bring continued attention to the group's agreements about how members would work with one another.

To allay concerns that they were continuing to devote too much time to process issues, the group agreed that the mediators would call members between meetings to "check in" with them about group functioning. The mediators could then raise any important concerns, as appropriate, with the whole group. In addition, midway through the process Frank and his partner developed a survey that members answered between meetings. Discussion of survey results still needed to be done during the meetings, but the use of the surveys meant that such discussion was more focused and therefore less time-consuming than it would otherwise be.

Eventually group members became committed to good process and took over many of the group leadership functions themselves. That was a welcome sign to Frank and his colleague.

FROM THE TOOLBOX

- *Evaluation pit stops:* As the group concludes the development of ground rules, propose that they evaluate their performance at preset times, such as just before or after the lunch break and at the conclusion of a meeting. This can be done through a facilitated discussion or by using special tools developed for this purpose.
- *Assign process observers:* Seek volunteers in the group who will serve as process observers. Give them a template for evaluating the group, or brief instructions on their role and how to perform it. At various points in the meeting, ask the process observer to offer insights and observations about the group's performance.
- *Incremental change:* Have each group member identify one ground rule they would like to modify or delete. Next, have each person identify a possible new ground rule. Instead of focusing on the specific changes, use the two lists of rules to focus on how the ideas relate to the vision or general principles of the group. Encourage reflection on how all the "uncontested" ground rules fit with the vision or desired outcomes, and how people see the potential changes as strengthening the vision or outcomes. Only then should you turn to specific ideas to change the ground rules.

We have described six elements applicable to a wide variety of groups for turning the principles of RHG described in Chapter Four into practical work. We have just described in detail how to get started and have outlined the steps of keeping on track. Ah, but we know the toughest part lies ahead. After the initial interest and excitement wear off, how do you keep going? When there is significant distrust or lack of commitment even at the beginning, how do you handle that? We turn to these slippery rocks on the path to higher ground in the next chapter.

Chapter Six

Putting Ground Rules to Work

Keeping the Group on the Path

We acknowledged in Chapter Four that reaching for higher ground (RHG) is a challenge. Here we discuss in detail one aspect of that challenge: maintaining an atmosphere in which higher ground is continuously pursued, even as the group's dynamics grow complex or conflicted. It is a challenge to hold one another accountable for principled behavior, in which truth and integrity are expected and rewarded. It is a challenge to strive continuously for that enlarged vision or for that view of the whole picture that can come only from understanding one another's perspectives, values, needs, and desires.

As circumstances evolve in group settings, the initial desire to seek new ground becomes elusive. Sometimes deep into a process the sense of safety begins to erode and group members begin to doubt the promise and possibility of creating a shared journey. Many of us have some experience in groups where desire for higher ground was expressed early in the journey. Fewer of us have the experience of staying the course. That is why we have written this chapter.

In this chapter we demystify the magic of skillfully managing groups and their unfolding dynamics. We offer practical advice on how to use the group's shared expectations as gentle guides, and we suggest ways of using as touchstones the deeper values expressed in covenants. We offer you the insight and advice you need for helping a group avoid danger and, when necessary, recover from distractions and detours. Here you will find practical advice and real-life examples that will help you keep the group on the path to higher ground. The benefits of engaging a group in self-critique are explored, and tools for evaluating group functioning are provided along with tips on gathering and using such information.

Here we address the often-overlooked issues of how to:

- Continuously encourage a group to reach its full potential and encourage peak performance from each individual.
- Step into the breach when promises have been broken.
- Maintain your composure when the unexpected—and undesired—occurs.
- Monitor a group's performance.
- Use information regarding performance to strengthen and stabilize a group.

Preventing unproductive behavior is a compelling reason for creating shared expectations for constructive engagement. But it may not even be the best reason. Increasingly we understand that human performance is enhanced when personal and psychological needs are respected and responded to. Therefore, intentionally creating a positive atmosphere that signals to all participants that the group's experiences will be productive and safe can prevent behavior problems and enhance individual and group performance. In a real sense, a group's best possible work is tied to creating the best possible atmosphere in which to do the work.

Some groups' priorities are clearly centered on their task more than on their relationships. However, these two aspects of group work—task and relationships—can never be completely separated. Whatever the past or future relationships among group members, inviting shared responsibility for the conduct of the group's business is one avenue for drawing people into recognition of their interdependence. It is so important to cultivate a sense of shared purpose and shared expectations in groups because no individual can manage a group as effectively or as legitimately as the whole group can.

Preparing for Success as You Plan for Trouble

A good group leader or facilitator is ready for the worst possible developments while working for the best possible experience. Many group leaders are comfortable with their leadership role as long as things are going smoothly. However, true leaders can lead in tough times as well. Recognizing this aspect of your leadership role is an important part of preparing for it mentally and emotionally. Some of us never seem to have the problem of groups becoming unproductive. Others of us are regularly challenged by the groups we work with, like pulling a stubborn mule that defies your guidance about the right path to take. While the differences in experience may be based in differences in technique, or in the groups themselves, they likely have as much to do with facilitators' manner of expressing confidence and competence in themselves and in the group.

FROM THE TOOLBOX

- If you're not trained as a mediator, *get trained as a mediator*. The experience of dealing successfully with people in conflict is particularly empowering and confidence building.
- *Practice using active listening*. Reassure the group that should things start to bog down or get unproductive, together you will be able to stay the course. Saying this out loud will help everyone believe it, including yourself.
- *Refer group members to "The Diamond of Decisionmaking"* (Kaner and others, 1996) and their likely encounter with "the Groan Zone." The Groan Zone is that awkward phase of a group's work—the result of diverse views—when ambiguity and complexity abound and clarity and consensus seem elusive. According to Kaner and his coauthors, the Groan Zone naturally precedes convergence and consensus. Groups seem to be comforted by this information. It encourages them to see the periods of struggle as necessary for eventual success.

What Will We Do If . . . ?

Once the group has developed and adopted its shared expectations, it is time to agree, as a group, on how best to handle behavior that challenges or threatens those agreements. We offer a number of suggestions that gradually move the facilitator or group leader from a passive to a more active role as the perceived threat to the group escalates.

The approach to intervening in unproductive behavior on the part of an individual or group should model what some facilitators, like doctors, call the first law of professionalism: "First, do no harm." For facilitators, the best interventions are brief. They redirect or extinguish the unproductive behavior. They are psychologically, emotionally, or spiritually nontoxic to the group as a whole and to the individuals involved.

Whatever the plan, it needs to be just that—a plan, laid out in advance and understood and accepted by all. The plan offers the group and the facilitator or group leader confidence. It can also serve as a deterrent by making it clear to group members that the group is serious about its agreements and will act to protect them. That delicate moment in which a group's agreements are first challenged or violated is no time to wing it.

The Good, the Bad, and the Ugly Moments in Groups

If the substance of a group's work is important, members of the group are often understandably more focused on the work than on the way they are working. Choosing strategic moments to remind a group of its agreements, to recognize its effort, to point out a risk you are observing, or to acknowledge outright when something is amiss is an essential function that a facilitator or group leader performs. How do you figure out what to do and when? This section provides guidance for three distinctly different situations that call for a leader's touch: when it's good, when it's getting bad, and when it's downright ugly. How do you interrupt unproductive or destructive behavior, ac-

> ### FROM THE TOOLBOX
>
> - *Ask group members about their experiences with broken agreements in groups.* Explore how violations were handled and what they liked and disliked about the corrective actions. Use the collective experiences of the group to build a plan with which everyone agrees.
> - *Help people to understand why such a plan is needed.* Reassure them that the plan is designed to work like a car safety belt or health insurance—you don't wear safety belts or purchase insurance because you *expect* the worst. Such things are there in case you need them. Unless and until the time comes that you do need them, they are there to give you a sense of security. When they are needed, they help to minimize damage.
> - *Ask the group to suggest a plan.* If group members are unresponsive or seem to be having trouble with this task, nominate a plan that is comfortable for you and ask the group to modify or improve on it.
> - *But beware!* When groups are asked to nominate consequences for inappropriate actions, adults, like children, can be rather harsh and punitive in their recommendations. They sometimes recommend that violators of the group's rules pay a fine or be asked to leave the group. While such serious penalties are sometimes appropriate, it is best if such action is taken only after careful deliberation of the consequences to the individual, the group, and the task at hand.

knowledge and productively channel the emotions, redirect the behavior, and then check for damage by monitoring and evaluating the overall health and well-being of the group?

Recognize the Good

Recognizing the good in a group can serve many important functions. Recognizing the positive can comfort and calm anxious individuals or groups, offering them encouragement to stay the course. It can teach the group what it means to be good and effective.

Offering specific feedback can be very instructive and reinforcing of productive behavior. If your approach to working with groups places a priority on helping them become more self-managing in the future, then the use of positive feedback or praise builds confidence. At the same time, it builds knowledge about what behaviors and attitudes are supportive of the group's efforts to accomplish its task. It can also be a gentle form of team building.

People tend to attribute their success or failure to four things: ability, effort, luck, or difficulty of the task (Anderson and Prawatt, 1983). If people can be encouraged to attribute their success or failure to effort, then they will believe that the matter is within their control. If they attribute the outcome to ability, luck, or difficulty of the task, then they believe it is beyond their control. Recognizing effort and accomplishment derived from effort motivates and inspires people.

Effective praise has three qualities. First, it follows the desired behavior immediately. Second, it is specific and describes the behavior. Third, it is credible and appropriate to the situation and the individuals involved. This is perhaps the most important of the three qualities in that adults recognize praise as an intentional motivator, which causes them to feel manipulated and resentful. However, even adults like to know that others recognize their efforts and accomplishments. Handled judiciously, praise can be powerful and can strengthen a group's experience.

Interrupt the Bad

Unproductive behavior in group settings among adults is usually a signal that something is amiss for one or more of the participants. Sometimes the behavior is unintentional and unconscious, done out of habit. In such circumstances, gentle reminders, intentional cueing (with eye or hand signals), or even helping the group to accept the behavior are all possible and appropriate. Other times, unproductive behavior is intended to be a message to you as facilitator or to some or all members of the group. Such concerns could in-

> **FROM THE TOOLBOX**
>
> - Regularly take time at the end of meetings to acknowledge the contributions of participants, whatever those contributions may be. This acknowledgment may range from appreciation for just attending the meeting—a significant contribution, particularly for people with many other demands on their time—to preparing presentations, to asking difficult but important questions, to offering new ideas, to showing up on time, to taking on new tasks.
> - Sometimes, for difficult discussions acknowledgment of the persistence it takes to work through such situations is offered. Such appreciation not only conveys gratitude, but it also creates or reinforces the expectation that if such behaviors are *valued*, then they are *valuable*. That is, attending meetings regularly, showing up on time, asking difficult but important questions, and persisting through uncomfortable situations, and related behavior, are important to the functioning of the group.

clude, "I don't like this conversation," "I don't feel like I'm being listened to or heard," or "I'm feeling frustrated by our lack of progress." These and countless other messages could be the underlying point of the behavior. Such behavior as interrupting others when they are speaking, shuffling papers, shifting in one's chair, rolling one's eyes, and appearing to do paperwork unrelated to the meeting are some of the many behaviors exhibited in groups when trouble is afoot.

There are many ways to intervene, but knowing which means to use when is a matter of professional judgment. There are some things to consider in choosing your approach.

❖ *Snapshot.* During a meeting, a previously absent member arrives. As he sits down he takes out a piece of paper with something printed on it and passes it to the person next to him. She reads it silently and looks to him in apparent amazement. They exchange knowing glances. Immediately attention in the room

> **FROM THE TOOLBOX**
>
> - Make sure the room setup is conducive to the task and relationships you are trying to support. For example, if people are seated outside the group, they may feel less a part of it.
> - Scan the group frequently to notice and respond to potential problems or minor disruptions. It is difficult to do many things at once, but that is in fact what a group leader or facilitator must do. At a minimum, group leaders must monitor the group's task and its relationships.
> - Your response to disruption should be no greater than the disruption it is intended to reduce. If the problem is with an individual or two or three people, deal with it privately, away from the attention of the group. If the problem has had an impact on the majority of the group, take it up in a group context. Even then, be efficient by using as little time as necessary and be effective by ensuring that the intervention does no harm to the group.

turns to these two individuals and lots of gesturing begins to occur among the group members. The paper begins to travel around the room as people anxiously try to "get the scoop."

Now it's obvious that the group is having trouble focusing on the topic at hand. So the facilitator asks the group if they would like to take a moment to talk about whatever is the source of the distraction. The group affirms this suggestion. The facilitator gestures with an open hand toward the person who initiated the paper passing and he proceeds to share the news of reorganization and new hires—decisions that had been expected for weeks by the group. Upon hearing the news, the facilitator poses an open-ended question: "So, what *is* your reaction to the decision?" She invites responses from everyone.

When it appears that everyone who wanted to speak has spoken, the facilitator suggests a sequence for getting back to the main topic. "What if we spend just a few more minutes on this, then take a short break and return to the main topic after the break? OK?"

Subdue the Ugly

There are ugly moments in groups when things turn personal and emotionally dangerous. Most people have not had to facilitate such a moment, but we bet most everyone has been witness to at least one such moment. Recollections of such events are vivid and compelling. Somewhere in the back of their minds facilitators live in fear of those moments when they are leading groups. You know those moments—the ones when the group members turn on each other, or turn on you; or when inflammatory language is hurled across tables. Here are a few tips for crowd control.

FROM THE TOOLBOX

- A calm but immediate response to a problem will produce a ripple effect in the group. Other members will calm down and seek to assist you in regaining control by controlling their own behavior.
- Remind everyone of your agreements. Ask or tell which shared expectations are being broken.
- If the problem involves only a couple of people, invite them to take up the issue outside with you while the rest of the group continues, or call a break. Once outside, listen, listen, and listen! Probe for the underlying concerns or issues that prompted the behavior. Engage in a negotiation focused on meeting everyone's needs, including your own as the facilitator. Engage the group member(s) involved in problem solving and consequential thinking, posing "What then?" questions. Generate options.
- If the preferred options to the problem require agreement or support from the group, then it is the group's decision, not yours. In these moments you'll want to have clear prior agreements about how to handle such matters. How will the group decide? By majority rule or by consensus? If the group declines the suggested changes, does the individual have to stay and comply or is he or she free to leave the meeting? If the person leaves, what is the cost to the group?

❖❖ *Snapshot.* A group that Marina was facilitating had been meeting every month for the previous three months to build a better partnership between parents and school personnel. They had established community commitments. Things had been progressing nicely. One day she sensed tension between one of the parents and one of the school administrators. The administrator was uncharacteristically silent during the meeting. His body language was hostile and included loud sighs, eye rolling, and pushing his chair back from the table when the parent spoke, signaling that something was amiss. Marina called for a short break and approached the administrator, who was a vice principal.

She learned that the parent had written a letter to the editor that had been published in the local paper. The letter criticized the administrator and the school district, quoting an admission by the vice principal that had been made at the previous meeting about a failure of the district. The vice principal said the parent's letter was a violation of the community commitments or ground rules regarding confidentiality and a violation of the entire effort that was designed to repair strained parent-community relations. He said he would not speak again in the meeting because he didn't trust that it would be safe or that he would be treated fairly.

Marina asked the vice principal what he wanted to do about this. His initial response was "Nothing." Marina expressed concern for him and for the group, which would lose his participation because of his vow of silence. The vice principal suggested that he drop out of the group. Marina asked him if others knew of the article and were troubled by it. He said yes. The two of them discussed the impact of this situation on the entire group's comfort—their feelings of trust and goodwill. The vice principal acknowledged that it affected everyone. Marina asked if he was willing to raise the issue in the group so they could discuss it openly. He was unsure. They decided that Marina would ask the group to do a self-critique of their performance upon returning from the break. If he wanted to, he could raise the issue. Marina hoped that if he didn't raise the issue, someone else would.

In response to her suggestion that the group do a self-critique and evaluate their collective performance against the ground rules, the vice principal took up the cause. The discussion that ensued was delicate and heated. School personnel wanted an apology and a promise that it would never happen again if they were to continue with the effort. The parent took a firm position and argued her right to use whatever means were available to her to advance her reform cause outside the group. She acknowledged that she might have made an error in quoting the vice principal, given the commitment to confidentiality. However, that was the extent of her remorse. She said that her involvement in the partnership project should in no way impinge on her personal freedom outside of group sessions.

This exchange led to a principled discussion about the feasibility of people engaging collaboratively in one context and as adversaries in another simultaneously. The majority of those in the room felt it could not be done and that a new community commitment was needed. They recommended the following: "For the duration of this partnership project, participants' actions outside the meetings should be consistent with the spirit of collaboration that the project is trying to foster." All but two of the group's members endorsed the addition. The parent who had written the letter and another parent rejected the proposal. The majority took the position that if this commitment was not adopted they would disband the group because it had no chance for success. The letter-writing parent suggested that they adopt the agreement and that she would leave the group.

The discussion was very awkward in the end. No integrative solution to the problem was found. New parents were recruited to fill the spots on the committee. Those who remained were enlivened by a new sense of community and the work progressed at an accelerated pace.

❖   *Reflection.* Sometimes, despite one's best efforts at preparation, conflict is still unresolvable. Perhaps there was no better way of handling the situation. Without the community commitments, this dispute would have been a more personal and bruising battle. The prior agreements were the group's best strategy for judging the offense, and for suggesting how to recover from the detour—through adding ways to address the problem to the list of community commitments. The group had agreed that process decisions could be made by a two-thirds majority if consensus was not possible. In the end, it was this point of prior agreement that allowed the group to move on. The process was messy and uncomfortable, but relatively efficient and not wholly destructive for the group.

Evaluating Group Performance

Although a sixth sense about group dynamics is a handy thing to have if you're a facilitator or group leader, not everyone is so lucky. Even if one does have a certain knack for sensing the emotional temperature in a room, there are great benefits to using other tools and techniques for collecting and sharing information from the group about its performance.

Feedback, evaluation of group process, self-critique—these terms are all used to describe a process of seeking candid, thoughtful descriptions of observed behavior (speech or actions) from group members, and determining how best to use the consequences of the critique to inform the group's efforts. Evaluation is a process of accounting for what has and has not occurred. It is about making sense of the lived experience of the group. It is about recognizing strengths and correcting mistakes. It is about personal and shared responsibility. It is about getting stronger and smarter. It is the only way to ensure continued learning, yet it is something that groups seldom do.

In a sense, taking time to evaluate a group's performance is like stopping to check your compass while hiking and charting progress or redirecting your path to your destination. Hikers recognize the wisdom of taking stock. Group members, however, often question the value of such activity, claiming that it takes precious time away from the "real" work. Yet there are compelling reasons for doing so:

to facilitate error correction, to promote intimacy, and to promote team learning.

Feedback for Error Correction

Gathering feedback from group members is an essential tool for making adjustments and midcourse corrections to both the task and the process. This approach is often referred to as a "feedback loop" whereby outputs of a system are fed back into the system as inputs so that adjustments and corrections can be made. The RHG approach encourages the group to consider the need for corrections not only to the task or procedures but to the governing values or goals as well.

❖❖ *Snapshot.* A group facilitated by Marina established shared expectations that favored task over relationships. They claimed that in the past people were too worried about hurting each other's feelings and work suffered as a result. The work was too slow. Things that needed to be said were not. Decisions that should have been made were avoided. Having achieved a clear consensus on this point, the group drafted shared expectations that encouraged "tough talk" and "honesty" over individuals' feelings.

During a feedback session at the conclusion of the second meeting, a group member explained that she was quite happy with the group's progress on its task but she was concerned that people's feelings were being trampled. She offered examples of specific incidents. Others in the group were asked whether this view matched their perceptions. Several people agreed with the woman and several others disagreed.

The people who disagreed correctly pointed out that the incidents described were perfectly consistent with the shared expectations they had developed. The progress they had accomplished on their task was evidence of the correctness of their position on this matter. The woman raising the concern conceded that much had been accomplished, but she suggested that, based on this experience, she personally no longer felt committed to the shared expectations. She didn't like the rules and didn't want to play by them anymore. It became apparent that the group was divided on this point. To resolve this difference of opinion, the group needed to revisit its shared expectations and examine statements that expressed their shared values.

A negotiation ensued that led the group to revise its shared expectations in a manner that was acceptable to everyone. Group members agreed to speak the truth, but in a soft voice. Specifically, they committed to acknowledging up front when their comments were likely to be difficult for others to hear. They agreed to ask those who were most likely to feel the sting of a comment to acknowledge what had been said and how it made them feel. They recommitted to their shared value of discussing the undiscussables, but they found a way to reconcile this value with the value of caring for each other in the process. To resolve this matter, the group had to revisit not just their behavior but the values guiding their behavior as well.

❖ *Reflection.* Could the group have been spared this conversation? Could Marina have pointed out the likely consequences of privileging task over relationships early on, when the shared expectations were being developed? She must have known it was going to cause problems down the road. Why wait?

Marina waited because she trusted that the group would self-correct. She also knew that nothing she could have said at the beginning of the process would be as meaningful to them as their own experience. Developing shared expectations allowed the group to surface a theory they collectively held to be true—that being considerate and caring in the past had cost them something even more valuable: accomplishment. They had inferred that considerate treatment of others and task accomplishment were in competition and incompatible. By expressing this perception, the group empowered itself. They were discussing an undiscussable. They were taking charge. Marina would have been foolish to try to redirect that energy. Multiple opportunities would exist for revisiting their shared expectations and for inviting expression about the group's experience. Marina trusted the group's collective wisdom and the wisdom of the RHG approach.

Feedback to Promote Intimacy

Promoting intimacy is another benefit of self-critique. Most people typically think of intimacy as emotional closeness, which is not necessarily a bad thing in many group settings but it is certainly not a necessity. We are using the word in a different sense. The word *intimacy* stems from *intimatus*, the Latin word meaning "to make something known to someone else." In this case, intimacy refers to a willingness to share honest information. This willingness to be honest—to be intimate—is a powerful leverage for dissolving barriers to collaboration and reinventing relationships (Roberts, 1994).

Engaging in self-critique as a group invites individuals to speak the truth. Being authentic in this context does not mean sharing personal secrets. Instead, it means sharing your true opinions about your experience of the meeting, acknowledging your uncertainties and your opinions about your own (or others') failures, and exploring the group's barriers to success (Roberts, 1994). Evaluation of group process offers people the opportunity, and then places on them the responsibility for authentic engagement and full participation. So many of us have had the experience of shutting down in the middle of a meeting because something started to go amiss. We disapproved of something that was happening that felt beyond our control, so we controlled what we could—our own level of engagement with the group.

Sharing your true opinions invites vulnerability. As you share your opinions, you expose what you think, feel, and value. This act of disclosure is harder for some people than for others. It is also harder for people in some settings than in others. Being intimate and expressing yourself honestly is a skill that can be strengthened with practice.

There are ways of inviting intimacy in groups that respect different levels of comfort and skill. By using the right tools and techniques for a given context or setting, a group leader can help increase a group's skill and comfort levels. As the level of intimacy increases in a group, the urge to be trustworthy will become stronger because members will realize they are bound to the team in the long run by a shared purpose.

FROM THE TOOLBOX

To illustrate how to match the tool or technique to the group's comfort and skill level, we offer three ways to modify the same technique. The technique is the "plus/delta" feedback technique, which invites everyone to candidly express their perception of "+"—what worked well or what was positive—and "Δ" (delta, the Greek symbol for *change*), expressed as things to improve.

- *For low-skill or low-trust settings:* At either the midpoint or the end of a meeting, or both, pass out a prepared sheet divided lengthwise down the middle with a + at the top of the left-hand column and Δ at the top of the right-hand column. Collect the information anonymously from each individual. Compile and report the information after the break or at the next meeting. Invite discussion about the meaning of the contributions and the appropriateness of the recommended changes. Seek consensus on important changes. Recognize strengths and celebrate successes.
- *For moderate-skill, moderate-trust, or time-sensitive settings:* The + and Δ columns are displayed on a flipchart page or pages for people to respond to as they leave the meeting. Assess the results in the same manner as in the previous approach.
- *For a high-skill or high-trust group:* At the end or midpoint of the meeting, invite both + and Δ feedback through brainstorming in the full group. You can use either "popcorn style" participation, in which people randomly take turns, or a "structured go-around," in which there is an explicit order and everyone participates. Assess the results in the same manner as in the previous approaches.

Learning as a Group

Groups are where people to try to get things done together. The poor performance of groups accounts for much of what people fail to get done—in families, communities, committees, and organizations. The main idea behind team learning or organizational learning is for people first to become conscious of what they think and how they interact, and then to develop capacities to think and interact differently. When this is done, people begin to change their group or organization for the better. With each improvement borne out of this self-study and improvement process, people grow more capable and more confident both as individual participants and as groups or organizations.

Team learning should be a highly valued outcome of group experience. Regardless of the intended life span of a group, there are sound reasons for nurturing team learning. If the group will meet over a long time, the learning produced from each meeting can facilitate individual growth and accelerate group accomplishment. If the group is to meet only once, then the effort to promote learning can be justified as an investment in the future. These individuals will in time go on to become part of other groups. They can take their learning with them and be more confident and competent participants in their next endeavor. Chances are that these individuals are members of your community, your group, or your organization. The issue at hand won't be the last issue they deal with. What they learn will reap benefits later, even if you aren't around to experience it.

Skills for Delivering Feedback

Feedback is most powerful when the information gathered is discussed by the group and shared meaning is created. Whether the facilitator shares the results of information gathered anonymously from the group or each group member speaks up on his or her own, success is highly dependent on the skills of giving and receiving feedback.

Giving and receiving feedback are complex skills that depend on other skills such as paraphrasing, checking impressions, describing another's behavior, describing one's own feelings, describing one's own behavior, and stating one's own ideas (Schmuck and Runkel, 1985). In short, knowing yourself, knowing your subject, and being able to effectively communicate are requisite skills for giving and receiving feedback effectively.

Most people experience positive feedback as easier to give and receive than negative feedback. Easier does not necessarily mean more effective. Promoting honest self-critical reflection whereby all individuals hold themselves accountable can be a very effective tool for a group's growth and improvement.

Publicly acknowledging positive performance—one's own or others'—can strengthen relationships and sharpen the performance of a team or group. Such a strategy focuses on the positive in order to create favorable expectations that members will work to live up to.

In the next section we offer a number of tools and techniques that rely on providing feedback. When critical feedback needs to be shared in a direct way, it is important that it be done responsibly. Feedback is a tricky business because it often implies the desire to change another person's behavior. For this reason, conditions should be nurtured that place feedback in a context of mutual and genuine concern for one another and the shared task. It is tricky for another reason as well: one's feedback to someone else says as much about oneself as it says about the other person. Everyone wishing to give critical feedback would do well to consider their own values and to explore the possibility of accepting the behavior before offering the information. The RHG approach, with its emphasis on shared expectations and responsibility for continuous improvement, takes some of the guesswork and risk out of feedback.

By establishing up front that feedback is an integral part of the group's process and something to be taken on as a shared responsibility, the task is ritualized and, consequently, depersonalized. The RHG approach further simplifies the process by focusing the feedback on matters of prior agreement—the group's shared expectations for constructive agreement. As agreements, these expectations constitute a legitimate focus for feedback. Regardless of the benefits of focusing feedback on matters related to the ground rules, community commitments, or covenant, it must be recognized that feedback is a skill that requires effort and that can be improved with practice.

According to Schmuck and Runkel (1985), feedback is best when it meets the following criteria:

1. *Noncoercive.* Feedback should be given in a manner that makes it clear to the recipients that they are not being coerced to change their behavior. Any decision to change behavior is a matter of personal choice.
2. *Considerate.* Feedback should be given after a careful assessment has been made of the recipient's feelings. This does not mean, for example, that you should not show anger toward the other person; it means that the person giving feedback should prepare the other person through choices such as timing and tactful expression.
3. *Descriptive.* Feedback should involve a clear report of the facts rather than a subjective judgment of another's actions or motives.
4. *Proximal.* Feedback should be given close to the time of the events causing the reaction. Festering grievances can grow and burst at inopportune times. In addition to using feedback at predetermined times, group leaders and members alike should be on the lookout for necessary ad hoc emergency feedback sessions.
5. *Doable.* Feedback should be given about behavior that can be changed. It is not helpful, for example, to tell people that you are bothered by their voice or the clicking sound their dentures make when they talk.

With these guidelines in mind, we offer a number of techniques that might be useful for facilitating the gathering and sharing of feedback and the making of shared meaning.

FROM THE TOOLBOX

Determining how best to gather feedback within a group is an important decision. The decision should reflect knowledge of the group's diagnostic skills, level of candor, and effective interpersonal communication. Other factors, such as time, come into play when deciding how best to gather the information. There is no set number of ways to gather such feedback—the possibilities are limited only by one's imagination. Following are some of the things to be considered in choosing an existing tool or when developing your own.

- *Focus of attention:* What is the focus of the feedback? Do you want participants to provide feedback regarding each of the group's shared expectations or do you want people to comment only on those things that they as individuals find noteworthy? Should they limit their comments to their own performance in the group or should they comment on the performance of others and the group as a whole?
- *Anonymity of process:* How public should an individual's feedback be? Do people have to express their opinions and perceptions publicly or would confidential contributions be better?
- *Investment of time:* How much value does the group place on this aspect of group process? How much time is available for gathering, sharing, and processing this information?
- *Intended use:* Does the group simply need to make midcourse corrections or are they interested in learning how to be a better group or team?

Selection of tools and techniques for gathering feedback should be based on the answers to the preceding questions. A variety of methods can be used, even with the same group, as circumstances change. For example, time-efficient, anonymous, and directed feedback techniques may be most appropriate in a large group or in the early phase of a group's experience. Over time, more attention to specific aspects of group functioning can be used, along with techniques that require direct communication among members.

The following are tools for groups with little experience in conducting feedback:

- Use a standard survey of meeting or team effectiveness. Ask for no identifying information. Gather and summarize the results.
- Create a survey based on the group's own shared expectations. Create two separate rating scales for each item, where one scale is focused on members' individual performance and the other is focused on the total group's performance. Summarize and report only the composite group performance scores. Keep information about individual performance confidential and use it as diagnostic information to help plan the work and facilitate the group.
- Create a team performance web. This is a method for graphically displaying evenness of attention to the group's shared expectations. Begin by drawing a circle in the middle of an 8.5-inch by 11-inch blank page placed horizontally (as in Figure 6.1). Label each line at its far end with one behavior, goal, or criterion to be assessed. Give all participants their own page and ask them to reflect on and then judge performance on each item.

Have members place a dot on each line at the point that corresponds with their view of how well the group has performed on that dimension, beginning from the center circle and moving outward. Better performance merits a dot farther away from the center circle. When the participants have judged each item in turn, ask them to connect the dots between the lines and color in the entire space inside the continuous line connecting the dots.

Following these instructions will create a spider web–like image, like the one shown in the figure, that depicts performance. Team performance web feedback can be especially interesting if similar items are placed next to each other (such as items related to task accomplishment versus those that address relationships, or those that address behaviors during group meetings versus those that address between-meeting behaviors such as communicating with constituencies, completing assignments, and so forth). The feedback can be focused on either the group's performance or individual performance. Over time a group may decide to alternate its focus from the group to individuals' actions. Another option: collect each person's completed web, calculate a mean and range for each dimension of the web, and then report the results to the group.

Figure 6.1. Graphing a Group's Performance

Instructions
1. Place the name of your group or meeting in the center circle.
2. Label the end circles by placing one shared expectation or ground rule in each.
3. Place a dot on the spoke leading to each end circle to represent your perception of the group's performance. The closer the dot is to the outer circle, the higher the rating of performance will be.
4. Drawing a line from one spoke to the next, connect the dots you placed on each spoke.
5. Shade the entire region inside the line you drew that connects the dots.

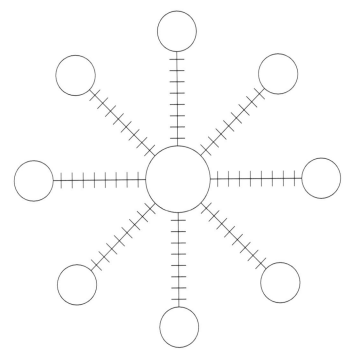

Source: Adapted with permission from Bailey Alliance, 1994.

Any of the methods just described can be handled in a more open and direct way by processing the information as a group. Following are a couple of ideas for making private perceptions a matter for public discussion:

• Reproduce the survey items on wall charts or enlarge a copy of the survey to poster size. Give all participants sticky colored dots and ask them to place a dot in the appropriate place on each of the scales on the chart. If appropriate, different colors can be assigned to different groups—such as role groups, constituencies, departments, length of tenure, and so forth—providing rich fodder for discussion.

- Place a twelve- to fifteen-foot strip of masking tape along the floor. Using shorter strips of tape, divide the first line into evenly spaced units representing a Likert-type scale. Identify the anchor points of the scale (that is, + or –, "not at all" or "to a great extent," and so forth). Read the first survey item aloud. Invite people to walk to the spot on the line that corresponds with their perception. Invite people at various points across the range of responses to explain the position they took.

A variation is to find the median point in the group based upon their responses to an item. Those at the median should stay stationary while the others fold the line in half by having those at the two extremes meet. Invite people to talk to those at the other end of the scale regarding why they perceive things as they do.

- Display the finished group performance webs on a wall. Place them in random order or group similar individuals on the basis of role or some other criterion. Invite people to study the display and then process the observations and patterns as a group.

For groups with considerable competence in working together, other tools may be suitable as well:

- Ask one or more people to serve the group as a process observer. Their job is to observe the group as it goes about its work and prepare to share observations with the group members upon request. The focus of the observations could be based on the shared expectations, it could be based on a few areas deemed by the group to be especially important, or it could be left to the process observer's discretion.

- Ask simple, open-ended questions about people's experiences in the group. How are people feeling about the meeting? The task? The group? To promote full participation, use a structured go-around in which each participant takes a turn responding to a question. Alternatively, introduce into the group a "talking stick" or any lightweight, graspable object that can be passed from individual to individual to designate who is speaking or who is next in line to speak.

- Learn from the last experience (that is, from last week, the last meeting, or before the last break). Ask people to recall anything that made them feel uncomfortable. Ask them how it might be addressed in the future. Some issues are better treated as awareness issues rather than as action issues. Ask the group which type it is.

- Give each participant a set of 3" × 5" Post-it Notes or index cards. Each person should receive one less card than the number of people in the group. For example, each person in an eight-person group would receive seven cards. If the group is large, then divide the members randomly into smaller groups. Ask everyone to write down one thing they appreciate about each group member in terms of the way they serve or contribute to the group. The more specific the feedback is, the more powerful the results will be. When everyone has written their notes, ask all members to stand up, move around the room, and place their notes on the appropriate chair or at the appropriate place at the table. When everyone returns to their place, have them read the comments to themselves.

A variation is to have participants share one point of feedback from the cards that they find most meaningful to them and why. They could then also be invited to offer one area in which they recognize the need to improve or increase their effort in order to be a better team member or group participant.

- Invite feedback in pairs. Ask everyone to find a partner. Allow each person three to five minutes to give feedback in the following forms: (1) "Something I *observe* about you in this group is . . ."; (2) "What I conclude from this observation is. . . ." When both partners have given feedback, redivide the group into new pairs and repeat the process. After a few rounds, return to the large group and debrief.

- Invite feedback by the entire group. Begin this activity by explaining it fully and reviewing the characteristics of constructive and balanced feedback (keeping in line with the group's shared expectations, where appropriate). One person at a time will ask the group, "How do I come across in our meetings? What are my strengths and weaknesses?" People will respond with comments like, "You always make an effort to be sure you understand someone before you challenge their comment or disagree with them. I really find that helpful." Unless the members of your group are very secure with one another, limit this feedback to positive behaviors or attitudes.

Using Feedback to Refine the Group's Shared Expectations

One aspect of keeping the group on the RHG path is to make wise use of the information gathered through discussion or other means of feedback and evaluation. Three questions should guide a group's response to feedback:

1. Is the feedback valid?
2. Is the feedback likely to have an impact on our ability to fulfill our covenant?
3. How can we best use this feedback to optimize our chances of success?

These questions are for the group rather than a group leader or facilitator to answer. If the answers to questions 1 and 2 are yes, then some effort must be put into answering question 3. Sometimes all that is necessary is clarification of one or more of the shared expectations already agreed to by the group. Sometimes what is needed is an elaboration of a point so that the shared expectations are more comprehensive and written to address the kinds of experiences that proved to be the basis of the corrective feedback.

Sometimes a problem has been identified to which no obvious or simple solution presents itself. In this case, it might be best to engage the group in a mini problem-solving session in which the problem is clarified, several options for solving it are generated and evaluated for their merit, and agreement is reached. If it seems unwise to involve the group in open-ended problem solving, due to resistance, time constraints, or group size, then it might be appropriate for the facilitator to offer a possible solution. However, this should be done in a nondirective way. For example, ask the group members what they like about the proposed solution and what they don't like about it. Their comments can be reframed as solution criteria. Using the criteria as parameters, the group may begin to see solutions emerge that meet their needs better than your proposal does.

Integrating New Members into the Group

The arrival of new participants into a group or team setting can be especially challenging for a group struggling to stay the course toward higher ground. Orientation of the new members is appropriate and advisable. New members need a certain grounding in both matters of process and substance of the group's work. In terms of process, new members should know the names and roles of other members, the shared expectations developed by the group, a general impression (offered by volunteers) of how the group has been performing in terms of its expectations, and any critical incidents that have been defining moments or developments for the group.

In terms of substance, new members need to be clear about the group's charge or purpose. They should understand the responsibilities for work between meetings and the typical approaches being used to get work done. It would be useful to share a complete history of meeting documentation, minutes, or group memory.

If changes in membership of the group are likely to occur, you may want to determine, before the fact, how such transitions will occur. In the event that no provision has been made in advance, the facilitator may want to welcome the new participant (or participants) and raise for the group the need for orientation of the new member. The group may decide to devote a limited amount of meeting time to do the orientation as a group. Alternatively, one or a few group members may volunteer to meet with the new person outside the group.

As for those already in the group, they may need some information about the new member. For example, it may be helpful for them to learn the reasons for the new member's arrival, information regarding the person's personal style that might be relevant, the person's aspirations or hopes, or even their fears and concerns. Creating a public and safe space for the inclusion of new members into the group is well worth the investment.

In this chapter we have explored ways of continually pursuing higher ground in the face of challenges to promised expectations. Specifically, we have described how to encourage a group's full potential, how to intervene when promises have been broken, how to anticipate the unexpected and undesired, how to make evaluation a key element of a group's task, and how to use that evaluation to strengthen and stabilize the group. We continue this theme in the next chapter, as we take a closer look at the many variable characteristics of groups, such as size, diversity of membership, and aspirations, that need to be considered when reaching for higher ground.

Chapter Seven

Too Big? Unbalanced? Quiet? Seething?

The Art of Working with Less-Than-Perfect Groups

As we have said, groups come in different shapes, sizes, and temperaments. The six elements of the path to higher ground described in Chapter Five are the common stepping stones, but there is no single way to lay them out. One size will not, and should not, fit all. Knowing how to recognize the important features of a group and then responding accordingly is an essential skill for a group leader or facilitator. Developing shared expectations is one of the group's important tasks and it requires the same thoughtful consideration and judgment as any other task. Good group leadership means continually adapting processes to accomplish that task.

Taking a lesson from the three little pigs, easy groups with simple tasks can probably afford to build their houses from straw. Adopting a proposed set of ground rules, getting the nod, and then moving on may be all that is called for. Given the sunny, calm atmospheric conditions of the group, anything more may seem—and indeed may be—too much.

However, many groups will face stiff winds and temperature fluctuations between hot and cold. Given such conditions, a house made of wood should serve them better, even though it will cost a bit more and construction will take more time. Such groups need a more solid foundation of shared expectations that includes clear meanings of each expectation and plans for how to live by their agreements. Such a task requires more effort of the facilitator or group leader, and more of the group.

For especially important work, it is more likely that groups will need a house that will last a very long time. They will want assurance that it will withstand the most extreme conditions and protect and serve the group's deepest needs. Such a job requires a substantial investment in materials and time. The amount and type of labor changes, requiring not only more labor but also more skilled labor. Encouraging a group to think into the future and imagine building something that will serve members in both the best and the worst of times requires information, inspiration, commitment, and imagination. Then it takes time and effort to build, and a sharp eye for continuing maintenance.

This chapter is about working with what you've got: the needs, values, abilities, and other characteristics of your group. Here we describe special features or characteristics of groups that deserve consideration when the group is reaching for higher ground. These characteristics influence the group's dynamics and chances for success. For each of these characteristics we share a set of techniques and tools. These tools offer creative approaches to addressing a group's special features. Designed to minimize the challenge posed by those special features, these tools simultaneously seek to maximize the benefits of enacting higher ground.

Finally, we offer a model for assessing where any group is on its path to higher ground. Knowing the group's level of enactment provides members with information needed to judge how high they can go—to decide at what level they can and want to perform. We contend that groups will be richer for the effort invested in the principles and techniques of reaching for higher ground (RHG), regardless of where they may actually end up by choice or by chance.

Group Characteristics Deserving Special Consideration

Although we advocate the ideal of reaching for higher ground by creating shared expectations, we recognize that actual circumstances in groups can make this ideal more or less appropriate and more or less possible. Consideration of the key characteristics of the group and the group's task can help determine the type of investment that is appropriate when it comes to reaching for higher ground.

Some of the characteristics that influence the decision about what investment is appropriate are as follows:

- Group diversity
- Duration of the group
- Complexity of the tasks or problems
- Group size
- Significance of the issues
- Levels of trust
- Power distribution
- Level of aspirations

These eight items do not exhaust the characteristics of groups, but they are characteristics that most commonly need attention. The approach used for generating and discussing possible shared expectations in a group of ten people won't work the same way in a group of one hundred. The honest conversation that can occur in a group of colleagues of equal rank and position is more difficult to achieve in a group that involves multiple levels of organizational hierarchy, from entry-level employees to division managers and everyone in between.

A high degree of difficulty in helping a group reach higher ground is not a sufficient reason to lower your expectations. It is our belief that facilitators and group leaders should invite high expectations for a group, educate and inspire the group's members about what is possible, and let the group determine the level of effort and investment it wants to make in reaching for higher ground. But when group members say they want to make the journey, you will want to be ready with strategies to help them accomplish the goal, in spite of the fact that the group may well be big or unbalanced or quiet or seething—or all four!

We share here a couple of tools for each of the characteristics, hoping to spark your imagination about how best to accommodate the unique features of the group to which you belong or with which you are working, while still helping them reach for higher ground. Then, with an ever-expanding toolbox, you can mix and match techniques to fit both you and the group.

Group Diversity

Common views among people in a group can be the result of shared special interests. Such interests can derive from racial or ethnic identity, political affiliation, religious doctrine, social cause, or shared rank, role, or position within an organization. Individuals who share such affiliations do not always share the same views, of course, but the more diverse the group is, the more you can expect them to have divergent views when it comes to a particular issue—whether it be new taxes, abortion, a neighborhood's house appearance standards, or an organization's plan for employee benefits.

Common views can also be the result of a shared culture, especially how the culture defines notions of the "right way" for people to relate to one another and solve problems. The accepted culture among a group of firefighters may be different from the culture experienced among faculty at a university. Both of these cultures may in turn be quite different from the culture of a group of farmers. Thus your RHG approach will need to account for who is in the group, how varied the group members' approaches to problem solving are, and given the issue at hand, how similar or dissimilar their views are likely to be.

FROM THE TOOLBOX

- *Homogeneous groups:* Have members who are similar to one another on some feature relevant to the task or setting form small groups to discuss what is important to them, what their expectations are, or what principles or values they would like to see guide the group's work. This can be very effective if trust is low or if people are not yet comfortable with members of the group who are different from them.

- *Heterogeneous groups:* Have the groups "jigsaw" by creating small groups that represent the full diversity of the large group (that is, small groups made up of one member from each homogeneous group). In this formation, cross-group dialogue is emphasized and group integration is accelerated. This can be very effective when trust across groups is not a known problem but lack of contact and familiarity is.

Duration of the Group

Some groups are here today and gone tomorrow. For example, the community members who attend a public meeting one week will not be exactly the same members who attend the meeting the next week. Other groups—such as a city council or a cross-function work team created as part of a company's reorganization—may be together for weeks, months, or even years. The duration of the group can make a difference in how much effort needs to be put into creating shared expectations. It's a matter of return on investment. How much benefit are you likely to get for the time you must invest in reaching for higher ground given the amount of time the group will be together?

FROM THE TOOLBOX

- *Group process prework:* When the optimal level of effort is moderate to great but the expected life of the group is short, front-loading work related to group process is very helpful. Using pre-meeting data-collection tools can prompt reflection and provide you, as facilitator or group leader, with much needed information about group dynamics and desires. Possible data collection methods include paper-and-pencil or e-mail methods, focus groups, or individual face-to-face or phone interviews before the group gathers for its task.

- *Spiraled conversation:* This approach is similar to the previous example but is more appropriate for a group of moderate to long duration and when time is on the group's side. In this situation, expanding over time the group's conversation regarding its process is an option. Stage the conversation so that discussion of process is always seen as subservient to the necessary focus on tasks. As the group members encounter one another through the work, how they work invites reflection. With experience, over time the group can be inspired to appreciate more deeply the importance of attending to group process issues.

Complexity of the Tasks or Problems

Simple tasks are less likely than complex tasks to put a strain on the individuals involved. If the path between the problem and the solution is clear and the distance is short, too much attention to process could be an unproductive investment of people's time. But complex tasks for which no solution is obvious or that require the cooperation of many actors can put a great strain on people's attention, emotions, and comfort in a group. The greater the complexity of the task or problem, the more likely it is that a substantial RHG effort will help the group.

FROM THE TOOLBOX

- *Create explicit agendas.* Attend promptly to task-related group issues. Build agendas for the initial meetings that invite the group to make decisions about how important process matters will be handled. These matters typically include, among other issues particular to your group, the following:

    Meeting attendance

    Mode of participation

Responsibility for sharing work and leadership

Agenda development in advance of the meeting

Use of data

Responsibility for evaluating efforts

Use of expertise external to the group

- *Task analysis and performance contracting:* It is possible to anticipate several of the subtasks involved in completing a larger task. Ask the group to make explicit its understanding of those subtasks. For example, an effort to forecast sales for a given product may involve forecasting trends in several major markets where the product is sold. It is also possible to clarify understandings about whether or not a particular approach will be used, such as whether a particular problem-solving process or set of specifications will be followed, or whether a specific measure or standard of judgment will be employed. For example, some external funding sources will require evidence that certain groups of stakeholders were involved in planning programs or that the approaches to be taken represent the use of "best practices" in a certain field.

- Working with these parameters in mind, ask group members to articulate the work behaviors necessary for successful completion of the project or task. Use the work behaviors as the basis for a performance contract—holding all group members accountable for a certain type and level of performance. Such work behaviors for a group forecasting sales on a particular product might include "having major market data available for discussion in meetings" and then assigning the task to various group members. In groups that need to provide evidence to funding sources that certain stakeholders were involved in planning programs or that best practices will be used, an example of work behaviors might be "hold meetings during those hours and on those days when the greatest number of key stakeholder groups can be present," or "research best practices to guide discussions," or "prior to finalizing plans, evaluate proposals in light of best practices."

Group Size

The dynamics of small groups are different from those of large groups. At a minimum, the effort to create full participation is a challenge in large groups and needs careful consideration. However, beyond the logistics of simply making room for everyone in the group, size introduces many of the other elements discussed in this chapter, such as trust, diversity, and balance of power.

Size itself is not a primary determinant of the value of an RHG approach, but it does make a difference in how a group seeks higher ground. It is likely that the larger the group is, the more diverse will be the views of its members, the more unevenly will the power be distributed, and the lower will be the level of trust. All of this can serve to complicate a task and could contribute to extending the amount of time a group will need to work together. Also, the RHG approach requires substantial participation and gaining it can be a challenge for large groups.

> **FROM THE TOOLBOX**
>
> - *Nested circles of consensus:* To accommodate everyone's participation in a large group (twenty or more members), use small groups (four to eight people) within the large group. Small-groups could be created by assignment, randomly, or by self-selection. Have the small groups work on ways they wish to work together and then, in the full group, have each small group offer one expectation it considers important and that has not already been mentioned by another group. Repeat the process until all expectations from the small groups have been nominated. Next, use a three-step refinement process: (1) clarify the statements, (2) discuss the value of the nominated expectations, and (3) discuss what important expectations are missing. Finally, seek full-group consensus by polling the group for its support using a technique such as *Fist to Five*.
> - Fist to Five asks every person in the group to respond to a specific proposal by communicating their level of support for it ranging from a

fist, which shows "no support," to five fingers extended for "full support." Have everyone show their hand at the same time to avoid having some people choose their response in reaction to how others in the room have responded. Find the individuals signaling the least support for the proposal and ask them, "What would it take to get a five from you on this matter?" Continue this process until all major concerns have been addressed and either discarded or incorporated.

Significance of the Issues

This characteristic may be obvious, but it is worth noting. If the group's issues are of modest importance to its members, discussion is unlikely to produce much conflict because members will feel that "it just doesn't really matter." But when it does matter—when people's values are at stake—then watch out! The emotional climate may fluctuate wildly. Disagreements can flare over small details or seemingly simple procedural questions. Certain individuals may dominate discussion while others recede into the background, unable or unwilling to do battle. As a general rule, the more significant the issues are, the greater the attention to RHG should be in order to help the group accomplish its task while nurturing relationships.

FROM THE TOOLBOX

- *Personal impact and personal promises:* When the stakes are high, it is helpful for people to understand the variety of impacts the issue and its possible solutions have on themselves and others. Taking others' perspective is an essential component of the RHG approach. Recognizing what each person has at stake can motivate people to be on their best behavior. It can also inspire people to protect one another and the group's process by working hard to establish shared expectations. Three questions to help raise this information are as follows:

1. "The way this issue impacts me is. . . ."
2. "I will likely be affected by any solution because. . . ."
3. "Given the importance of this issue, we should work hard to. . . ."

- *Probable versus preferred future:* Sometimes the significance of a task is so overwhelming that it stymies people, leaving them locked into inaction or dysfunctional behaviors such as finger-pointing. One way to motivate a group to step up to a difficult task in a seriously collaborative way is first to allow them to consider the consequences of doing nothing beyond what is already being done—in essence, to imagine the probable future. To do this, invite people to imagine that events will unfold exactly as they are now unfolding, with no interruption and no change in direction. The question becomes, "What do you see when you look to the horizon? What will happen if we do nothing different from what we are now doing?" It can be very helpful to record all brainstormed contributions on newsprint posted on the wall.

- *Hint:* draw a line across the paper to signify a horizon. When participants have exhausted that vision, ask them what they would prefer to see on the horizon. On a new set of newsprint sheets containing a horizon line, construct their preferred future in words. To conclude, ask them to imagine the principles or values that need to be enacted to turn away from the probable status quo future and toward the preferred future.

Levels of Trust

A skilled facilitator or group leader works hard to discover the conditions of trust among people in a group. Knowledge of these conditions is essential to group functioning. In high-trust groups, people can say what they think and they can expect that others will seek to understand and value their opinions. Trust is the group process equivalent of gold. But not all groups are wealthy, particularly at the outset. Trust must be earned through trustworthy behavior. If trust is high, creating (or in high-trust groups, enhancing) shared expectations for higher ground can be approached up front. If trust is low, the search for shared expectations must be carefully nurtured for a long time. Creating and explicitly acknowledging the development of these shared expectations need to occur slowly as understanding and trust develop.

FROM THE TOOLBOX

- *Ongoing evaluation:* Build into your meetings ways of assessing your group's progress and process. For low-trust groups, this effort must begin slowly and not take up much time. At the end of each session, do a simple "plus-delta" exercise of the sort discussed in Chapter Six to determine what people liked and what should change. Encourage people to discuss process problems and ask for the group's suggestions, if any, for ways of addressing those problems together.
- *A shuffled deck in large groups:* Give each person five or six index cards. After educating and inspiring the group about the value of reaching for higher ground, invite them to nominate principles by which the group should operate and to suggest a behavior that illustrates that principle. Participants should put only one principle and at least one behavior related to that principle on each of their cards. For example, one person could list "respect" as the principle and "No sidebar conversations" as the behavior. Another could list "respect" as the principle but "Ask for clarification when you don't understand something someone has offered" as the behavior. Collect the cards and shuffle them. Sort the cards by placing similar principles in the same pile. Make a list of the principles and the illustrative behaviors. Discuss the list by looking at the range of principles valued by group members and the variety of behaviors that illustrate those principles. Identify those items that have broad support and those that might conflict with each other. This approach makes it possible for people to raise issues anonymously that they might feel uncomfortable saying directly to the group. It also allows people the chance to speak to an issue without having to claim personal responsibility for it. Finally, it invites more thoughtful discussion about the behaviors we want in groups and about the values those behaviors represent for us.

- A *shuffled deck in small groups*: Invite people to form small groups of four to six people. Chances are that individuals will gravitate toward those people with whom they already feel comfortable. Invite them to nominate guiding principles and supportive behaviors, recording one principle and one behavior per index card. Collect the cards from each group and shuffle the deck. Pass out the index cards, giving each person at least one card if possible. Invite people to read the principle and illustrating behavior on the card they received. Ask all other participants with a similar principle to offer any additional behaviors that illustrate that principle. Then move to a different principle and repeat the process of capturing behaviors. Do this until all unique principles and behaviors have been captured for the group. Refine the list using the "three C's" refinement process: *clarify*, *comment* on what is there, and *comment* on what is missing. Finally, test for consensus using the Fist to Five polling for consensus tip discussed earlier, or some other method.

- *Anonymous postmeeting feedback*: Sometimes a group is not ready to admit that there will be challenges in working together. In such a circumstance, it is possible to avoid up-front attention to such matters so that the need will present itself naturally. When it seems that group members have formed an opinion about the group's performance, distribute feedback forms that invite people to assess the meeting on a number of key features, addressing both matters of task accomplishment and group dynamics. Gather the data, summarize the results, and display the summary of the results. Ask how the members' perceptions of the meetings are likely to affect the groups' accomplishment of its goals. Discuss what might be done to improve the group's functioning. This can be a great time to invite more serious attention to RHG.

Power Distribution

Groups in which power is distributed unevenly typically find it difficult to promote full participation. Differences in power can be real, as in an organization in which one person in the group has the power to fire another. Power differences can also be a matter of perception, such as when one group member is intimidated by the experience, poise, or intellect of another. Such differences can create a destructive dynamic in a group. Like trust, the dynamic of power influences not only the need for shared expectations for higher ground but also the approach used.

FROM THE TOOLBOX

The tools presented for dealing with low trust will also help compensate for power differences in groups. In addition:

- *Get in Line:* If the group is of good humor, you may want to try breaking familiar patterns of who speaks first and who speaks the most by playing Get in Line. Ask people to line up according to verbosity, with those who speak least taking their place at the beginning of the line. Then invite people to contribute to the discussion by going around the group in order from the least talkative to the most talkative. Often the most powerful people also talk the most. If that is the case in your group, this is a simple way to interrupt the all too familiar dynamics and invite some new voices into the discussion.

- *Is there anything I'm not saying?* This idea comes from Sam Kaner and his colleagues at Communities at Work (Kaner, 1996). After generating a set of expectations in a large-group setting, invite people to break into pairs or triads. Ask each partner to answer the question, "During this discussion have you had any thoughts you haven't said aloud?" Assure people that they are not required to say anything they don't want to say. Next ask the partners or triads to answer the question, "Would the group benefit from hearing your partner's thinking?" Return to the large group. Ask for volunteers to share any thoughts from this exercise that might be useful for others to hear.

Level of Aspirations

Some groups form only to get a piece of work done and then they disband. People in such groups want to make a limited investment of time and psychic energy. Thus they expect a limited return. In these groups, encouraging members to reach for higher ground through reflection on the values and principles that define individuals' actions may be asking too much. The members' aspirations are functional, meaning they have come together to perform a particular function or accomplish a particular task—nothing more, nothing less.

However, some groups know from the start that their aspirations are transformative. They intend to accomplish more than a mere task. They intend to change themselves as individuals or as a group through working together. Perhaps it is even their intention to serve as agents of change in their community. A group with such change-oriented or transformative aspirations would likely be more open to and is better served by an RHG approach.

FROM THE TOOLBOX

- *Individual metaphor metamorphosis:* Another clever tool from Susan Bailey of Bailey Alliance is to invite people to describe their typical behavior in groups using a metaphor, such as a common household tool, an appliance, or an animal. Then invite them to suggest a more ideal metaphor (from the same genre) that captures their preferred way of being in a group. Help them compare and contrast the two metaphors by asking, "What are the essential characteristics of the preferred metaphor? How does it suggest certain perspectives about aspirations, group guidelines, or behavior?" For example, a person using animals for their metaphors might choose the turtle to characterize their typical behavior, implying that they are slow moving and have a protective attitude, that they withdraw quickly at the first sign of trouble, and so forth. For their preferred metaphor, the person might choose the monkey to convey agility, quickness, and the ability to solve problems. By comparing

their typical behavior to their desired behavior, individuals and groups can aspire to better performance.
- *Write the book jacket of a best-seller:* Help the group envision the future, a future in which all they hope for their group and from their project will come to be. Imagine that a major publishing house wants to publish a book about the group's experience and accomplishments. The group's task is to write a blurb for the inside flap of the book jacket that explains what it took to get the job done.

Level of Attention and Commitment Needed

The eight characteristics just illustrated and the accompanying toolbox items are not meant to be a complete compendium of possibilities. Rather, they are offered to enlarge your vision of what is possible and appropriate, to expand your imagination, and to create your own toolbox. As we have said, the specific techniques can be modified or merged. The challenge is to find a way to help your group reach for ground higher than they thought possible, and to do it in a manner that respects the unique features of the group.

In a group characterized by common views, high trust, relatively equal power, functional aspirations, a simple, low-stakes task, and an intentionally short-term effort, less time and effort are needed to create and maintain shared expectations for higher ground. However, for a group whose members have diverse backgrounds and views, in which power is distributed unevenly, and who have transformative aspirations, a complex task, and an expectation that the group will continue to work together over time, it would be well worth striving for a peak level of enactment of shared expectations. The path to getting there, however, may be steep and will likely test the resolve and resourcefulness of everyone involved.

A skilled group leader will assess the critical features of a group and its task by considering issues such as those raised in this chapter. Having considered such matters, it may seem obvious that the six elements of the RHG approach we offered in Chapter Five are unlikely to work unless they are modified to be consistent with the group's needs.

As the snapshot that concludes this section illustrates, few groups belong at one extreme or the other of the ranges suggested by the features or characteristics summarized in Table 7.1. Also, group dynamics change over time. In reality, things are not so neatly partitioned or so black and white, as you will see.

❖ *Snapshot.* Marina had an opportunity to help a group of state-level public agency administrators come together for the happy task of deciding how to spend millions of dollars they anticipated receiving from a court settlement. Large installments of money would come to the state over a number of years. The funds were to be spent on a set of priority community issues. The group

Table 7.1. Level of Attention and Commitment to Shared Expectations Needed for Higher Ground

	Low Effort	*Medium Effort*	*High Effort*
Group diversity	Homogenous	Some diversity	Highly diverse
Duration of group	Short-term	Medium-term	Lasting
Complexity of task	Simple, clear task	Medium complexity	Very complex
Group size	Small	Medium	Large
Significance of issue(s)	Low	Fairly significant	Great significance
Level of trust	High	Uneven	Substantial distrust
Power distribution	Equal	Somewhat disparate	Highly stratified
Level of aspirations	Low	Medium	High

responsible for the task was a cross-division team from the state agency.

In interviews with participants, a number of things became clear to Marina. The group would number about eighteen people, chosen to participate because they represented different aspects of expertise. Although everyone was part of the same organization and the same field, they would bring to the group a variety of perspectives about priorities and approaches.

The group was to be long-term—the project would last several years—and members intended to work together for a long time. Even at the end of the project, these people would still be colleagues in the same organization. The task was complex. They were trying to do something neither they nor anyone else had ever done before. The stakes were high. They had to perform well or they would risk losing millions of dollars for the state—a state with a bottomed-out economy. This money was the best chance their citizens had for a significant infusion of resources. The group had to show results or risk the money and their credibility.

The group membership would span three levels of organizational hierarchy (that is, some people would be in this group with their boss and their boss's boss). Although the whole group had never worked together as a group, many of the individuals had personal and professional relationships, some good and some quite bad. Marina was told that no one was about to be honest with her about the relationships among people in the group for fear of retribution by powerful group members. People felt threatened and trust was low.

The group had a big task to do—disburse the money in a way that would accomplish their goals. Group leaders also believed that the money and the group's effort represented an opportunity to transform the state. To do so, they needed to create a shared vision, transforming themselves in the process, both as individual managers and as an organization, by overcoming divisional boundaries, partnering with the community, and finding new ways of working together.

Among the tasks that had to be accomplished was the task of creating shared expectations for constructive engagement. Marina had to determine the best way to approach that task given the characteristics of the group. How much effort was appropriate and what approach might the group most appreciate and support? Using Table 7.1 as a diagnostic aid, and with the guidance of the group, Marina determined that medium to high effort was needed.

The level of effort needed was a matter separate from the question of approach. The approach would be determined by the specific characteristics of the group. In this case, the low level of trust and the group's anxiety about the complexity of the task required a somewhat indirect and incremental approach to reaching for higher ground. Marina decided to introduce issues of group process part way into the first meeting, a five-hour retreat, rather than at the outset. She also decided to deal with shared expectations in a basic way at the first meeting, knowing that there was not sufficient trust to have a truly open discussion of these group issues. Additionally, an atmosphere of anxiety and impatience about the amount of work to be done would leave little tolerance for long discussions of process issues.

A deep discussion of how best to reach for higher ground would have to be worked into the conversation, over time and in the right way. Until then, Marina would have to work hard to create a safe and productive atmosphere for everyone. Her tools were the meeting's agenda, the composition of small work groups, and the process tools she deemed appropriate to get the work done.

Basically, Marina decided to order the agenda in response to the group's priority concerns. The agenda had four items: (1) the task: givens and knowns; (2) the vision: inspiration and aspirations; (3) the team: the players and their parts; and (4) the issues: problems and proposed actions. Marina determined that placing issues of group composition and group process behind the issue of vision for the project or initiative would likely place people in a reflective and motivated frame of mind. While she would not deliberately speak of reaching for higher ground in the first meeting, Marina hoped that the group would begin to recognize the significant role that their relationships would play in enacting the vision for the project and accomplishing the task. She relied heavily on small-group work to increase participation and a sense of safety. Marina also assigned membership in the small groups to minimize the power differences and the influence of negative personal histories between certain group members.

Because of trust and time factors, Marina limited the discussion of the team and group functioning to two types of reflection. First, she had people describe their understanding of their role in the project given their place in the larger organization—a question of function. Second, using a simple tool for discussing work style preferences, Marina invited each person to assess his or her own preferences and then share that information with the group by marking their response to each of six items she had drawn on flipchart paper (see Figure 7.1). The group looked at patterns in the members' responses and discussed the likely impact of those patterns in terms of the work to be done.

Marina wanted each person in the group to leave the meeting wanting more attention to group process at the next meeting. She wanted to create an appetite for concern about the team and about how to optimize its performance and chances of success. Marina needed the group members to feel safe with her and with each other. She sought to inspire hope that, in time and with effort, relationships could be strengthened and everyone could feel good about their work and about one another.

◆ *Reflection.* Marina's plan was wholly successful. The group accomplished its task while recognizing that more work needed to be done, both in terms of the complex problem they had come together to solve and in terms of their ability to work together in more efficient and collaborative ways. Evidence of this conclusion was visible in the appreciation they expressed for the way the meeting had gone and their conviction that they needed a facilitator for future meetings. The shift was under way. The task quickly became one of helping the group establish productive work habits and relationship-building routines. This would in time afford them less dependence on an outside facilitator.

Figure 7.1. Work Styles: What Can We Expect from You in a Group?

In a meeting, while working with colleagues, you generally . . .

1. Amount of time you talk during a meeting on a new topic:

|―――――――――――――――――+―――――――――――――――――|
| Very little | Medium amount | Talk a lot |

2. How you deal with conflict:

|―――――+―――――+―――――+―――――|
| Avoid | Accommodate | Compromise | Compete | Collaborate |
| Deny, avoid all conflict. | I give up something to satisfy you. | We both give up something to get something. | I get what I want. | We can work together. Your needs and my needs. |

3. During a meeting, you think about . . .

|―――――――――――――――――――――――――――――――――|
| Task | Relationships |
| Let's get the work done. | Let's make sure everyone feels comfortable. |

4. How much information do you need before making a decision?

|―――――――――――――――――――――――――――――――――|
| Everything | Nothing |
| I need to know it all before I can decide. | Why let information get in the way of making a decision? |

5. Decision-making style:

|―――――――――――――――――――――――――――――――――|
| Let's talk to everybody and make a detailed plan. | Just do it! Don't talk about it! |

6. Attitude toward implementation of plans:

|―――――――――――――――――――――――――――――――――|
| Cheerleader | Analyzer |
| This is great! Let's do it! | This is what will go wrong with the plan. |

Assessing Your Location on the Path to Higher Ground

In this final section we offer lenses through which to judge how far along the path to higher ground your group is. As we have stated, we believe that every group can and should aim for the next higher rung on the ladder in order to strengthen relationships and become more productive.

Evaluation of groups should include attention to the following elements:

1. Scope of attention to rules and expectations
2. Process of development of expectations
3. Process of accountability to the rules and expectations
4. Level of enactment of shared expectations and higher-ground principles
5. Refinement and renewal of rules and expectations

We also offer four general levels at which a group may be judged in terms of their performance:

1. *Subgrade:* There is no effort or awareness of the role of shared expectations, even in the basic sense of ground rules, much less a higher-ground approach.
2. *Basic:* The group takes a traditional approach to ground rules.
3. *Rising:* Some effort is made to move from using directive, traditional ground rules to making a higher-ground effort.
4. *Peak:* The group tries consistently to enact higher-ground principles; the peak is not a final accomplishment but instead, a goal and a continuing commitment.

How groups are likely to behave at the four levels is summarized in Table 7.2. How they perform on each of the five elements may

Table 7.2. Assessing a Group's Path to Reaching for Higher Ground

	Subgrade	Basic	Rising	Peak
Scope of attention	No attention given	Behavior only	Values and behavior	Vision, desired outcomes, and behavioral ground rules
Process of development	Expectations are implicit	Rules are given by group leader or borrowed from other settings	Some group members participate in the development of rules	All group members are invited to engage in development of rules
Process of accountability	Varies; depends on quality of leadership, effort	Group leader	Group leader, with some group members sharing responsibility	Group leader helps group members hold one another accountable
Level of enactment	Varies, generally low	Varies, generally low to medium	Commitment to enactment is often realized	Full commitment to enactment
Refinement and renewal	Rules change according to group and individual whim	Rules are rarely reviewed	Renewal occurs during crisis or challenge	Periodic renewal

not be in the alignment suggested, but we think the summaries are useful.

The *scope of attention* is the range of concerns explicitly addressed by a group. At the subgrade level there is no discussion. At the basic level they consider specific behavior only (as in "don't interrupt," "be on time," or "ask questions before criticizing"). The rising level builds on more general values or shared expectations—the principles that guide behavior. Finally, at the peak stage the group holds a broader shared vision of explicit values and principles about how it does its work.

The *process of development* is how the rules or expectations are created. The process ranges from only implicit rules and expectations at the subgrade level to open participation and full agreement by the group on the shared expectations at the peak level. You can never guarantee participation but you can invite and encourage it, consistent with the general principle of educating and inspiring for higher ground.

The *process of accountability* is whether and how compliance or correction occurs in relation to the rules. Most often people expect the group leader, committee chair, or facilitator to be the monitor or even the traffic cop when people move away from the rules. We judge that in a rising group the group leader and the other group members share the responsibility, whereas in the peak condition the group members themselves monitor compliance and correction, for the most part.

Assessing the *level of enactment* of shared expectations or higher ground principles requires a hard look at not only accountability but also overall performance. Commitment as well as accomplishment count in this dimension. Of course at the subgrade level you can't enact what is not discussed or decided. At the other end of the spectrum, a peak level is reached when there is full commitment and high accomplishment of the vision, values, and behaviors adopted by the group.

Refinement and renewal call for attention to how rules are reviewed and changed. There is a big difference between the rising and peak levels of seeking higher ground. In the rising situation, review and change occur only when prompted by a crisis or challenge. In essence, there is a reaction that questions how people understand a rule or expectations and whether they think it should be modified or abandoned. In the peak condition, there is proactive, periodic review of the vision, desired outcomes, values, and behavioral guidelines. The group need not wait for a crisis to do maintenance.

Some of the elements just presented will become clearer as we compare a small work group under the "rising" and "peak" conditions in the next chapter. We recognize that the six dimensions of reaching for higher ground cannot always be easily followed in a step-by-step process. While educating and inspiring is logically the first step, other group needs may take precedence. We think that understanding the characteristics of groups covered in this chapter will help you apply the principles in real life for your group. We have offered specific tools for addressing characteristics that make applying a higher-ground principle difficult—when the group is too big, unbalanced, uncommunicative, or seething. Finally, we have provided two different sets of lenses for judging where your group is on the path to higher ground. Let's take a look next at how different approaches to higher ground might affect an actual group.

Chapter Eight

Reaching for Higher Ground in Action

A Hospital Department Management Team at Work

By now you may be wondering what reaching for higher ground (RHG) looks like in real life. Can you get a picture of it in your mind? We intend to help you do just that.

In this chapter we demonstrate the RHG approach by contrasting two distinct approaches to the same scenario. Our setting is the management team of a hospital radiology department. By showing a team using first typical ground rules then an RHG approach, we hope to add color to the principles, toolbox items, and illustrations discussed previously.

The scenario is fictitious so that we may carefully draw both obvious and subtle differences that result from using RHG. The people and issues are the same in each scenario. We'll move through three meetings, showing each meeting first in a typical environment of ordinary ground rules in a good-faith effort, and then using an RHG approach. Throughout we'll demonstrate the importance of being flexible and creative as you respond to the unique needs and characteristics of a group while remaining true to the elements of RHG. Notice that in the second and third meetings the elements of higher ground are reintroduced to the group, only this time they are not in the order in which we presented them in Chapter Five. Instead we have combined elements and attended to them in a fluid manner designed to support the group's work in the most natural and unobtrusive way.

The group we present in this scenario is not exactly enthusiastic about attending to matters of group process. One strategy for dealing with a group with a heavy task orientation or a low tolerance for discussing matters of process is to engage the group in thinking about matters of process on a specific high-stakes issue or on an issue with high potential for conflict. Even a group that is loathe to expend any effort discussing group process can become more open to the need to do so when focusing on a particular hot topic. Principles and shared expectations that are useful for guiding the discussion of the hot topic can then be recycled for their value as guidelines for the group's work more generally. This is a sort of backdoor entry into the discussion of shared expectations. We demonstrate this technique in the second meeting using the RHG approach.

Now, on with the show!

The setting: A university hospital radiology department

The meetings: The first three meetings of the new business manager and his management team

The people: David—business manager of the department; Delores—head of equipment and film processing; Juan—director of scheduling; Peter—supplies coordinator; Margaret—chief attending physician, supervises residents and medical students

---

David is the new business manager (that is, the director) of the radiology department of a university hospital. He began work two weeks ago after serving for three years in the same position at an out-of-state hospital. He reports to the vice president of finance. David also reports to and coordinates with the chair of the radiology department of the medical school affiliated with the hospital. David is white and in his late forties. He was raised in a conservative rural community. He finds expressions of sexuality uncomfortable and has always thought that expression of matters related to sexuality was inappropriate for the workplace.

Delores is head of equipment and film processing. She manages the work of the technicians who perform the X rays, CT scans, ultrasounds, and so on, and oversees vendors who service the machines. Delores has been with the department for ten years, the last four in her current supervisory position. She had some run-ins with the previous business manager and has only met David twice: in a group during his job interview visit two months ago and a brief private session last week. Delores is Asian American and in her late thirties.

Peter is in charge of supplies. His position was created one year ago after a big scandal in the central purchasing and warehousing department of the hospital. One result of the scandal was the distribution of the purchasing and warehousing responsibilities to different sections of the hospital. Peter often has to do swaps with supply coordinators in other parts of the hospital when something gets delayed in the ordering and delivery system. He has a bachelor's degree in history and followed his partner Leo to town when Leo got a job with a software firm.

Peter has been with the hospital for two years. He spent his first year in a part-time writing and editorial position in community relations but did not receive benefits. He took his current position to ensure health benefits for Leo, whose employer went through a downsizing that made health insurance premiums unaffordable. Peter organized a book club at the hospital that meets biweekly. He is in his late twenties and is a first-generation American—his father is Romanian and his mother is Scottish. Peter has been active and vocal in his support of gay rights. He brings Leo to hospital social functions and has made it comfortable for other staff to be more open in the workplace about their gay or lesbian lifestyles.

Juan is head of scheduling. His duties cover everything from supervising the receptionists to managing patient appointments, radiologists' and technicians' schedules, and equipment downtime for maintenance in order to coordinate daily operations. Juan is in his early forties and is second-generation Hispanic American. Two years ago he received a health administration certificate from the community college; he has been in his current position for the last eighteen months. Juan liked the previous business manager, who was Hispanic and, with Juan, founded a monthly brown bag lunch group among Hispanic employees. Juan and Delores discovered they both love the Marx Brothers, and they often throw funny lines from the movies at each other to lighten the mood.

Margaret is the chief attending physician for radiology. She supervises the board-certified radiologists, the residents, and the medical students, and she works with the chair of the radiology department scheduling other medical school faculty to supervise the residents. The residents do the bulk of the hands-on, routine work in the department. Margaret is in her late fifties and is African American. She likes Delores a lot—they share a lot of girl-talk humor in the hallway.

Given the rapid changes in health care and hospital administration these days, it seems that the management team is always dealing with uncertainty and with decisions forced upon them. David's predecessor made it clear that he called the shots and he saw everyone, except Margaret, as a subordinate.

The First Meeting

Using Regular Ground Rules

David has had separate brief get-acquainted meetings with Delores, Juan, and Peter and a group meeting with the hospital business managers, the chief attending physicians (including Margaret), and the dean of the medical school. He just got back from a two-day orientation in which he divided his time between a couple of vice presidents at the hospital and state agency medical insurance people at the state capital.

David learned the hard way a few years ago that conflict could be productive and strengthen relationships if handled properly or destructive and cause misery if ignored or dealt with improperly. In his experience, sometimes the ground rules work and sometimes they don't. But what's the alternative? He figures it's worth trying to find out, so he begins his first department management team meeting by laying out ground rules he picked up from an effective manager training he attended two years ago. These rules include the following:

- Agenda items must be submitted to David forty-eight hours in advance and he will distribute an agenda twenty-four hours ahead of the meeting.
- Meetings must begin and end on time.
- Don't interrupt.
- Focus on interests, not positions.

David indicates that he tries to seek consensus but is ambiguous about what that means and about his own authority when consensus is not reached. He notes that he is responsible to the hospital's CEO for making all necessary decisions on time.

David asks, "Are these ground rules OK with everyone? I just want to be straight with everyone." People nod their heads or murmur their agreement. David thinks, "I'm glad that's settled; now let's get down to business."

Peter asks, "How long will this meeting be?" David replies, "Ninety minutes."

However, Delores thinks, "While the rules sound OK, the last business manager always interrupted and treated me disrespectfully, and I heard similar things from the two other Asian Americans in the department. I hope David is different."

Peter thinks, "It's good to have some basic rules. I don't mind if he is 'straight' with everyone, as long as he's not narrow-minded. If the on-time rule would ever *really* work with doctors, I'd be astonished!"

Juan thinks, "I've never heard of this ground rules stuff before. Don't people just know how to behave? Well, he's the boss—no problem from me."

Margaret thinks, "What's the big deal? He should show leadership and get down to business. Lord knows how long I have until I'm paged."

The meeting proceeds through three main topics: handling intakes received from two outpatient clinics, the recent damage of some equipment, and the hospital board's guidance to top management to prepare a budget assuming a 5 percent reduction from this year's spending. David reports that he'll have more information about how and when each department must submit its budget in time for their next meeting in two weeks.

The ninety-minute meeting is coming to an end and there is tension around the budget cut. At two minutes before the time to end the meeting, David suggests, "Let's go ten more minutes just to lay out some budget questions to research before our next meeting." He does not see Delores roll her eyes as a private message to Juan. Margaret shifts in her seat. The meeting does end ninety-eight minutes after its start.

As people leave the room, Delores thinks, "So much for staying on time. Get ready for marathon meetings—ten extra minutes this time, twenty minutes the next. Ugh."

Peter thinks, "He seems pretty cool, ran a good meeting."

Juan thinks, "I'm going to hear it from Delores. Doesn't David pay attention to body language? Maybe he just doesn't care. Oh well."

Margaret thinks, "I wonder what Delores makes of all this? Maybe I can catch a minute with her. Nope—there goes my beeper."

Using RHG Techniques

David learned the hard way a few years ago that conflict could be productive and could strengthen relationships if handled properly, or destructive and cause misery if ignored or dealt with improperly. As part of his first round of introductions to individual staff members, he mentioned his hopes and expectations about being able to work together productively and in ways that support one another as well as the hospital's mission. On the basis of his one-on-one talks with Margaret, Peter, Juan, and Delores, David senses some tension among them. Peter was the only one to note explicitly some friction between himself and his coworkers and other members of the management team, but he said he thought it might self-correct with a new business manager. David noticed a picture of Peter and another man on Peter's desk. It made David stop, but he did not say anything. David thought to himself, "Don't go into people's private lives; treat everyone professionally. The less I know, the better."

David considers the two most important groups for his work environment to be his management team and the department head group chaired by the vice president for finance. He decides it's worth the effort to engage his management team in thinking about how they can work together effectively using the six elements of RHG introduced in Chapter Five:

1. Establish the need
2. Educate and inspire
3. Begin by envisioning desired outcomes
4. Promote full participation
5. Be accountable
6. Evaluate and revise

Element 1: Establish the need. As he opens the first meeting, David expresses his appreciation for the chance to have met everyone individually prior to the meeting. He explains that it gave him a better understanding of the members of the team and convinced him of their collective potential. He says he considers this group to be essential to the hospital and to his success and he therefore wants to invest some effort in making sure they are highly effective at working together.

He tells the group, "Working in a group can be really challenging, but I also realize that if we do it well, it can be really rewarding. It seems to me that my arrival creates an opportunity for everyone to have a fresh start. But that's all it is—an opportunity. The question is whether we want to use this opportunity to our best advantage. As I see it, we don't have to let habit or history dictate to us what our experience will be in this group. I'd like to think we can invent this together, that we can be open and straight with one another. But I recognize that what I'm talking about will take some creativity and commitment from each one of us. I've had time to think about this. I'd like to use a few minutes of our meeting time to let you think about this and then we can decide together whether or not it's worth any serious investment."

Peter thinks: "Straight with one another: innocent or with a message? I don't mind if he is 'straight' with everyone, as long as he's not narrow-minded."

David looks around the room and sees a mix of expressions ranging from curiosity to skepticism to enthusiasm. He decides to wade in with a question: "What might the benefits be of trying to work together in ways that exceed our wildest expectations for both cohesion and productivity? What would it get us?" There is a long silence. Then, just as David is rethinking his question and this approach, Delores offers, "Better decisions?" David, grateful for any response, nods and follows with another question: "OK, better how?" Delores hesitates and then adds, "Better because they are based on information, not just opinion." David says OK and writes her comment on a flip chart under the heading, "Benefits of Investing in the Way We Work."

Juan timidly says, "I'm not sure I know what you're after here but I was thinking that if we really started clicking as a group, we might see decisions that make sense to everyone—decisions that I support and can justify to the staff." Margaret quips, "That would be nice, now wouldn't it?" David says, "That's just the kind of thing I'm looking for." He writes Juan's comment below Delores's on the flip chart.

Margaret follows with, "One benefit worth working for would be meetings that are brief and to the point!" Before David can finish writing down that comment, Peter suggests, "Better coordination of resources." Other comments follow, including "reduced costs from better use of resources," "better attitudes," "better communication with staff," "better use of our time—focusing on important rather than trivial stuff." This exchange goes on for some time and David records every comment. After about four minutes, the group grows quiet. Peter, reviewing the list, says, "Sign me up! Who wouldn't want those things?"

Delores cautions, "Don't get too excited, Peter. There's got to be a catch. If this were easy, we'd all be doing it, right?" David steps in and acknowledges the truth of Delores's statement. "You're right!" he says. "There is a catch. We have to *make* this happen. So what would it cost us? What would it take?" Juan jumps in immediately with, "A willingness to change old, unproductive habits—which is much easier said than done."

David pins the first flipchart page on the wall and starts a second one titled "Cost of Investing in How We Work." Delores comments, "I guess it wouldn't just happen. We would probably have to put some time into the whole issue of how we work together—and time is something we don't have much of. We need to be realistic." Margaret says, "I get your point, David, but I don't see where it's going and we're already fifteen minutes into the meeting. I mentioned that I have to leave on time, right?"

David steps back from the flipchart paper where he has been recording the group's ideas and says, "What do you conclude from this cost-benefit analysis?" As he looks around the room, he sees people reading over the two lists and nodding knowingly. Juan says, "It's a no-brainer but how do we deal with the issue of time?" David pauses and then offers his thoughts.

Element 2: Educate and inspire. David explains, "I'm really interested in experimenting with just how good we could get at being a group. I think if we put a bit of effort into this up front and then just enough to maintain things along the way, it could save us time in the long run—you know, time wasted in unproductive conversation or costly conflicts, time wasted in decisions that never get made or, worse yet, that get made and then are never successfully implemented." Everyone nods—some enthusiastically, others cautiously. Peter says, "So what did you have in mind?"

Element 3: Begin by envisioning desired outcomes. David replies, "I thought we could ease into this by reflecting on our meeting experiences in general. What has worked well or poorly for you in this group or in other management meetings?" Once again David stands ready to record the others' responses on the flip chart. Delores mentions the need to begin and end meetings on time as important to her. Peter suggests that if there is a conflict or misunderstanding, it should not go outside the group—that is, there should be no gossip. Juan isn't sure what David is looking for. He says he has always given his view when asked by the business manager, but he knows that David has to make the decisions. Margaret immediately jumps in and asserts that she wants to be able to make decisions quickly; she doesn't want to discuss things over many meetings.

As David reflects on these ideas, he says, "Well, let's list some of these things as guidelines." Margaret interrupts, "David, no disrespect but I'm concerned about how long we're going to take to talk about this procedural stuff. We've heard people's concerns and as adults we should already know how to be productive in a meeting."

Juan just cannot hold back—a rude interruption just when they are getting to know the new business manager! Although he knows how doctors and residents can make his life hell, it is time to speak up. "Margaret, I have to say that what really did *not* work well for me in our meetings with the previous business manager was interrupting people when they are speaking—and you just interrupted David. I'm willing to take a few more minutes to lay out some rules we can live with—it doesn't have to take long. Not interrupting people—just as a basic courtesy—is important to me."

Element 4: Promote full participation. David responds, "Margaret, how about we take ten more minutes to create some rules of the road for our meetings and then move to other business? And Juan, thanks for expressing your concern about interruptions." Margaret relents but clearly is not engaged in the ground rules discussion.

The group takes an additional ten minutes and agrees on the same ground rules as in the previous version of this meeting, but about a third of that time is focused on decision making by consensus. David suggests that reaching consensus is a good goal. "It's less likely that people will feel they lost on an issue."

"But the problem is that trying to get a full consensus can take a long time and often it is just a compromise rather than a well-reasoned decision," Margaret says. The agreement they reach is, "Seek consensus but David has the responsibility if a decision is needed before consensus is reached."

To address Margaret's concern about prompt decisions, they set a two-meeting rule: a topic can be discussed at one meeting but can't go beyond the second without a decision. David notes that the group may have to revisit this rule. In his experience, many matters are interrelated and may need to be revisited from a different angle or with new information not long after the initial decision has been made.

The meeting proceeds through the three main topics: handling intakes received from two outpatient clinics, recent loss and damage of equipment, and the hospital board's request to prepare a budget assuming a 5 percent cut. The ninety-minute meeting is coming to an end and there is tension about the possible cut. At two minutes until the end David says, "Let's go ten more minutes just to lay out some questions to research before our next meeting."

The ground rules discussion had been really invigorating for Delores, but now she wonders if it's just for show. "I thought we agreed to end meetings on time," she thinks, but here is the guy in charge trying to get ten more minutes. I really have to go!"

Element 5: Be accountable. Delores takes a chance: "David, I know we might be able to get a bit more accomplished by going overtime, but didn't we agree to the ground rule of ending meetings on time? Not going overtime is important to me, especially today."

David says, "You're right. How about this: tomorrow I'll distribute a list of options and questions for research on potential budget cuts. Each person can modify or add to it. I will make clear who will investigate which questions or options between now and the next meeting. OK?" Everyone agrees with David's proposal and the meeting ends on time.

Element 6: Evaluate and revise. As they leave the meeting, Peter thinks, "I really want to iron out the problems among ourselves. But I worry about Margaret and her arrogant MDs, and then certain staff always need something to gossip about. I don't know how David is going to keep everyone in line."

Margaret thinks, "Ground rules, quality improvement, managing by objectives—Geez, I've seen it all before. Procedures without action. I hope this is the end of the "What do you think this meeting should be about" junk. I have work to do!"

As Delores and Juan leave, they duck into an empty room. "He actually followed his own rules!" Delores says excitedly but quietly.

Juan replies, "His rules? I think he thinks they're *our* rules. Anyway, you showed some guts to challenge him on extending the meeting. Good for you! And I only counted two interruptions, and both times the people knew they were in the wrong. Maybe this is the start of something a bit more civil for our meetings. I just wish Margaret didn't have such a sour face so much of the time. She is so uptight, watching the clock and counting the minutes. What is that, anyway? It's really getting on my nerves!"

"It looked like she ate something that disagreed with her. Maybe an animal cracker?" joked Delores. Juan shot back, "Or a bowl of duck soup with lots of quackers?" They laugh quietly.

Reflection on the First Meeting

David could have called an extra meeting to lead his group through creating a covenant. A covenant is a more ambitious undertaking focused on values and needs that are much deeper than the ground rules established in either of the two versions of the first meeting. David decided against doing this because of his limited knowledge of the dynamics among his four colleagues and of their willingness to take such a process seriously. To properly prepare a covenant, it is important to know how trusting and open people are. In the second version, David built the group's interest and then invited the members to create ground rules together instead of simply presenting a list of ground rules as he did in the first version. This is a good first step toward a process that can deepen over time.

We have kept most of the ground rules the same in order to make fair contrasts in the second and third meetings. (See Exhibit 8.1 for a list of both sets of rules.) David also kept his word about the rule to end on time—a very important precedent to set. Nonetheless, as you can see from Margaret's comments, not everyone loves this "process stuff." We think this response is typical, and we will show you one way to handle Margaret's "let's get down to business" focus.

Exhibit 8.1. Comparison of Regular Ground Rules to RHG Ground Rules

Regular Ground Rules

1. Agenda items must be submitted to David forty-eight hours in advance and he will distribute an agenda twenty-four hours ahead of the meeting.
2. Meetings must begin and end on time.
3. Don't interrupt.
4. Focus on interests, not positions.

RHG Ground Rules

1. Agenda items must be submitted to David forty-eight hours in advance and he will distribute an agenda twenty-four hours ahead of the meeting.
2. Meetings must begin and end on time.
3. Don't interrupt.
4. Focus on interests, not positions.
5. Consensus must be sought but David has the responsibility if a decision is needed before consensus is reached.
6. Two-meeting rule: Discussion of a topic must not go beyond a second meeting without a decision being made.

Between the First and Second Meetings

In both versions of the story, two days after the meeting David e-mails his team with research assignments:

> Delores and Peter: Explore sources of cheaper film for CT and MRI work.
>
> Juan: Report on any likely savings from changing two receptionists from full-time to part-time positions, and consult with Delores about having a "floating" technician position.
>
> Peter: Identify the three most expensive supply categories and compare the department's costs with those of the radiology departments of three other university-based hospitals and two area private hospitals, and do some Internet research on costs of supplies.
>
> Margaret: Research the possibility of more weekend time for residents' work hours to reduce personnel costs.

A week after the radiology management team meeting, David and his fellow business managers are told by the vice president of finance to prepare two budget submissions: one for a 5 percent cut and another for a 7 percent cut. The vice president cannot yet say what the specific time frame will be for submitting a budget, because revenue estimates are being held up for two weeks due to questions about grants and contracts.

One of Peter's gay friends at the hospital, George, reports to Peter that he overheard David while in line at the bank machine. David was talking with someone George took to be another department administrator. They were talking about personnel matters when David said, "Boy there are a lot of benefits here: child care subsidies, gym access—even bereavement leave for, um, same-sex couples. That's way out there." George asks how Peter is doing with David. Peter says, "No problems, but I'm still figuring him out."

Three days before the team's second meeting under David's supervision, the resident and med student rotation turns. Margaret receives a new batch of residents to get up to speed, which always takes a lot of her time for about two weeks.

The Second Meeting
Using Regular Ground Rules

The day before the meeting, per the ground rules, David sends out the following agenda:

Agenda: Sixty-Minute Meeting

1. Budget planning—possible 5 percent cut, possible 7 percent cut

   Reports on assignments

   Additional research needed

   New ideas, options

   Timeline to a decision

2. Updates on other topics

Peter arrives at the meeting two minutes late, rushing in and offering apologies. "I had been trying to track down this lead for cheaper paper since last week and finally the woman called me back." As Peter sits down, he inadvertently brushes against David's back. Peter feels David stiffen.

After a brief review of the agenda, Juan, Peter, and Delores report on their research on how to cut costs. Each of them has proposals for cutting 5 to 8 percent of the costs in their areas of responsibility. David probes them about their information. Peter explains he created two lists: tier 1 substitutions would save 5 percent, tier 2 substitutions, when added to the tier 1 items, would yield a total savings of 8 percent in supply costs. Peter and Delores respond that they think they could move things closer to a 10 percent savings in each of their areas, but it would be very tight.

Turning to the cost estimates for residents and medical students, David and Margaret say they have each heard rumors about the medical school planning to increase the rate it charges the hospital for residents' work. Things become very quiet because such an increase would make it virtually impossible to get to a cut of 5 or 7 percent. Margaret reports that she does not have any figures, nor does she know if there is much possibility of scheduling the residents more on the weekends to reduce costs. She explains to the group about the new set of residents and med students she is dealing with, and how that has been taking almost all of her time.

> *Peter:* Without figures on the med school charges to the department, how can we think about the other options? That's a real hole to me.
>
> *Delores:* Me, too. David, what is this budget exercise about if we don't have the information we need to give our input?
>
> *Margaret:* Don't look at me; this is beyond my control. I do think the current rates for residents are far too low, but it's not my call.
>
> *Peter:* Rates too low? I know the rates at three other university hospitals and ours is at the top end of the scale.
>
> *Margaret:* Peter, I don't think you know what you're talking about. I've seen a peer-reviewed study of forty-five university hospitals and we stink!

Things are getting hot!

David interjects, "Hold on just a minute. I know budget cutting puts everyone on edge. Peter and Margaret: I want to hear each of your opinions, but do remember that we set a rule of no interruptions. When someone gets interrupted, they get frustrated and sometimes angry. It is a natural, human reaction, but we need to try to use the rules to put forward the 'better angels' of our human nature."

Delores thinks, "I'm glad this didn't get out of hand. David seems to have a nice touch."

Margaret ponders, "Just when we are getting at the meat of something, David tries to smooth things over. Supposed peace, but no fairness on residents' salaries; just a way to keep me from speaking. Peter does like to try to show he is a policymaker and is more intelligent than the other staff. But he always goes off half-cocked. If it mattered, I'd find the article and stick it under his nose."

Juan reflects, "Peter does like to act like a know-it-all, and Margaret just has a typical physician's 'I'm in control' attitude. I'm glad David cut off their spitting contest, but its not going to go away."

Peter fumes silently, "Peer-reviewed, schmeer-reviewed. Doctors are just trying to boost their fat paychecks without any accountability. What's the point?"

David returns to the residents' weekend work question and asks if he and Margaret could research this issue together through a joint phone call to a couple of other departments at the hospital that David thinks use a heavy weekend schedule. Margaret agrees. They set a time for the next day to make the calls.

Turning to the new ideas or options agenda item, Juan says, "David, as much as I'm willing to continue to think about some way out of this fix, isn't it up to you to make a decision? Two weeks ago we talked about consensus, but in my mind this is the kind of decision in which it is impossible to reach consensus."

David asks if anyone disagrees. There is silence from the group. "Well," David says, "this is important, and I need all the input I can get, but I guess that at the next meeting I'll put forward the 5 percent and 7 percent proposals and get your reaction."

Margaret thinks, "Yes, Mr. Business Manager, you *do* have to make the decision. Enough of this consensus malarky. Let's keep moving."

Delores thinks, "Gee, we don't have all the information at this moment and here he goes saying consensus isn't worth it. Sigh."

Juan reflects, "I think Peter has a point. I really wanted to say something about trying to work toward consensus. I've seen it happen in even tougher circumstances. But I didn't want Margaret to bite my head off. I wish someone would let her have it. Maybe if we knew less about what Peter did in his free time his opinion would carry more weight in this group."

Peter thinks, "So he really *doesn't* value consensus—and on something that will affect everyone in the department! Now that 'straight' comment he made back in the first meeting might mean more than I thought. I think we deserve to be a part of the decision rather than just to feed information to straight-laced David. I can see that Juan agrees with me. Why doesn't he speak up? I'll try to give David a bit more time."

Using RHG Techniques

The day before the meeting, per the ground rules, David sends out this agenda:

Agenda: Sixty-Minute Meeting

1. Budget planning

    Clarify the big picture, desired outcome

    Possible 5 percent cut, possible 7 percent cut

    Reports on assignments

    Additional research needed

    New ideas, options

    Timeline to a decision

2. Updates on other topics

Peter arrives two minutes late, rushing in and offering apologies. "I had been trying to track down this lead for cheaper paper since last week and finally the woman called me back." As Peter sits down, he inadvertently brushes against David's back. He feels David stiffen.

David blinks a couple of times, then says, "Thanks for letting us know why you were delayed, Peter. Before we get to the agenda, I think it's important to look at the big picture and work backwards. Unless we can agree on a clear vision of our goal, it's hard to know how to get there. I know that budget cutting raises lots of anxiety, so let's briefly go around and share where we want to come out on this meeting. Juan first, then around the table, OK?" (*Element 3: Begin by envisioning desired outcomes, and Element 4: Promote full participation*)

> *Juan:* Hmmm. It's unclear to me if a decision will be made today, and if it will be the group's decision or yours, David. I need to know that in order to get a clear view of this meeting's goal.
>
> *David:* Good point, but I'd like to hear from everyone first and then respond to questions. My presumption is to try to reach consensus, but we don't need a final decision today.
>
> *Delores:* I want to feel that whatever the decision is, we understand how it will affect each of our areas. I also want a feeling that David is fighting for our needs as the department's budget proposal gets picked apart as it goes up the ladder.
>
> *Margaret:* I want a clear and quick decision. I think it is David's call, but we need to know why he decides whatever he decides.
>
> *Peter:* Hmmm—I like the idea of trying to reach consensus because this affects all of us and the people we supervise. I also understand the need for a timely and firm decision. I want our goal to be like Delores put it: we understand it and feel we are getting the best shake possible.
>
> *David:* I see that Peter and Delores lean toward clear understanding and seeking consensus, while Juan and Margaret see this more as input into a decision I solely control. Margaret sees a need for a quick decision. Margaret, we do have the two-meeting rule on reaching a decision. But because we are limited somewhat by the directions I get from the vice president for finance, I'd like to try to use this and the next meeting to get to budget proposals within the limits set by the vice president. Is that OK? (*Element 5: Be accountable*)
>
> *Margaret:* Fine. I'm likely to get paged in about twenty minutes and I will have to respond. That's why I'm eager to move on.

Juan, Peter, and Delores report on their research on how to cut costs. Each of them has proposals for cutting 5 to 8 percent of the costs in their areas of responsibility. David probes for more information and Peter and Delores respond that they think they could move things closer to a 10 percent savings in each of their areas, but it would be very tight.

Turning to the cost estimates for residents and medical students, David mentions the rumors he has heard about the medical school planning to increase the rate it charges for residents' work. Margaret says she has heard the same thing but does not know if it is a real proposal or a trial balloon. Things become very quiet because an increase for residents' charges would make it virtually impossible to get to a reasonable cut of 5 or 7 percent. Margaret then reports that she does not have any figures and she doesn't know if there is much possibility of scheduling the residents more on the weekend to reduce costs. She explains to the group about the new set of residents and med students she is dealing with and how that has taken almost all of her time.

> *Peter:* OK, without figures on the Med School charges, how do we think about the other options? That's a real hole to me.
> *Delores:* Me, too. David, what is this budget exercise about if we don't have the information we need to give our input?
> *Margaret:* Don't look at me; this is beyond my control. I do think the current rates for residents are far too low, but it's not my call.
> *Peter:* Rates too low? I know the rates at three other university hospitals, and ours is at the top end.
> *Margaret:* Peter, I don't think you know what you're talking about. I've seen the peer-reviewed published study of forty-five university hospitals and we stink!

Things are getting hot again!

David intervenes: "Hold on. Let's take a short pause to see where this is going." (*Element 5: Be accountable*)

Peter fumes silently: "Peer-reviewed, schmeer-reviewed. Doctors are just trying to boost their fat paychecks without any accountability."

After about fifteen seconds, David continues, "Peter, Margaret—you both did the right thing. I need to hear what you know or have heard so that everyone can examine the same information. Although arguing about something that is beyond what we can control is not worth much time, I don't want to squelch anyone asking questions about costs and ways to prudently cut costs.

Peter ponders, "Was there a touch of condescension in David's voice? Speaking up is not acting up!"

David continues, "I know budget cutting puts everyone on edge. So, because we have ten minutes left, and because Margaret still might get paged, here is what I propose. I'll start two sheets of paper going around the room. If we run out of time, I'll make copies for people to ponder before the next meeting. On the first sheet is written, 'The outcomes to avoid in our work on preparing a budget are. . . .' Fill in the blank. Sometimes it's easier to say what we don't want to have happen than to say what we do want.

"The second sheet has at the top, 'Three values for how we work together in the management team.' Put aside the immediate budget problem if you can and list some values that should guide us. Beyond the specific rules on interruptions and time-outs, what are some big picture things? I haven't heard what you liked or didn't like about how things worked under my predecessor. I assume there are some things I'm doing differently, and that may be fine or it may be bothersome. Let's lay out some key values so that as we address this budget crunch and then the next problem, we have a good sense of direction."

Each person writes a few points and passes the paper on to the next person. After Margaret finishes the values sheet, her pager goes off. David asks if he and Margaret could research the weekend residents' work together by calling a couple of departments that seem to use a heavy weekend schedule. Margaret agrees and they set a time the next day to make the call. Margaret leaves. Peter, Juan, and Delores leave as they finish filling out the two sheets of paper.

Reflection on the Second Meeting

Even with the focus on the budget crisis, David tries to weave in ideas about how to work together for the long term. After some effort to create ground rules jointly, he asks for attention to larger values. His use of the sheets may help raise views that Peter, Delores, or Juan might have withheld in a direct, oral approach. David also does not choose between Peter and Margaret on the relative salary of residents but tries instead to focus on affirming both of them for bringing opinions and information to the table. There is growing tension in how Peter sees David behaving, and this kind of important and volatile relationship issue will be treated differently in the two versions of the third meeting.

Between the Second and Third Meetings

Rumors, rumors, and more rumors! They seem to breed like rabbits. Although everyone has heard some things separately, there is one hot rumor everyone has heard, albeit in various versions: There was a shouting match between the dean of the medical school and the hospital's vice president of finance. After an increasingly acerbic exchange of e-mails, one of them burst into the office of the other (accounts differ) and issued an ultimatum about the proposed increase in the charges by the medical school for residents serving at the hospital.

One day before the third meeting, George has another story about David for Peter. George was in the lunch line near David, talking with Greg. Greg, George, Peter, and Leo go dancing together from time to time. Greg and George were talking about some new people they saw at a gay club and George said that David quite deliberately turned his back on them. Greg said he saw the same thing. Then they saw David blush when the straight couple in front of him patted each other on their tushes and kissed. Peter tells George that he is beginning to share some suspicions about David being homophobic, or at a minimum really uptight about sexuality.

But Peter has not felt excluded from anything in the management team. In fact, Peter says that he thinks David is working hard to have the management team work together. Still, Peter privately ponders, if David has such a strong reaction, it is likely eventually to be directed at Peter.

The Third Meeting
Using Regular Ground Rules

The day before the third meeting, David sends out the agenda:

Agenda: Ninety-Minute Meeting

1. Budget submission

    Final reports on research: possible savings

    How potential cuts would affect operations

    Create detailed proposals on two options: a 5 percent cut, a 7 percent cut

    Attempt to reach consensus

2. For the final five minutes of the meeting: set an agenda for a next day stand-up update meeting not to exceed thirty minutes

David opens the meeting, checking that everyone can stay until the end. Margaret says she has a colleague covering for her and hopes not to get beeped.

Margaret reports that she and David made their calls and found that the pediatrics department saves 4 percent in labor costs for medical positions by using a heavy weekend schedule for residents. David notes that should the budget cuts come, he wants to try this system because it has been battle-tested at the hospital. Margaret is more cautious. She is still trying to get more details from her counterpart in pediatrics to see if their arrangement is really comparable to the residents' work in radiology.

Returning to the previous 5 to 10 percent cuts in other areas, Peter, Delores, and Juan describe how the cuts would affect their operations. Juan anticipates a grievance from the union if the receptionists' positions are reclassified from full-time to part-time. Peter summarizes the risks of using some lower cost supplies that Margaret, Delores, and Juan say their people would find pretty hard to swallow. Delores asks for some way to recognize the technicians' sacrifices to take some of the sting out of how the cuts she has offered would affect them.

The six-hundred-pound gorilla in the room is the med school–hospital tension over the residents' pay rate. David says, "Despite a variety of rumors, we do not have a decision on the proposal for a 3 percent increase for residents' pay. Since this begs bigger questions about the hospital's budget, we will not plan on this increase but will work within the other parameters we can control."

David then offers the following combination to reach a 5 percent cut:

1. Supplies substitution: Peter's tier 1 list.
2. Receptionists: change one position from full-time to part-time.
3. No later than two months into the budget year, switch the scheduling of residents to the heavy weekend model.

The proposal for the 7 percent cut is as follows:

1. Supplies substitution: Peter's list combining tier 1 and tier 2 items.
2. Receptionists: change two positions from full-time to part-time.
3. No later than two weeks into the budget year, switch the scheduling of residents to the heavy weekend model.
4. Pick smaller items off of Peter and Delores's 10 percent cut lists to make up any difference.

Delores speaks first: "David, it seems like you've taken a hard but fair look at the budget. I just want to hear how you would advocate for us to reduce these cuts or sound the alarm bell to the vice president about what the cuts mean to our work."

David summarizes the trade-offs of the changes to save money and how it will strain material, morale, and coordination. Delores is satisfied.

David then looks at the others. "Any other comments or questions? Last call to say something to me that you might want to say about me after the meeting." People laugh quietly and nervously.

Delores thinks, "No one backed me up on the need to do something for the technicians on morale. We always get the short end of the stick. If David doesn't get it now, he'll just have to see how things get worse. So much damage, but that is what it takes to get the muckity-mucks to pay attention."

Juan thinks, "I just remembered that the receptionist I want to keep full-time will be going on maternity leave in about five months. But it seems the decision is made; we'll just handle that when it comes up."

Margaret thinks, "That 4 percent savings on the weekend scheduling of residents is unlikely. That's OK; I'm sure there are other areas to cut."

Peter thinks, "David didn't look at me as he asked for final input. In fact, he has only glanced my way a couple of times throughout the meeting. He concentrates on the other three. I may regret this, but. . . ."

Margaret says, "Good work, David. Bet you did not expect this budget crunch so soon after coming here! Can we move on to the quick list of items for tomorrow's meeting? There are some other policy and procedure things that need attention, but I don't think they have any financial impact."

Peter interjects: "David, I need to say something. You've referred a few times to being straight with us. I need to be direct with you. You haven't looked at me in this meeting; you give your attention to Delores, Margaret, and Juan. I'm beginning to feel that you don't value my opinion, maybe because I'm gay and you have a problem with that."

David sits up straight. He focuses on Peter and holds his gaze for a few long seconds. "Peter, I value your opinion. I don't care about your or anyone else's private life. I think I've given everyone a fair hearing. I don't like being accused of prejudice. Can we move on?"

David turns to the others. "Do we have consensus on the list of the 5 percent and 7 percent budgets I'll submit by the end of the week? Last call!" He looks at everyone.

There is silence. Although no one speaks, people are thinking:

Delores: He wants to move on; I'm not saying anything. I'll talk to Peter after the meeting. I know that being direct about homophobia is best, but I'm not sure doing it in front of the group was the best way to go.

Juan: Hail Freedonia! All Hail Freedonia! [From the Marx Brothers' movie *Duck Soup*] I know Peter needs to raise the issue, but it sure is not comfortable here.

Margaret: Let's move on.

Peter: Well, I may have made my life hell but I won't be silent. I'll check things out with Delores after the meeting. Margaret and David, two charioteers for the price of one—the rest of us are the horses.

David proceeds, "Ok, moving to the list of topics for our no-sitting meeting tomorrow, Margaret you go first."

Using RHG Techniques

The day before the third meeting, David sends out the following agenda:

Agenda: Ninety-Minute Meeting

1. Review worksheets from last meeting *[Element 5: Be accountable]*

    Outcomes to seek and avoid on budget matters

    Values to guide our work

2. Budget submission

    Reflecting on key items to preserve

    Final points of research and information

    Clarify how potential cuts would affect operations of the department

    Detailed review of two options: a 5 percent cut and a 7 percent cut

    Pros and cons of packages David offers

    Trade-offs and changes

3. For the final five minutes of the meeting: set an agenda for a next day stand-up update meeting not to exceed thirty minutes

He also distributes the two lists made at the last meeting:

Possible Values to Guide Our Work

- Treat people equally
- Respect one another
- Share information, rumors
- Make decisions on time
- Don't repeat points
- Always look for ways to improve morale
- Create opportunities for employee development
- Humor is the best medicine

Outcomes to Avoid on the Budget-Cut Decision

- Delaying a decision until it is made for us rather than by us
- Rushing before we have needed information
- Having one person feel like all the cuts fall in his or her area
- Not cutting enough and having to go back for more midyear

- Letting the information leak out: once a decision is made, send an e-mail or have a meeting so everyone in the department knows what's going on as soon as possible

David opens the meeting, checking that everyone can stay until the end. Margaret says she has a colleague covering for her and hopes not to get beeped.

David turns to the two lists. "I know our minds are focused on the budget, but here is what I propose," he says. "Two brief go-rounds: First I'd like you to comment on the list of outcomes to avoid, if any item is unclear or if you don't agree with it. The goal will be to clarify and then see where we agree on what not to do."

David continues: "The second go-round won't be for everyone to comment on each value on the list. Instead, each person can cite one value from the list that was well supported when you worked with my predecessor, Jose, and one value that was not well supported in how things got done, if there is one. Is that OK?"

There is silence.

David continues: "I know that most times silence is OK, but I don't want to push something you don't think will work. Can we do about twenty minutes on the outcomes and values discussion and then move to the details on the budget?"

David looks to Delores on his left.

Delores: Yes, this is OK.

Juan: Sure. I'm not sure what the values stuff will do for us but I'm open to doing it and seeing if there's anything more to do. Seems simple to me.

Margaret: I'm not crazy about this values stuff, but since we can give some feedback on what went well with Jose, that makes sense to me.

Peter: Sure, let's go. There are some things from last year related to the values that I'd like to speak to; don't worry, Margaret, I'll be brief and I won't repeat. (*Element 4: Promote full participation; Element 5: Be accountable*)

The discussion on outcomes to avoid proceeds and the group agrees that David will prepare a memo for their quick review and then e-mail it to the whole department once the budget submission is set. David says that a decision is needed today to retain control over the choices of where to cut. The discussion on not having information that is needed prompts David to report confidentially that if the residents' pay rate increases to the level desired by the medical school, the vice president for finance will cover the difference from the hospital's contingency fund for three to six months. That would offer some time for more budget adjustments in the department.

Finally there was more discussion on how to handle the concerns: "Not cutting enough and having to go back for more midyear" was a tough call. Although they were adding to the pain, the management team agreed to target 5.5 percent and 7.5 percent cuts to ensure actual savings of 5 and 7 percent.

Turning to the values list, Delores talks about the need to feel respected and says she feels that Jose didn't set the right tone. She tells how Jose referred to Margaret and himself as "professionals" but did not put Juan, Peter, and Delores in the same category.

Juan praises Jose for being open to ideas to improve morale, but he also says that Jose repeated himself a lot. Margaret says she did feel respected by Jose. She is unsure whether the "treat people equally" value—very useful in general circumstances—can work in the hospital setting due to specialization and different levels of responsibility.

Peter says he wrote "Create opportunities for employee development" because of his experience of moving from one section of the hospital to another. He shares some specific ideas and David takes note of them. Peter continues, "I also wrote 'Treat people equally.' I think that is no surprise to anyone given my involvement with the hospital's Allies for Gay-Positive Education—AGAPE." Peter thinks he detected a reaction from David. He continues: "Equal treatment in word and deed is essential." David makes some notes and then observes that they are almost out of time on this agenda item.

David says, "Here's a suggestion. Peter, could you start with the values sheet and fill in more specific items about what the values mean to you? I have the, let's see, six things you mentioned for opportunities for employee development, so why don't you pick two or three we might address as a group in two weeks. Then circulate it to Margaret, Juan, and Delores—any order will do—so I can get it back forty-eight hours before our meeting, or earlier if possible."

Peter knows that David is trying hard, but he has to interject, "David, I also said how important it is for people to be treated equally regardless of sexual orientation. Are you saying I shouldn't write on that?"

"No, that's not what I meant," David says. "I agree about treating people equally, but I think there are larger issues about what is private and what is appropriate for the workplace."

"So equality means not sharing certain things about who we are?" Peter probes.

Juan interjects, "Hold on. Isn't it better to think about this in terms of the broader values: a willingness to be inclusive and the need for everyone to share a perspective?"

David sighs and says, "Yeah, you're right. OK, let me see if I can talk about my perspective without us getting too bogged down. I was raised in a way that nobody talked about gay or lesbian things and we were private about all sexual topics. I do have a hard time sometimes when people are open about being gay. I'm not sure it affects my behavior at work, though, because I really can say that I don't care what anybody's private life is about when I'm here. I can't help the way I was raised, but I know I can be fair to everyone and I don't think I let anyone's sexual identity or lifestyle affect my work decisions. But I'm willing to put the topic on the table if you think we need to discuss it."

> *Delores:* Peter: Juan, Margaret, and I already know about your dedication to equal treatment for gays and lesbians. I'm glad to join you in that effort. Attitudes can affect how we work,

so it could be something the five of us need to talk about. I don't want to put it off if you think it has to be dealt with now, but I want to be sure that if we talk about it, we do so in a safe atmosphere. And one part of being safe is having enough time and doing it at the right time.

Peter: David, Delores, thanks. We don't have to put it on the table now. Your honesty, David, is more than enough for me for our work today, tomorrow, and this week. I'm OK to wait and see. I know that how people are raised follows them around, regardless of what they want. At the same time, I don't assume a gay-positive environment is appropriate for the purposes of our group. I judge people not by their foibles but by their actual deeds. Thanks, everyone. I know many people think you can separate the personal from the workplace. I can't and don't want to. I want to live my life whole. So let's go back to this nice and easy decision we have on the budget.

They all laugh.

Margaret: I have something to add on a different topic. Delores, I know you made some jokes to me about Jose treating you in a, hmmm, this may be too strong, but in a "subservient" role. I didn't think it was that important to you.

Delores: Yes, it was. I know we try to keep things light around here, but it did not make me feel respected.

Peter: I only saw a little bit of it. When Margaret, Jose, and I were at a book club meeting together, there was good give and take and I felt like an equal. But back at work I did feel talked down to sometimes by Jose.

David: OK, this is getting rolling and we have come to the end of the twenty minutes we set for discussion of outcomes to avoid and values to support. Do you want to go five more minutes and adjust the other topics, or continue this in two weeks at our regular meeting?

They agree to hold off for two weeks—with a sense of common movement on an important topic that feels a little exhilarating and more than a little unusual. (*Element 3: Begin by envisioning desired outcomes; Element 4: Promote full participation; Element 5: Evaluate and revise*)

Back to budget realities! On the final reports, Margaret says she and David made their calls and found that the pediatric department saved 4 percent in labor costs for medical positions by using a heavy weekend schedule for residents. David notes that should the budget cuts come he wants to try this system because it has been battle-tested at the hospital. Margaret is more cautious: she is trying to get more details from her counterpart in pediatrics to see if their arrangement is really comparable to the residents' work in radiology.

Returning to the previous 5 to 10 percent cuts in other areas, Peter, Delores, and Juan describe how the cuts would affect their operations. Juan anticipates a grievance from the union if the receptionist positions are reclassified from full-time to part-time. Peter summarizes the risks of using some lower cost supplies that Margaret, Delores, and Juan say their people would find pretty hard to swallow. Delores asks for some way to recognize the technicians' sacrifices in order to take out some of the sting of how the cuts she has offered will affect them.

The group puts the pieces together to reach a 5.5 percent cut:

1. Supplies substitution: Peter's tier 1 list
2. Receptionists: change one position from full-time to part-time, and one part-time position to a temporary position
3. No later than forty-five days into the budget year, switch residents scheduling to the heavy weekend model

The proposal for the 7.5 percent cut is as follows:

1. Supplies substitution: Peter's list combining tier 1 and tier 2 items
2. Receptionists: change two positions from full-time to part-time, and one part-time position to a temporary position

3. At the start of the budget year, switch the scheduling of residents to the heavy weekend model
4. Pick smaller items off of Peter and Delores's 10 percent cut lists to make up any difference

David checks with Juan and Margaret to see if they need input on item 4. They do not, so the group agrees that David will set the final amounts under item 4 in consultation with Peter and Delores. Delores speaks first.

> *Delores:* David, it seems like you've taken a hard, but fair look at the budget. I just want to hear how you would advocate for us to reduce these cuts, or how to sound the alarm bell to the vice president about what the cuts mean to our work.
>
> *David:* Well, because one of you noted a value of not repeating points, do you want me to summarize the trade-offs and the main points for preserving us from all or some of the cuts, or would that be repetitive? *(Element 5: Be accountable)*
>
> *Juan:* I think it could get repetitive. How about if each of the four of us hit the high points in a minute or less and then we'll know you have the key points?

They do the review as Juan suggests and finish in two minutes. What are the others thinking?

> *Delores:* I'm glad I got one more chance to lay out my concerns about the cuts.
>
> *Margaret:* Jose would have moved on. But it seems we are clicking more as a team. Not bad for so early with David as the new boss.
>
> *Peter:* David is sharp, and even Margaret seems to be on board. Will wonders never cease! *(Element 2: Educate and inspire)*

David then looks at the others and says, "It's good to work with you. I sense that this talk about outcomes and values is different for you. I'm trying to work out a way of not always handling immediate crises to the exclusion of keeping focused on good working relationships. I know we have to get the right mix of substance and process, but I think we're doing very well."

> *Margaret:* Good work, David. I learned some things about how Delores, Peter, and Juan want things to be different with you here. You can tell I'm not a process person, but this has been good. We made—you made, I guess—a tough decision, and we looked longer term. However, can we move on to the quick list of items for tomorrow's meeting? There are some other policy and procedure topics that need attention, but I don't think they have any financial impact.
>
> *David:* I'm about ready for that but I want to see if we have consensus on the list of the 5.5 and 7.5 percent budget cuts I'll submit to the VP tomorrow. Also, tomorrow I'll draft the memo to go to the whole department and send it to the four of you by e-mail for comment by the end of the day. OK?
>
> Peter, Delores, Margaret, and Juan say yes.
>
> *David:* OK. Moving to the list of topics for our no-sitting meeting tomorrow—Margaret, you go first.

Reflection on the Third Meeting

As you can see, commitment is being built over time to keep process issues an important focus of the group's work. David is also helping the group excavate its past to uncover deeply held values and reframe them as aspirations that can guide the group rather than as a rehash of gripes and slights. With a growing commitment to and sense of safety about their values, David shared a difficult feeling about his upbringing and sexuality. Peter replied that he appreciated David's honesty and then Margaret noted how she had just realized how Delores felt treated by Jose.

Using the specific challenges posed by a high-stakes issue such as budget cutting gives the group a much needed opportunity to recognize the real conflicts that can and will surface. In other groups, such high stakes and potentially high-conflict items might be questions about group membership, decision making, confidentiality of meeting discussions, leadership roles in the group, use of experts, expectations for work between meetings, and so on. In time, and with guidance from David, the group's aspirations for how the budget-cutting should be handled will provide valuable insight into general aspirations for how they want to work as a group.

It is also worth noting that all of the elements of the RHG approach were repeated in this meeting, though they were not approached in a sequential or lock-step fashion. Instead, David wove them together in a seamless fashion while still attending to each of them. Again, over time the elements will become familiar to the group and the group members will begin to share responsibility with David for supporting the group's need for attention to process. Exhibit 8.2 summarizes values and goals the group has developed.

Using the basic elements of RHG, we've seen how a group can deepen its commitment to effective working relationships and enhance the quality of not just process but also outcome. Matching the unique characteristics of a group with well-chosen tools and techniques allows a leader or facilitator to guide a group gently to greater awareness and to commitment to tending their relationships while accomplishing their tasks. Once that awareness and commitment are built, it takes consistent effort to sustain it. One of the things that poses a threat to a group, even after the internal commitment and capacities are built, is interference from the outside.

Groups are often nested within a larger context—departments within divisions, committees within agencies, and task forces within the context of neighborhood and city politics. Just because one group decides to live up to its potential and aspirations does not mean the rest of the world is prepared to follow along the RHG path. Groups can get pulled off course by outside forces. The challenge is real. The next chapter looks at promising efforts being put forward by whole organizations and whole communities to reach together for higher ground. Whole communities reaching for higher ground is perhaps the best way to ensure the long-term viability of any single group's efforts.

Exhibit 8.2. The Group's Products, Using the RHG Approach

Underlying Values [from Meeting #1]
Investing time in how the group works can bring great benefits
Productive, strong relationships are important for the group's success

Budget Decision: Values and Goals [from Meeting #2]
Clarity on how the decision affects the department's operations
David being willing to fight for the department's needs
Reach a quick and clear decision

Possible Values to Guide Our Work
[from Worksheets Done at the End of Meeting #2 and Presented in Meeting #3]
- Treat people equally
- Respect one another
- Share information, rumors
- Make decisions on time
- Don't repeat points
- Always look for ways to improve morale
- Create opportunities for employee development
- Humor is the best medicine

Outcomes to Avoid on the Budget-Cut Decision
[from Worksheets Done at the End of Meeting #2 and Presented in Meeting #3]
- Delaying a decision until it is made for us rather than by us
- Rushing before we have needed information
- Having one person feel like all the cuts fall on his or her area
- Not cutting enough and having to go back for more midyear
- Letting the information leak out: once a decision is made, send an e-mail or have a meeting so everyone in the department knows what's going on as soon as possible

Chapter Nine

Beyond Boundaries

Bringing Higher Ground to Whole Communities

Imagine the following situations:

1. You are upset to learn that a new subdivision planned for your community will require a new road across a dam, thus spoiling an area used by hundreds of people for quiet walks and fishing. You want to protest this proposal but you dread speaking at a public hearing that you assume will be lengthy, contentious, and an exercise in futility.

2. Your daughter's new school is rocked by accusations from parents that the administration has tolerated several racially motivated incidents of harassment. You want to do something to help but you don't know any way to get involved that would be productive.

3. The company you work for has directed your division to absorb another division. Although no jobs are being lost, it is inevitable that some individuals will have less authority than they do now. You have some ideas for sharing authority that you think may please people in both divisions. In most companies you would never get a chance to offer those ideas given the atmosphere of suspicion and distrust that would accompany this sort of reorganization.

Each of these situations may benefit from the reaching for higher ground (RHG) approach we have discussed to this point. But what if instead of needing to engage people in creating higher ground you found a very different atmosphere as you became involved:

1. You receive a notice in the mail prior to the public meeting describing the issues, offering a list of the pros and cons of different

views of the road, and detailing several ways in which you might let your views be known as well as learn from the views of others. These ways range from a confidential hot line to a collection of postings on a Web site, a series of informal neighborhood discussions with your area's representative to the town council, and the formal public meetings required by law. The notice includes the phone numbers and mailing addresses of local elected and administrative officials. It also describes the ground rules for the public meeting as well as the ways in which your input might be used. The notice includes a promise to respond to your questions or ideas within five days of your first contact—and just as important, printed on the front of the notice is the reason that your locality values your input, and a pledge to make use of such input.

2. When you call the school, you are invited to attend an open meeting of parents and other community members concerned about the accusations. At the meeting you are surprised to see not just school officials but a facilitator from the local community mediation center who pledges to ensure that all participants will be given sufficient time to ask questions and make their concerns known. You are even more surprised to learn that the community-wide parent-teacher organization and school administration have already created guidelines for dealing with difficult situations. The meeting is run according to this process and you are impressed that the difficult issues are not put aside. Instead, they are handled with candor and with little rancor, despite the emotions aroused by the incidents and the accusations.

3. Your company is not like most companies. When you went through the last organization-wide visioning process, your company invested a substantial amount of time engaging all employees in thinking about conflict—how it can be valuable, why it is often unproductive, and how the company can help people handle conflict in a productive and people-affirming manner. With the assistance of an employee from a third division who has been trained in group facilitation, you and the merging division identify your needs and concerns and generate several unexpected but exciting options for

the new structure. Although implementing these options won't be easy, most people express exhilaration at the challenge and at the opportunity to work together in new ways.

To this point much of this book has focused on the workings of individual groups in defined contexts, in settings where arrangements for shared expectations for higher ground could be worked out face to face. This chapter looks at the power of creating shared expectations for whole communities—be they religious, civil, social, organizational, political, or cultural. Individual groups, regardless of how committed they are to working together for higher ground, operate in a larger context. That context may not support the highest aspirations of an individual group; indeed, it may even obstruct an individual group's efforts to reach for higher ground.

Dare we think about, dream about, whole communities reaching for higher ground? Is it conceivable that a single family, a single committee, a single organization, or a single community could reach for higher ground in a supportive and nurturing environment where reaching for higher ground is the norm, not the exception?

We think so. But more important, many others seem to think so, too. In this chapter we look in on works in progress from around the United States, Canada, and Australia.

A variety of initiatives are under way to raise the expectations and standards of conduct in whole communities. Examples of this work range from political arenas, such as the Enlibra project in the American West, to civic settings, such as the Quandamooka Lands Council Aboriginal Corporation and Redlands Council in Australia, to whole school communities, such as the Kamehameha Schools Bishop Estate in Hawaii. Here we take a look at what each of these projects is about, what motivated their creation, and how each is going about the task. Then we'll offer observations about how the work of these groups might inform your own efforts to advocate and work for whole-community commitment to reach for higher ground.

The scale of these examples is much larger than the groups we have used to illustrate most of this book. The context, number of people involved, and expectations vary widely from one situation to another, but the leaders involved in each of the examples we describe here are all seeking the same higher ground.

In each of these situations, severe conflict has been exacerbated and prolonged by the absence of shared expectations about how conflict may best be addressed. In each situation, leaders began by invoking a set of values or principles in which to anchor their efforts—in other words, principled ground. The groups in each of these situations attempted to provide a forum for exchange of information and dialogue, a forum that was safe and welcoming of different, sometimes sharply conflicting perspectives—in other words, a refuge. In each situation, the groups realized the need to bring people together, not in spite of but because of their differing views—a shared ground that is essential to creating an enlarged perspective. In each case, leaders recognized that existing ideas were insufficient to deal with problems, and in each situation, some of which are ongoing as this book goes to press, it is certain that reaching for higher ground was, and is, a challenge requiring continuing effort and renewal.

Let's look at the examples.

Native Title Process Agreement

In 1996, Australia saw one of the most significant decisions ever handed down by its Supreme Court. In what is called the *Wik* case, the Court affirmed that the grant of a pastoral lease to individuals raising sheep or cattle does not extinguish what is called *native title* on those same lands. As identified in the 1993 Native Title Act, *native title* is the term used to describe the traditional uses of land by the Aboriginal people based on indigenous law and custom. Native title is extinguished by grants of private freehold land and cannot displace privately owned homes, backyards, farms, or any other such land. But it may continue to exist on a broad variety of lands where the Aboriginal people had use of such land.

As you might imagine, the affirmation of such rights has provided fertile ground for conflict at the state and local levels. The conflict may be traced to the initial settlement by the English in the eighteenth century and the clash of cultures between the English and the Aboriginal peoples that settlement engendered. The 1993 Native Title Act and the subsequent decision in the Wik case may be thought of as forms of conflict resolution because they provide a legal and institutional framework for settling claims and disputes. But the Act and the Wik decision left the question of exactly where and how native title may be enacted to be determined on a case-by-case basis. That decision caused considerable consternation from all sides—among advocates for native title who wanted a clearer and stronger statement of aboriginal rights, among landholders and public land lessees worried that their property rights could be abrogated with minimal warning, and among local government officials wondering how they could make land use decisions in the face of such uncertainty.

One imaginative community decided to face the challenge of native title by first staking out higher ground. The Quandamooka people of Moreton Bay, encompassing three major Aboriginal clans, had repeatedly claimed a role as traditional custodians of Minjerribah (Stradbroke Island). In 1994 an application claiming traditional uses of the land, much of it under private ownership, was made by the Quandamooka Lands Council Aboriginal Corporation (QLC) to the national tribunal responsible for overseeing the determination of title. The QLC rejected the arbitration process that was available through the Native Title Tribunal in favor of mediation. The Redland Shire Council, the local authority with responsibility for strategic planning for areas affected by the claim, and the QLC then entered into negotiations about how they might address that application. The parties agreed that their first task was to seek a *process* to determine how the claims for native title would be resolved. They spent many months preparing together a seven-page native title process agreement. This agreement included not only the issues involved in the native title claims but also a set of principles that would provide the basis for these negotiations.

The principles are brief but impressive. They include acknowledgment of the possible need for mediation to resolve any impasses, respect for the cultural decision-making processes of the Quandamooka people, and a goal of reconciliation between Aboriginal and non-Aboriginal people.

Eventually, a strategic plan and management framework agreement was reached that included a planning and management study. This agreement provides the aboriginal community with a shared role in planning for the future of the island while allowing the Redlands Shire Council to fulfill its obligations under the Environment Protection Act (R. Neumann, e-mail message to E. Franklin Dukes, Jan. 7, 2000).

When the agreement was signed, a community-wide celebration brought forth exultation and many tears of joy. Although the search for *principled* ground is prominent in this case, perhaps the most significant element of higher ground in this circumstance was the agreement to develop this ground together—*shared* ground. This process has served as a model and, perhaps more important, as an inspiration for a number of other indigenous land-use agreements currently being negotiated (R. Neumann, e-mail message to E. Franklin Dukes, Jan. 7, 2000). For the Aboriginal people who for so long had seen their identity very nearly destroyed, this agreement represented recognition of that identity in a manner—publicly and in print—that could never be taken away from them.

Common Ground Network for Life and Choice

"We believe that there is a space—it could be for dialogue, it could be for work on issues—where pro-life and pro-choice can come together in a nonadversarial way. We also believe that such coming together is a good thing. It produces positive outcomes for both the individuals and groups involved and for society" (Jacksteit and Kaufmann, 1996, p. iv).

Who said this? Some wild-eyed idealist who does not understand the abortion conflict? A cloistered academic with some special dialogue model seeking to experiment on people? A well-meaning but out-of-step handful of pro-life and pro-choice advocates who are wishy-washy on their values?

The statement comes from the founders of the Common Ground Network for Life and Choice. The statement was crafted in 1993. It is not merely a nice idea. It has been applied, tested, and refined in more than a dozen communities across the United States. These local efforts have gained notice on television shows, in *Newsweek* (Lemagie, 1998), and through many newspapers.

The participants are never asked to "check their values at the door" regarding abortion and their pro-choice or pro-life activism. Instead, the efforts grew from an interest on the part of many pro-choice or pro-life activists in engaging one another in ways other than vituperative rhetoric, clinic confrontations, or legislative battles.

The organization Search for Common Ground (SFCG) has been working since 1982 to promote dialogue among antagonists on a variety of issues and in many places. In 1992, local abortion activists in Buffalo, New York, approached SFCG for help in creating a model for community-level pro-choice–pro-life dialogue. The need for such dialogue grew out of increased division stemming from Operation Rescue's choice to hold several direct action demonstrations at abortion clinics in Buffalo in the summer of 1992. Other ad hoc abortion dialogues had been taking place in St. Louis, Missouri, and in a few other communities.

In 1994, a modest network linking six local efforts was established under SFCG's rubric. As of fall 1999, with ten local groups still active, the network ceased to be a project within SFCG, but its resource materials and some assistance were being provided through the National Association for Community Mediation.

The network pursued three main strategies (Jacksteit and Kaufmann, 1996, pp. 1–2):

1. Provide forums and processes enabling pro-life and pro-choice supporters to come together for constructive dialogue and for the exploration of cooperative activity in areas of joint concern
2. Assist and support local community efforts to create and sustain pro-life and pro-choice conversations and collaborations
3. Provide resources, publications, and national-level activities to support local activities and groups

All local efforts are voluntary. More than twenty communities—from Pensacola, Florida (in the aftermath of the shooting death of a doctor who performed abortions), to Cleveland, Ohio, to Davenport, Iowa—have been touched by private and genuine pro-life and pro-choice conversations.

On matters of violence, justice, human will, and other foundational values, the point is never to imply that someone's values are wrong; instead, it is to engage opposing advocates on values they hold in common.

For example, the Life and Choice Network's statement of purpose reads (Jacksteit and Kaufmann, 1996, p. 2):

We [wish to]

- honor the humanity of those with whom we are in conflict, respecting them in spite of their differing values and beliefs;
- acknowledge that we are in relationship as members of the same society and therefore need to come together, at times, to work on common concerns.

We emphasize that when we come together as a common ground group we are not engaged in making compromises or seeking changes in people' positions on abortion.

Karen Swallow Prior is a pro-life advocate and co-founder of the Buffalo Coalition for Common Ground. "The process allows me to maintain the consistency and commitment to my values on abortion while working toward mutual goals with people who don't support my views. Divisive debates, like [those about] abortion, are often played out in the public arena. Those confrontations mask possibilities for more positive change. I've found that the pro-life/pro-choice dialogues in which I've participated have allowed for measurable steps toward better understanding and some areas of agreement" (K. Swallow Prior, e-mail message to and conversation with J. B. Stephens, Nov. 20, 1999).

The network's description of its approach to ground rules is a shining example of a higher ground approach: "Each common ground group requires a set of ground rules that reflects its own special needs. Group participants are encouraged to ask of each other and potential participants: (1) 'What do you need to make this conversation comfortable to you?' or (2) 'What kind of agreements do we need to make with one another to create a safe environment?'" (Jacksteit and Kaufmann, 1996, p. 20).

Outcomes of these dialogues include joint projects as well as more civil and humane relationships between advocates of opposing views on abortion. Adoption has emerged as one response to abortion that pro-choice and pro-life advocates can support and strengthen while remaining fully consistent with their values. The Life and Choice Network published *Adoption as Common Ground* (Puzder and Isaacson-Jones, 1995) and local groups have jointly educated the community about adoption.

A four-person pro-life, pro-choice group articulated seven points of common ground on teen pregnancy in *Common Ground on Teen Pregnancy* in 1996 (Common Ground Network for Life and Choice, 1996). This paper and a pilot common ground forum on teen pregnancy in Buffalo led to a partnership between the network and the National Campaign to Prevent Teen Pregnancy to address values-based conflicts in that arena. By 2000, two structured community-wide dialogues on teen pregnancy and values differences—one in Arizona and another in California—had occurred.

The network's third coauthored paper, "Common Ground on Clinic Activism" (1998), saw a reproductive health clinic director and pro-life sidewalk counselor-activist reach agreement on such things as opposing violence and intimidation and supporting full and accurate information for women facing unplanned pregnancies. The coauthors carried out a speaking series at four major universities in the 1998–99 academic year.

Viewing religion as an area of common ground led to collaborative programs with religious institutions such as the National Council of Churches and the Washington National Cathedral, and a meeting cosponsored with the Aspen Institute, "Common Ground/Faithful Ground?" For local common ground groups, a major area of action has been publicity and public outreach (to "spread the common ground message") through local radio, newspapers, television, public forums, press conferences, and events. For example, in the wake of a physician's murder in 1998, and in response to fears of escalating tensions about a scheduled Operation Rescue event, the Buffalo Coalition for Common Ground and the central office of the network cosponsored a series of forums and dialogues. One result of the exchanges was a "New Way" statement that, when made public, drew activist support and received wide local news coverage.

However, even the strongest advocates combine their optimism with caution. According to Swallow Prior, "Overall, within the pro-life community, there is not wide support for common ground dialogues. I don't think that it is a reason to be discouraged. The Common Ground approach represents the cutting edge of the movement. I hope that it eventually will change the dynamics of the discussion" (K. Swallow Prior, e-mail message to and conversation with J. B. Stephens, Nov. 20, 1999).

The pro-life, pro-choice dialogues exemplify reaching for higher ground principles of finding new and shared ground (adoption and teen pregnancy). Opposing advocates are not yielding their views on abortion but have journeyed together to affirm ideas and values they hold in common.

Canada's National Round Table on the Economy and the Environment

It is commonly accepted that *sustainability*—defined as the ability to use the Earth's resources in ways that do not impinge upon the needs of future generations—requires economic well-being as well as environmental protection. Yet when Canada convened its National Round Table on the Environment and the Economy in 1991, that acceptance had not yet occurred. Furthermore, even if one accepted the linkages between the environment and the economy, there was little guidance about ways in which people could integrate the two. Canada therefore began its search for sustainability by conducting a national effort to identify what it would take to build consensus about sustainability. That effort included an attempt to develop, by consensus, a set of fundamental principles on consensus building. Led by the National Task Force on Consensus and Sustainability, more than one hundred members of the national and regional round tables helped create those principles. They are represented in a substantial publication entitled *Building Consensus for a Sustainable Future: Putting Principles into Practice* (Cormick and others, 1996).

This effort to develop knowledge and agreement about how to bring competing interests together began with an acknowledgment that sustainability requires more than technical and scientific knowledge or resource management. In fact, the National Round Table affirmed that the main challenge to achieving sustainability was the need to resolve differences in culture, interests, visions, and needs. Because of that need, round table members concluded that only through consensus building could such differences be understood and addressed, and only through achieving consensus could people learn, appreciate, and develop the commitment to do what it takes to create a sustainable future.

The round table defined consensus as a process that includes all stakeholders who meet with a goal of reaching agreement on issues that advance sustainability. The key components of consensus-building processes are inclusion and representation, face-to-face discussion, equal opportunity to air concerns and needs, and the goal of meeting each representative's needs so that everyone is satisfied with the total agreement even if parts of the agreement may not be preferred.

The ten principles agreed to by every member of the round table are as follows (Cormick and others, 1996, p. 7):

1. *Purpose driven:* People need a reason to participate in the process.
2. *Inclusive, not exclusive:* All parties with a significant interest in the issues should be involved in the consensus process.
3. *Voluntary participation:* The parties who are affected or interested participate voluntarily.
4. *Self-design:* The parties design the consensus process.
5. *Flexibility:* Flexibility should be designed into the process.
6. *Equal opportunity:* All parties have equal access to relevant information and the opportunity to participate effectively throughout the process.
7. *Respect for diverse interests:* Acceptance of the diverse values, interests, and knowledge of the parties involved in the consensus process is essential.
8. *Accountability:* The participants are accountable both to their constituencies and to the process they have agreed to establish.
9. *Time limits:* Realistic deadlines are necessary throughout the process.
10. *Implementation:* Commitments to implementation and effective monitoring are essential parts of any agreement.

As S. Glenn Sigurdson, one of the round table facilitators who helped developed the principles, observed, the strength of these principles is not so much in what they say but in how they were developed—once again demonstrating the power of *shared* ground

(G. Sigurdson, personal communication, Sept. 24, 1999). These principles were crafted and agreed to by all the members of the regional and national round tables. The agreement of more than one hundred individuals representing business, community, environmental, and governmental interests ensures a degree of legitimacy that could not otherwise be developed.

Enlibra

Conflict over land use and protection of natural resources is endemic around the world. But it is hard to imagine anyplace where such conflict is more bitterly fought, and where it is so much a part of the daily lives of so many communities, than in the American West. There are many reasons for the nature and extent of such conflict. Among those reasons are the vast amount of publicly managed lands in the West, the competing demands for use of those lands (such as resource extraction, wilderness, and recreation), and the migration to the West in recent decades of people who bring experiences and values different from those in the places to which they relocate.

The conflict is played out in many ways. The courts are full of challenges to the decisions of agencies responsible for administering public lands, including the Bureau of Land Management, the Forest Service, and the Fish and Wildlife Service. Public hearings on proposed plans often attract hundreds of shouting antagonists. Newspapers, journals and magazines, and electronic media provide forums for demonization and degradation. Even more seriously, many threats and acts of violence have been tied to conflicts over how lands are being managed.

Enlibra is not a word you will find in any dictionary. It is, in fact, a neologism coined by two governors of Western states—John Kitzhaber (Democrat from Oregon) and Mike Leavitt (Republican from Utah). They developed Enlibra as a doctrine for environmental management designed to promote balance and stewardship, but also as a call for an end to the polarization and antagonisms common to environmental disputes.

Enlibra encompasses the following eight principles (C. Carlson, e-mail message to E. Franklin Dukes, Nov. 2, 1999; Bergman, 1999):

1. *National standards, neighborhood solutions:* This principle concedes—and in many circles in the West it is a major concession—that federal standards are a necessary step for environmental protection. However, "necessary" is followed by "but insufficient," because policies that provide incentives as well as penalties are more likely to garner support from local communities.
2. *Collaboration, not polarization:* This principle means that stakeholders representing a variety of views must be brought together with the goal of meeting one another's needs.
3. *Reward results, not programs:* This principle is a plea for regulatory flexibility and for rewards for innovation that achieves desired outcomes.
4. *Science for fact, process for priorities:* This principle encourages elimination of "advocacy science" by separating the development of information from the competition of subjective values and priorities. Furthermore, parties in disputes can be assisted so that their decisions take into account the possibility that those decisions will need to be adapted as new information becomes available.
5. *Markets before mandates:* This principle emphasizes the power of the market and financial incentives to achieve outcomes that command and control cannot.
6. *Change a heart, change a nation:* This principle reflects the need for public education on stewardship of the environment.
7. *Recognition of costs and benefits:* This principle means applying a commonsense approach that adds social and cultural factors to the equation of economic and environmental benefits and costs.

8. *Solutions transcend political boundaries:* This principle is an acknowledgment that for the many environmental problems that do not fit within a single political jurisdiction, cooperative agreements and partnerships across such jurisdictions will be necessary.

In contrast to the Canadian experience in developing principles for consensus building for sustainability, Enlibra was produced by two leaders recognizing and codifying what had worked on the ground—at least from some observers' perspective—in several prominent environmental disputes, including the Grand Canyon Visibility Transport Commission, which developed recommendations for improving visibility in the Grand Canyon area, and a coho salmon protection consensus building effort in Oregon (Bergman, 1999). Enlibra is most prominently an effort to create *new* ground in order to get beyond a continuing polarization of environment versus economy. To the extent that these two leaders represent the two major political parties, Enlibra does represent a limited *shared* ground. This limitation means that skepticism abounds that Enlibra can offer a way of resolving the very real differences and interests that are played out in environmental disputes. However, Enlibra has also been endorsed by many public and private groups, including most prominently the Western Governors Association, as providing a framework of shared expectations that can help bring people together to find ways of protecting both the land and the people who depend on the land for their livelihood.

Nā Kumu o Kamehameha: The Legacy of a Princess

The Kamehameha Schools is a private school that exists to provide educational services to children of whole or part Hawaiian ancestry. The children served by the school are the direct beneficiaries of the legacy of a Hawaiian princess, the last direct royal descendant of King Kamehameha I, Princess Bernice Pauahi Bishop.

Prior to the arrival of James Cook in 1778, an estimated 400,000 people lived in the Hawaiian Islands. With James Cook came increasing numbers of foreigners and diseases. In 1883, when Princess Bernice made her will, less than 40,000 remained among the kingdom's total population. The princess's inheritance came one year before her death and included a sizable amount of land, approximately 11 percent of the entire land area of the islands. Upon her death she willed that her estate be dedicated to the education of the children of Hawaii and governed by a board of trustees to be named by the state's Supreme Court. A school for boys opened three years after her death in 1887. One for girls opened in 1894.

The estate grew with the help of the princess's husband, an English businessman and philanthropist, Charles Reed Bishop. Eleven decades later it is said to be the single largest private estate in the United States, as a result of shrewd investments and the skyrocketing values of Hawaiian land in the 1980s. Now estimated to be worth more than $6 billion dollars, the Kamehameha schools are proof that money cannot buy happiness.

In 1997, Nā Kumu o Kamehameha, an organization of faculty and administrators, played a pivotal role in exposing existing conflict and charting a direction for the future. Convinced that the school was being governed and managed by trustees in a way that was detrimental to the students and the legacy, teachers and administrators came together to effect positive change. They accused the trustees of micromanagement, of the removal of faculty involvement in the planning and development of educational programs, and of the imposition of a climate of fear throughout the school. Like David battling Goliath, these two hundred educators stood up for what they believed, and did so guided by strong principles that shaped their actions.

In response to growing criticism from this and other quarters, including some administrators and alumni, two of the five trustees took action to have one of their fellow trustees removed by the attorney general, alleging mismanagement. The controversy that ensued spilled out beyond the board and into the courts, ran through every part of the school, and enveloped the community. In three short years, a proud legacy and a much-beloved institution had its identity redefined by court battles and front-page coverage, eventual criminal indictments of trustees, and an investigation by the Internal Revenue Service. By the time it was all over, all five trustees were removed or resigned and a new system of governance, including a new teachers' union, was put into place.

The controversy cut deep wounds. People took sides during the controversy. In the end, some won, some lost. Then came the reality that winners and losers alike were on the same team. As the publicity subsided, it was clear that it was time to take an inventory of the damage and to begin the arduous task of rebuilding. Fortunately, the creation of shared goals and values-based expectations by Nā Kumu showed the way. We excerpt here their 1998 *Statement of Visions and Goals*:

> We owe our greatest debt allegiance to Pauahi and to her beneficiaries, our past, present and future students. We express that allegiance by honoring the distinctive culture, traditions and history of Kamehameha Schools and by living the values adopted by trustees in our [school] mission statement: Pono [to be moral and proper]; Imiʻike [to seek knowledge]; Laulima [to work cooperatively]; Lokomaikaʻi [to share]; Naʻau Pono [to possess a deep sense of justice]; Mālama [to care for each other]; and Haʻahaʻa [to be humble]. All of these rest upon a foundation of Aloha, a sense of warmth and respect for others [Nā Kumu o Kamehameha, 1998].

Nā Kumu o Kamehameha exists to articulate the professional concerns of Kamehameha teachers and to express their strength and pride. In partnership with trustees, administration, and parents, and guided by the spirit of Pauahi's will, it places the educational needs of students above all other considerations. The members of this voluntary group concluded that respect for these values would lead to the following:

- An institution focused on the primacy of the teacher-student relationship
- A sense of community, mutual respect, and trust
- A tolerance for free and serious debate, with a regular reevaluation of policies, procedures, and strategic goals at all levels of the institution
- A supportive but hands-off relationship to education-related matters
- A respect for excellence and professionalism of the teaching staff, with corresponding respect for professional autonomy within the classroom
- A willingness to share responsibility for implementing the school's educational mission with the administrators and teachers, those closest to the students
- The ability to plan in matters such as budgeting in ways that address the needs of the classroom and therefore of the students
- A decision-making process that respects consensus
- The creation of structures and processes that allow for the free expression of professional opinions, and genuine participation by teachers in all decisions that affect the education of students

Building from the inspiration of this vision, efforts are being made by top management to build and sustain inclusive decision-making practices. Simultaneously, dialogues and facilitated problem-solving sessions are occurring to address deep divisions within and across role groups. Slowly and intentionally, emotional distance between people and groups is being bridged. Conversation and healing are being helped and encouraged. A widely inclusive strategic planning process is under way. A shared vision for the school is being forged.

Like a phoenix rising from its ashes, the school is using this opportunity to recreate itself. This time it hopes to cross new frontiers, to come to rest in a place of refuge where truth seeking and truth telling are honored and expected, and from that place to have a view of new vistas and new possibilities for the children of Hawaii.

Core Values for Public Participation

Have you ever thought that public hearings and meetings are a waste of time because public officials have already made up their minds before they go to the public? Have you ever wondered what would happen if you tried to get your community to make its public participation processes legitimate and effective?

You're not alone! A rapidly growing organization, the International Association for Public Participation (IAPP), has adopted seven core values that its members—a mix of public officials, consultants in public involvement, and academics—believe should guide any public participation process (Michaelson, 1996). The National Environmental Justice Advisory Committee, which advises the U.S. Environmental Protection Agency, included the core values in a model plan for community relations that they developed into a handout. The IAP2 offers an annual award for projects and communities that best exemplify the core values.

These are the core values:

1. People should have a say in decisions about actions that affect their lives.

2. Public participation includes the promise that the public's contribution will influence the decision.

3. The public participation process communicates the interests and meets the process needs of all participants.

4. The public participation process seeks out and facilitates the involvement of those who potentially are affected.

5. The public participation process involves participants in defining how they participate.

6. The public participation process communicates to participants how their input was or was not utilized.

7. The public participation process provides participants with the information needed to participate in a meaningful way (Michaelson, 1996, p. 80).

These core values represent most prominently an effort to create principled and shared ground. Can you bring this set of core values to your community? Of course. Should you expect your elected or appointed leaders to adopt these values wholeheartedly? Perhaps not—at least not yet. As the very first core value notes, people should have a say in decisions about actions that affect their lives. Your locality's leaders may be concerned about insufficient resources to fulfill these values, or they may have other values that they believe are more important, or they may share the views of many who don't believe that public participation is important.

Catron County, New Mexico— From Battleground to Higher Ground

Catron County, New Mexico, is one of the least populated counties in the United States. Fewer than three thousand people inhabit a jurisdiction the size of Massachusetts. The scarcity of people is a function of many factors, including rugged and high terrain, a large proportion of federally managed land (75 percent of the county), and little economic opportunity. But the few people who are there have had their share, and more, of notoriety. In the early 1990s, Catron County gained fame nationwide for what is called the County Movement, an innocuous term that in fact covers a wide range of plans and actions devoted to liberating local government from the yoke of federalism. The anti–federal government sentiment was exacerbated by the decline in the timber industry and the closing of a sawmill, conditions brought about at least in part by increased restrictions on logging on public lands.

The libertarian spirit that sparked the County Movement was not shared by all Catron residents, however, and bitter antagonism marked public and private interactions. The county was plagued not only by conflict over its battles with federal agencies but also by high unemployment and all the problems that often accompany economic suffering, including domestic violence, drug and alcohol abuse, and mental illness.

A family physician residing and working in Catron recognized that many of the health problems he encountered were, at their source, a product of the economic and social climate. In order to attack the physical and mental illnesses, the community itself needed healing. He therefore decided to engage community members in informal discussions about ways of reconciling their antagonisms and other county woes. He began by contacting the New Mexico Center for Dispute Resolution, a community mediation center in Albuquerque, which then helped convene a "dialogue group" of citizens and public officials. This dialogue group agreed initially to three simple ground rules (Smith, 1998):

1. Listen to all in a respectful manner.
2. Engage in open and honest discussion.
3. Talk to others outside the group in a way that respects all views.

The individuals who met at the inception of this process had no idea what the group might do, how long they would meet, or even whether they would be willing to meet together long enough to become an ongoing group. But after several meetings they created a mission statement along with a commitment to continue to work together. During the next several years, the group faced many challenges, but it continued to broaden its scope of work and membership. Eventually the Catron County Citizens Group (CCCG) received foundation funding to hire its own director.

One of the facilitators of this process who continues to observe the effort, Melinda Smith, reports that higher ground is very much visible even in the midst of conflict. Indeed, more recent economic downturns have come about by the reduction in herd sizes through the cutback of grazing permits on public lands. A number of ranchers have been forced to sell their private land and their herds. But the will of the CCCG to work together remains, as does the hope that collaboration will produce some economic benefit. As this book goes to press, the CCCG is working on the development of a woodlot and a small-diameter timber industry. This has given the community a sense of hope. They have also incorporated the CCCG, and the officers include the county extension agent, a local environmental activist who has been with the group from the outset, one of the county commissioners, and a forest service ranger.

Smith writes, "Higher ground is reached in several different ways. There are some group members who have internalized the conflict management process and have a deepened understanding of civil discourse and integrative solutions. Their voices seem to always come through during tense moments. Further, there is an ongoing commitment, driven by not only the hope for positive change but also by frustration and even anger, that keep people coming to meetings and working together. While individual transformation to higher ground does not always occur, the commitment to a forum for problem solving and dialogue has built a capacity for higher ground in the community" (M. Smith, e-mail message to E. Franklin Dukes, Dec. 12, 1999).

What does this Catron County effort say about higher ground? The continuing *challenge* to reach for higher ground is of course most prominent in highly conflictual situations, and Catron County is no exception. As we have observed in the last three chapters, the process of creating shared expectations for higher ground is iterative. While *safe* ground was initially provided by creating ground rules and using a facilitator, truly safe ground had to become the responsibility of group members. In low-trust and high-conflict situations, the only way to develop that sense of responsibility is by demonstrating through repeated behaviors that members are trustworthy. To do so requires time and concrete actions rather than dialogue alone.

The Chelsea, Massachusetts, Charter Consensus Process

In the early 1990s, the residents of Chelsea, Massachusetts, shared with those of Catron County a deep distrust for government (S. L. Podziba, e-mail message to E. Franklin Dukes, Nov. 29, 1999). But the context was entirely different. Chelsea is all the way across the country from Catron County, in the urban eastern United States. Its 28,000 residents include second- and third-generation Americans of Eastern European descent and a substantial proportion of recent Hispanic and Asian immigrants. The distrust of its residents was directed not at federal agencies controlling public lands but at local government officials who were running the city as their own fiefdom.

So mismanaged and corrupt was Chelsea's elected government that by 1990 two of its past four mayors had been imprisoned and a third escaped the same fate only because the statute of limitations for his crime had expired. In 1990, Massachusetts took the extraordinary step of placing the city into state receivership, with local government decisions needing approval by the court-appointed receiver. One significant duty of that receivership was to recommend a new form of government to the governor. Recognizing that the legitimacy of the new city government was at stake, the receiver brought in a mediation team to engage citizens in what became called the Chelsea Charter Consensus Process.

The mediation team began this literal reinvention of democracy by listening to Chelsea's citizens. As might be expected, they interviewed some forty community leaders, formal and informal, to learn of their hopes for Chelsea's future and their visions of what good government means, and to answer questions about the charter process and how they could participate in it. In an innovative departure from common practice, they trained Chelsea citizens as facilitators to run some forty-five community meetings in which all citizens could discuss what was wrong with the past and what form of governance would allow Chelsea to escape receivership, and more important, to become a functioning city. Other outreach efforts included a series of newsletters (in English and Spanish, the language of many recent immigrants) sent to all households, a survey, public forums, call-in cable television programs, and a telephone hotline.

The people who actually drafted the charter were the residents of Chelsea themselves. Again, the need for legitimacy shaped the representation. A team of three respected citizens was presented with some seventy nominees to the group that would draft the charter the community had recommended through interviews, meetings, and a hotline. Selection criteria included willingness to seek consensus and to think citywide rather than about parochial interests, and commitment to the best governance that Chelsea could design. The drafting of the charter's language involved an iterative process of proposed language, public input, and deliberation, as well as assistance from a consultant.

The state receiver retained the authority to recommend the proposed charter to the governor for final approval. The charter preparation team reached consensus. Because of the active public involvement process, the charter garnered 60 percent support in the referendum that followed—not unanimity, but in a deeply divided community it was a significant majority. The charter was approved by the state.

The charter lives in Chelsea, too. For example, when a police captain who had been convicted of tax evasion was elected to the city council, the city asked the Massachusetts attorney-general to enforce the charter's section that states that convicted felons are not allowed to hold elective office, and the captain was not allowed on the council. Perhaps even more promising for the long-term interests of Chelsea has been the increase of civic associations from two to ten (Podziba, 1998).

The Chelsea Charter Consensus Process represents an extraordinary example of democracy building. A charter of this sort represents codification of shared expectations about how a community wants to be governed, and it is hard to think of any of the elements of higher ground—principled, safe, new, enlarged perspective, shared, and most certainly a challenge—that did not mark the path of this process.

The examples we have described here are indeed extraordinary. Not all communities need or can afford an effort of the sort enacted in Catron County. Few efforts can begin, as did Enlibra, with the endorsement of two governors representing the Republican and Democratic parties. Yet each of you participates in a variety of communities—communities of place, such as your hometowns, villages, and cities; and communities of interest, such as church, school, and workplace. Each of these communities already has ways of addressing conflict. Sometimes these ways work fairly well. All too often they don't work at all. Your daily interactions are often shaped by how well these larger communities support positive expressions of conflict. The more the larger community supports a higher-ground approach, the more likely you will be able to call on those shared expectations to work through differences productively.

We have also offered these examples to show that reaching for higher ground is more than a pipe dream. None of these efforts necessarily represents 100 percent fidelity to the principles and elements we have outlined in this book. However, we are increasingly optimistic as we see large-scale efforts at conflict resolution and community decision making reflecting higher-ground principles.

In our closing chapter we turn back to those key principles and a very small-scale higher-ground effort: how we brought our own values to life through our work on this book.

Chapter Ten

Conclusion and Inspiration

The tobacco war.

The culture war over homosexuality and abortion.

A community split over how to decide which children go to which public schools.

A hospital management work team.

We have covered a lot of territory in showing you the meaning of reaching for higher ground (RHG). We have not claimed that the peak of these shared expectations is possible or appropriate in every situation. But we do believe that RHG can mean bringing to all your group experiences a vision for seeking the best that is possible.

In this last chapter, we begin by reviewing the RHG approach we have offered in this book. Then we turn to certain forms and examples of covenants that capture the elements of RHG. Because such creations must be unique to the group and its enterprise, the one covenant we can best talk about is the one we created—and struggled with—in writing this book. We share with you, warts and all, how we structured our own quest for RHG while writing about the same topic—the problems we encountered and how we labored to build respect and strength through our own differences. We conclude with a reflection to help carry you from the pages in your hands to the work of your heart and head at the next committee meeting, church board retreat, or workplace team gathering.

What We Have Learned

Higher ground is a metaphor for how people may work together through ordinary and not-so-ordinary problems and needs as they aim to become better—better family members, better citizens, better workers, and better group leaders. It is a way to build community through conflict. But higher ground has to be more than a wish or a general attitude of goodwill or a worthy goal. Moving toward higher ground means making a shared vision real. To continue metaphorically, the effort is indeed in the reaching, not in the gazing.

We opened the book by showing how much conflict within groups and committees comes from unspoken rules that are often unproductive. Moreover, because such rules often remain unspoken, people bring to groups competing ideas of how to address conflict and how to go about problem solving and decision making in the family, workplace, or community.

We then observed how people typically encounter shared expectations for addressing conflict in the form of ground rules—a list of dos and don'ts about behaving in a group. Many of these guidelines, such as "Don't interrupt," "Ask a question before criticizing," or "Start and end meetings on time," can be useful. They can move a group from unspoken and often conflicting expectations to basic and explicit guidelines for how people should work together.

Nonetheless, common practice with ground rules is often ineffective—or at least it falls far short of what groups need—for several reasons. Ground rules are typically presented by leadership without any preparation or input from group members. The ground rules are often presented—and accepted—as merely a preliminary step to doing the "real" work of the group. Enforcement of the rules is uneven and the rules usually focus on specific behaviors, missing the need to address higher expectations and values.

We introduced RHG as a more robust way of creating principled and productive behavior in families, the workplace, and the community. The metaphor of higher ground represents many aspirations, including principled ground, new ground, a refuge, a place of enlarged perspective, shared ground, and a continuing challenge.

Next we described six elements essential for making RHG a reality. We asserted that creating shared expectations for behavior can be more than a modest, pro forma exercise in establishing ground rules. Rather, the process can be a way for groups to envision together relationship-affirming and effective behavior. We observed how *covenants* can be created to link group members' highest aspirations to clear principles and specific agreements about behavior. The breadth of a covenant helps meld and reinforce a need for task accomplishment with a focus on fair procedures that strengthen a group's ability to work in the long term.

"From the Toolbox" sections presented many specific ways to enact the six elements of the RHG model. We addressed what you can do with a specific kind of group by identifying key features of groups (for example, duration, size, and diversity) and how to apply RHG in real, often messy circumstances. You can review the tables and figure in Chapter Seven to judge what level of enactment of RHG is appropriate for your group and how well your group reaches some degree of higher ground, with higher levels still to be attained.

To give a real-world view of the practical payoff that can be achieved using RHG, we showed a fictitious hospital management team and illustrated the difference between a new department manager using typical ground rules and using an RHG approach. Recognizing that a budget crisis called for some immediate actions, RHG principles were applied within tight time constraints. We think this scenario shows the opportunity for the group to work for broader and deeper shared expectations for the team's best performance in the long run. Finally, in Chapter Nine we raised the idea of creating communities and networks that support individual groups and organizations doing RHG. We presented real efforts, addressing a variety of needs and conflicts that are consistent with the RHG vision.

Making Higher Ground Solid Ground

More and more often people are recognizing the costs of unproductive conflict and taking steps to be proactive and prescriptive about how such things will be handled should problems arise. Here are some specific examples of processes for creating shared expectations for behavior that capture several aspects of the RHG approach. Not every example is a perfect fit with the principles and tools of RHG, but they illustrate businesses that are moving in the right direction.

These types of agreements do not routinely involve transformative outcomes for the parties. More likely the interest in formalizing agreements about how conflict will be handled is driven by bottom-line concerns, such as closing deals, continuing work uninterrupted, and concluding projects as planned. However, the proliferation of such practices does mark a collective awakening about the likelihood of conflict, the potential consequences for the parties if such conflict is not addressed productively, and the need to act in predictable and principled ways when the conflicts occur. These approaches to preparing for conflict may not bring about the higher ground we are advocating, but they do represent an important stretch in the right direction. With such agreements marking attention to the relationship and shared responsibility for the outcome, the mechanisms are in place to nurture the agreements and the relationships. Well-managed efforts at narrow functional outcomes today could give rise to fuller, transformative aspirations tomorrow.

Examples include the following:

- Partnering in labor-management relations
- Charters and protocols in groups charged with seeking consensus agreements on policy and regulatory matters
- Mediation clauses in realty agreements
- Agreements on conduct among adversaries in a common forum

Partnering in Labor-Management Relations

Relations between labor unions and company management have varied greatly since the legal recognition and protection of collective bargaining. Certainly there are opposing interests—workers wishing the highest compensation possible for their labor, and managers and stockholders seeking the lowest production costs possible. Nonetheless, there is a rising movement to look at general productivity and worker ability as areas of common ground, albeit with eventual hard bargaining about how productivity and profits are translated into wages, dividends, and investments.

Building on many local, regional, and national forums called *labor-management cooperation councils*, the idea of partnering has gained a foothold. As a way to create better relations within the structure of both contract negotiation and implementation, and to promote a general atmosphere of respectful problem solving, partnering agreements involve more than who does what when. They include statements of shared goals, general principles of fairness, and specific projects for mutual gain. They entail the spirit of RHG: general values, principles of behavior, and specific dos and don'ts.

Charters and Protocols in Groups Charged with Seeking Consensus Agreements on Policy and Regulatory Matters

The term *protocols* may remind you of complex, even convoluted language in some diplomatic document between countries, or it may imply a code of conduct related to diplomatic manners—how flags are arranged or seating at a state dinner. *Charters* may bring to mind a legal document, such as a town charter, or perhaps educational policy, because charter schools are now a hot topic.

However, we see these terms now being used for public policy dialogues and regulatory negotiations involving representatives of competing interests. For example, on questions of river water quality in North Carolina, the Stakeholder Advisory Committee for the Neuse River Buffer Rule was established in 1998. The committee reviewed regulations on buffers—defined areas next to rivers and streams designed to naturally prevent excess nitrogen from reducing the water quality in the Neuse River basin. The advisory committee's charter included a number of details regarding the group's approach to the task, such as the topics under discussion, how information would be shared, the basis for consensus decision making, how different stakeholders (people representing interest groups such as farmers, developers, environmentalists, local government, and cooperative extension) would be represented, and how they would work in the group.

Temporary or time-limited efforts to resolve a problem or propose a specific policy or regulation do not always aim at the higher values or principles that are most appropriate for long-term groups. However, the principles of fair participation and open and effective involvement are explicit in many of these documents.

By no means would these charters or protocols be confused with vision or mission statements adopted by ongoing organizations. While their statement of purpose focuses on the task, much of the document describes the process and relationships that need to be created and maintained to reach a consensus outcome.

Mediation Clauses in Realty Agreements

Another more nuts-and-bolts example, and literally close to home, in the real estate area are standard contractual agreements to use mediation if disagreements arise following the sale of land for residential purposes. In some ways these contractual provisions might be seen as a safety mechanism, like being sure there is a fire extinguisher in the kitchen in case a fire in the stove turns into a major conflagration. However, we see these kinds of mediation clauses as efforts to recognize the accountability results consistent with RHG and the need to preserve relationships if conflict arises. We distinguish between voluntary mediation in these circumstances, which provides a way for parties to understand one another's interests and seek mutually acceptable solutions, and mandatory mediation or arbitration, which can result in consumers being forced to accept a process that may undercut their interests.

Agreements on Conduct Between Adversaries in a Common Forum

We've covered many examples in which there is indeed a group with a common purpose, including the workplace, a nonprofit board, and a church. But what happens when there are clear and probably irreducible differences between people who can't get away from one another?

The best examples we've encountered come out of the dialogues on tobacco use and on faith and homosexuality. Not only did Frank see common cause grow from discussions he managed among tobacco farmers and public health advocates, but the groups themselves have seen a surprising form of higher ground emerge. Part of RHG in this instance comes from how the participants agreed to disagree on some things and yet work together on others.

One of the outcomes of the work done by the United Methodist Church on their bitter divisions over how their faith informs their policies on homosexuality was a set of guidelines for civility in the face of conflict. The opposing advocates—some firmly convinced that homosexual practice is sinful and that such sin must be faced by the church, others calling for change in church policy to support homosexual couples in committed, monogamous relationships—saw a need to avoid demonizing one another and to create a model for faithful discussion amid strong differences on faith. Their *Guidelines for Civility in the United Methodist Church* were adopted as part of a general consensus document after two sessions of deep and difficult conversation. The guidelines are evocative of higher ground:

- Respect the personhood of others while engaging their ideas.
- Be careful in defining terms, avoiding needless use of inflammatory words.

- Exercise care that expressions of personal offense at the differing opinions of others are not used as a means of inhibiting discussion.
- Be open to change in your own position and patient with the process of change in the thinking and behavior of others.
- Always remember that people are ultimately defined by their relationships with God—not by the flaws others discover or think they discover in their views and actions (General Commission on Christian Unity and Interreligious Concerns, 1998).

◆◆ *Reflection.* We've been talking about making the desire to reach for higher ground an explicit and intentional focus of group work. Formalizing these ideas into standing agreements, charters, and partnering arrangements means taking the idea to the next level of formality and commitment. The advantages of formalizing these agreements include the fact that it

- Ceremonializes the expectation and promotes accountability
- Communicates intentions to others both inside and outside the group making the commitment
- Protects against leadership transition or the deleterious effects of changing group membership
- Establishes clear norms for behavior
- Encourages regular attention to the relation between the general mission or vision of a group, medium-term priorities, and short-term objectives

What We Learned About Higher Ground by Creating This Book

When we first talked with friends and colleagues about our plans to coauthor this book and about working together long-distance, many offered their best wishes and condolences in the same breath.

Apparently no small number of people have lost perfectly good colleagues and friends because they thought it would be "fun to work together." Writing can involve high stakes and high demands, like many other ventures. These are the perfect conditions for conflict.

We decided early on to protect our shared investment in our relationships and the project. We set out together to define for ourselves what higher ground would mean. Along the way we learned a great deal about ourselves, each other, collaborative writing, and the value of our ideas on higher ground.

We started with the germ of an idea from Frank, in January 1998. He had worked with Marina and John in different settings and the three of us knew one another as friends as well as colleagues. As our ideas developed, Marina moved from Delaware to Hawaii in the summer of 1998. Undaunted, and perhaps a bit naive, we kept going, with the goal of approaching a publisher and getting a contract.

With a signed contract in hand, new trepidation arose. We believed that no one of us had sufficient knowledge or experience to write the book ourselves. But, we wondered, could we blend our experiences and build on each other's thinking in a way that produced a product that was bigger than the sum of our individual parts? Could it be a text that was more than the least common denominator across our three experiences? Could the demands of distance, full-time jobs, families, and civic responsibilities be balanced sufficiently to give ample attention to these important ideas? Could we write in a manner that was both inspirational and, at the same time, highly practical for the reader?

We engaged in significant face-to-face work only three times across the eighteen months of finishing the proposal for the book and doing the actual writing. Otherwise we used e-mail and conference calls to coordinate our work.

Knowing the challenges, we worked to develop our own covenant, which contained three sections. Since we viewed this as a living document, this version has been edited for clarity and grammatical purposes:

1. Aspirations: general statements of principles and goals that are, almost in themselves, the higher ground we seek to "do" as part of writing about it.
2. Guidelines: midlevel ideas with more specificity that are means to move toward the aspirations.
3. Ground rules: specific dos and don'ts that are the most measurable items. These should be clear to observe if they are followed, or their degree of use should be easily judged.

Aspirations

1. Use our work to apply, create, and understand more fully the concepts and concrete applications of higher ground.
2. Protect and build mutual respect and appreciation.
3. Mix humor and personal poignancy with task-oriented behavior.
4. Take the necessary time and contribute the required vulnerability and courage, creativity, iterative approach, and testing and retesting of principles.
5. Value our personal and professional relationships, and work to maintain and deepen both.
6. Seek agreement on a fair combination of individual responsibility, accountability, and credit.
7. Value one another's unique contributions and therefore demonstrate respect for one another's needs, ideas, and concerns.

Guidelines

1. Use effective communication techniques.
2. Focus on interests.
3. Guard against relying on past harmony and goodwill to resolve different views on small and large issues.

4. Beware the "Fate of Threes" rule whereby two align, thus alienating the third person.
5. Promote shared interest over self-interest.
6. Commit to agendas and time allocations for shared responsibilities.
7. Strive for parity in distribution of work.
8. Recognize interdependence—complete assignments on time and with quality.
9. If "off-line" conversations occur between two of the three regarding problems or concerns, coach, advise, and bring the discussion back "on-line" in a constructive manner.
10. Recognize that we are human and therefore give each other occasional permission to be cranky, obstinate, and otherwise fallible.

Ground Rules (Specific Dos and Don'ts)

1. Restate and summarize agreements, work assignments, and items for our next meeting.
2. Regularly test for meaning: offer examples, metaphors, and distinctions. The voicing of uncertainties or confusions should be rewarded.
3. At agreed benchmarks, have explicit discussions on our working relationships in which we review our rules and expectations, judge how well we (individually and collectively) are enacting them, determine whether behavior needs to change, and decide whether rules need to be added or revised. Following big-push periods, establish protected time to evaluate group functioning and revisit ground rules.
4. Clarify in writing all agreements and task assignments.
5. When offering critiques, state what you appreciate first, then what can be improved.

6. Know that problems often fester when left unspoken and therefore raise any concerns with philosophy, process, content, style, organization, or any other matter as soon as they arise.

Living Out Our Promises

The covenant and its three sections look impressive—at least we hope they do. Coming to agreement on these points took some time; we wanted to be sure we knew what we were talking about and to have a common view of the connections between certain aspirations, guidelines, and ground rules. But as we have observed throughout the book, goodwill alone is not sufficient for a smooth ride.

As we would recommend for any group, and in keeping with our third ground rule, on revisiting our own ground rules following big-push periods, the writing of the last chapter became another opportunity for reflection and taking stock. So we recently asked ourselves three evaluative questions:

1. Did we accomplish what we set out to do?
2. How well were we served by our covenant and how well did we serve it?
3. What have we learned from this experience?

In answering question 1 we need only look at a few simple facts. Our manuscript was mailed to the publisher within seven days of the original deadline. It arrived in a shape that left us content with our work and the publisher pleased with its quality. The three-way phone conversations that took place in the final week of readying the manuscript included laughter, playfulness, and clear evidence of solid relationships. Last but not least, no one has reported undue strife in his or her home or workplace as a result of this project.

As nearly anyone who has taken on such a writing project can attest, these data are compelling. It seems we did in fact accomplish what we set out to do. We accomplished our goal, nurtured our relationships, and in the end produced together something we all believe we could not have done alone.

So we turn to question 2: How well were we served by our covenant and how well did we serve it? Well, in reviewing the aspirations, guidelines, and specific ground rules carefully, it is a joy to report that by and large we honored all of our shared expectations. Only one guideline proved challenging to live up to—guideline 8: Recognize interdependence—complete assignments on time and with quality—and it is not surprising.

As we shared with one another our views of how well we did in relation to our covenant, we found several themes:

1. The discussions that brought about the written covenant, and the understandings that very discussion developed, were perhaps even more valuable than the finished product.
2. We behaved like most groups by delaying discussion of ground rules at the outset, knowing that it required us to talk of the most important, vulnerable parts of our selves and our project. Although the collaboration was not without its challenges at times, the covenant gave us a way of addressing the issues and staying on the path we had chosen.
3. Explicit agreements raise one's self-consciousness for performance and responsibility to the group.

Value of the Covenant Discussion

The process of discussing and writing our expectations was as valuable as, or maybe even more valuable than, actually having the covenant. We could have but rarely did rely on the written covenant as a touchstone, mostly because we all agreed that we were living out our aspirations, principles, and ground rules. When we were not, for the most part we knew it without looking at the written agreement.

Having shared expectations for reaching higher ground means that the tough conversations that sometimes need to occur have in a sense already been started. It is so often intimidating to initiate a conversation about very risky or undiscussable topics that surface in group work. The RHG approach means that those conversations have been sanctioned and are both expected and welcomed. Talking about the undiscussables becomes a matter of continuing forward, not beginning anew. This expectation may not make discussion easy, but it does make it more likely to occur.

Delaying Discussion of Important and Vulnerable Topics

"Let's face it: we delayed discussion about forming our own covenant," Marina comments. It was somewhere around our fourth phone meeting when we finally addressed the issue. In each of the first three calls we failed to get to that particular agenda item, agreeing that we didn't have time given the other pressing demands on our attention. The irony of this was not lost on us. We eventually did the necessary work to build our own agreements for how we wanted to work together and what we wanted to accomplish through the book project.

For our group, as for most groups, the time crunch is the reason given for failing to address such matters. We had both a time crunch and a bit of discomfort in addressing such matters directly. The insight we gained from this was the value of expecting that such a discussion of values, guiding principles, and specific dos and don'ts will occur. Without that expectation, the tendency is to believe that it isn't really necessary. In the end it was both necessary and valuable. Our prior commitment to reach for higher ground propelled us to follow through with the conversation. That is a value in and of itself.

We were very much aware of the importance of developing and making explicit our own expectations of how we would work together in ways that supported one another and that prepared us for difficulties and differences. But because we had been friends and colleagues for some time before writing, we had a sense that it was not necessary to devote significant time to formalizing the implicit expectations we had demonstrated in how we related to one another. So we found a way to build the agreements without investing excessive time. Giving our covenanting process the right amount of effort was smart. Trusting that we were good enough at working together or that our group of three was too small to need to work out these expectations would have been foolish.

Staying the Course Through Challenging Moments

Because we decided to all have a hand in the preparation of every chapter, one of our greatest challenges arose out of communicating via e-mail, John reflects. Two of us were far more comfortable working through e-mail than was the third coauthor. This difference, and what spun out of it, at times strained our working relationship.

One of us found the communication methods—e-mail plus periodic but rushed phone calls—difficult. That partner says, "The distance between us, the always time-pressured agendas, and the heavy reliance on e-mail were not optimal for my work style. The creative task of developing ideas into a book would have been more comfortably accomplished, for me, through face-to-face discussion and the free-flowing exchange of ideas prior to the assignment of tasks. I wanted dialogue about the key ideas. I was looking for the chance to think out loud with my two colleagues and friends. But the methods we developed for assigning the writing meant that we wrote first, individually, and then talked later, through the editing."

The mismatch between that one coauthor's thinking style and our team writing approach contributed to that partner missing some deadlines. The other two were perplexed, even concerned, when the third coauthor did not acknowledge with action or word that a deadline was passing. That left two coauthors caught between conflicting emotions: torn between the real need for and interest in being supportive of a person they respect and care deeply about, on the one hand, and being on the receiving end of violations of promises on the other.

We then turned to ground rule 6: We know that problems often fester when left unspoken and therefore will raise any concerns with philosophy, process, content, style, organization, or any other matter as soon as they arise. Thus we entered a discussion among us that was our first real encounter with the power of our own agreements for reaching higher ground. We discussed the matter in a supportive way and developed new arrangements to solve the problem. Our discussion was honest and constructive. We modified our writing process in a way that improved it for everyone. Without our agreements, we don't know how the problem might have been handled. It might not have been discussed at all and the patterns that were emerging could have spiraled into some real challenges to our vision of what we wanted for the book and for our relationship.

A second time that the covenant was used to keep us on the path to higher ground was when one of us felt that another was not giving the writing sufficient attention in the shared editing process. Ground rule 8 says that we will acknowledge our interdependence by completing assignments on time and with quality. A pattern was emerging whereby one of us was always on time in turning around the assignments, but often with too few additions, comments, or acknowledgments of what worked and what did not. Another of us was expecting clearer indications of deep thought in the editing process, more dialogue, and more original contributions as a piece of writing was passed around among us.

This can be a very sticky conversation to have among colleagues and friends because it is, at base, about subjective judgment of each other's work. There is no room for argument about whether a deadline was missed without word to others. But there is ample room for disagreement about what is expected in terms of quality of effort and whether or not something is in fact quality. However, having survived the delicate conversation from the first challenge of missed deadlines, there was greater confidence that this problem too was solvable. But perhaps even more important than whether or not it was solvable, the perception was that this problem could risk not just our relationships but the quality of the final product.

In honor of our agreements, the concern needed to be aired, and so it was. Perceptions were shared, wishes were expressed, and agreements were made. Greater appreciation for difference developed. Immediately changes occurred. Once again we had driven a bit close to the edge of the steep path we were climbing toward higher ground. Once again our covenant served as our guide and our guardrail, pulling us back to the middle of the path and assisting us in our efforts to stay the course.

Higher Self-Consciousness for Performance and Responsibility

Having explicit agreements makes one more self-conscious about one's own performance. This is a good thing. The shared expectations gave us values-derived, objective criteria for gauging and guiding our own actions. This means that each of us became more self-aware and self-regulating, leaving less responsibility to the group for managing or tolerating anything less than constructive individual behavior.

Because we knew that each of us was committed to our covenant, we did not feel we were nagging each other about missing deadlines or being unduly critical when we talked openly about expectations for quality. This candor was helpful and it modeled for all three of us the accountability that was central to our project. Valuing relationships can mean being direct, but being direct need not mean scolding.

A powerful lesson from this experience is recognizing that having the shared expectations doesn't mean that the appropriate behaviors are easy to manifest as the work progresses. Thoughtful shared expectations represent our best intentions and our rational understanding of appropriate behavior. Best intentions sometimes have little relationship to performance. Rational behavior is not always the chosen path.

Reaching for higher ground is indeed a continuing challenge. Group work is hard work, especially when the stakes are high and differences exist. That combination brings emotion and investment to the table. Using the RHG approach is the best strategy we know for ensuring success in group work, especially when the goals of the work represent not just expectations regarding the task but investment in relationships as well.

Our writing experience deepened our conviction that this approach is highly practical and well worth the investment. We have grown in our confidence through our own work together as well as through the work we've continued with other groups while working on this project.

We know that not every committee meeting or neighborhood forum is built for the aspirations and principles of higher ground we have described. Some groups or projects are short-term, narrowly functional, and without large consequence. However, we hope you work within relationships that guide your life—family, workplace, neighborhood, and volunteer endeavors—in a way that offers opportunities to travel up the mountain, up toward higher ground.

We hope we have given you both inspiration and the tools for the challenge before you. Change from familiar patterns is risky and may be uncomfortable. When you consider the alternative, however, you may find change less troublesome than continuing along a dead-end path. Your form and focus as you do a given exercise will make a huge difference in how effective the exercise is at accomplishing your goal. Five good sit-ups are worth more than twenty poorly done sit-ups. Not only are the five good sit-ups more likely to get you the firm stomach you want, but they are less likely to produce some unwanted damage, like a pulled muscle. Understanding your goal, using good form, and maintaining focus make all the difference. That is what the RHG approach is all about.

The twentieth century was one of staggering accomplishment, yet it was also a century of incredible and escalating violence. Violence is the outgrowth of conflict poorly managed at some earlier stage. We have written this book as an antidote to destructive conflict in all its forms. Solving problems while staying connected to one another makes destructive conflict behavior less necessary and less likely.

We hope for a more civil, just, and caring society as we move into the twenty-first century. Important work needs to be done that can only be done by people working together. We dream of families, workplaces, and communities capable of acknowledging the diversity of their members and their aspirations, talents, and needs. We wish for skilled and shared group leadership that harnesses the potential of the human spirit to lift us from where we are to where we want to be.

To those of you who have long been working for higher ground in the circles in which you live and labor, we hope we have affirmed your efforts. To those who desire to seek higher ground, we hope we have encouraged and supported your journey. And to those who remain uncertain of the value of the ideas and their application to your work, we would like to think that RHG has become a grain of sand in your oyster—in time producing a pearl—a pearl of personal wisdom, valuable to yourself and to others.

This has been a great journey for us and one we intend to continue. May all your shared endeavors be as fruitful and fulfilling as this has been for us.

Appendix A
Typical Ground Rules

Below is an example of typical ground rules offered to a group for their consideration and adaptation. Often, such rules are put forward by the facilitator or group leader.

Proposed Ground Rules

- Contribute.
- Do not dominate, so that everyone can participate.
- Treat others with dignity and respect.
- Expose and explore differences of opinion that impact the task.
- Be relevant and stay on task.
- Honor time commitments.
- Leave what is said here, in here, unless we agree otherwise.

Appendix B
RHG Covenant of the "Wannabe Better" School District's Education Management Team

Statement of Purpose

The purpose of the Education Management Team is to promote the welfare of the school community on issues that cross programs and departments.

This purpose is accomplished through planning and direction setting, thoughtful coordination of effort, and information sharing both inside and beyond the team.

As a team responsible for shaping the culture of the district, members seek to model inclusive decision making, collaborative problem solving, and conflict resolution.

Principled Guidelines

These guidelines are more general than ground rules and place our ground rules in a values-based set of agreements about how we, as a group, want to operate:

- We seek first to understand and then to be understood.
- We honor and reinforce the internal expertise of team members by referring people to appropriate others before attempting to handle issues ourselves.
- We leave room for people to make mistakes and make it safe for people to admit it when they do.
- All decisions are accompanied by a rationale.

- We challenge ourselves to abandon "sacred cows" or assumptions about the future based upon experiences of the past.
- We have defined priorities as a group and do not deviate from them.
- We honor the team's policy of keeping confidences while sharing information as broadly as possible, as often as possible.
- We respond to strong emotion by gathering and sharing information.

Ground Rules for Meetings

In the interest of consistently holding high-impact and high-involvement meetings where adequate attention is paid to both the tasks and the relationships of the group, we adopt the following ground rules:

1. Begin and end on time.
2. Develop the agenda inclusively and deliver it to participants at least one full day prior to the meeting. At the meeting, finalize and approve the agenda.
3. Remember the purpose of our meeting; only discuss items relevant to that purpose.
4. Conduct and conclude one piece of business at a time.
5. Participation is a right . . . and a responsibility. Preparation for meetings is expected.
6. Listen as an ally. Then, it is OK to disagree because conflict is an opportunity for positive change.
7. Give others a chance to talk. Silence does not always mean agreement.
8. Communicate authentically. A person should say what he thinks *and* feels.
9. Conduct group business in front of the group.

10. Conduct personal business outside of the meeting.
11. Develop conditions of respect, acceptance, trust, and caring. Nurture our relationships.
12. Respect time limits. Survey the group if you wish to extend the discussion.
13. Develop alternative approaches to the solution of a problem.
14. Test for readiness to make a decision. Respond appropriately if the group is not ready.
15. Make the decision.
16. Assign follow-up actions and responsibilities.
17. Summarize at the conclusion of each item and at the end of the meeting.
18. Document and distribute the meeting outcomes.
19. Be accountable to these guidelines to promote continuous improvement.

Appendix C
Negotiating Team
RHG Pre-Negotiation Preparation
Meeting Documentation

Desired Outcomes of Negotiations

1. To get a contract that works for everyone involved.
2. To rebuild trust in labor-management relations.
3. Work for our own and each other's needs.

Agreements

Adopted Principles of Interest-Based Bargaining (IBB)

The team has agreed to adopt and abide by the following expectations during negotiations:

1. Share information openly.
2. Identify information needed or wanted to facilitate discussion and decision making.
3. Gather information in a timely way to support the group's work.
4. Share, rather than conceal, internal differences of opinion.
5. Focus on interest, not positions.
6. Focus on issues, not personalities.
7. Focus on interests and assist in satisfying the other party's interests as well.
8. Focus on the future and do not dwell in the past.
9. Use creative brainstorming to develop creative, satisfying options and solutions that offer mutual gain.

10. Evaluate options and solutions against objective criteria as opposed to power.

Final Approval Before Ratification

Prior to going to union membership for ratification, the Negotiating Team and Management's *final* approval will be secured. Once ratified by the membership, no changes will be made.

Supporting Rationale

Both proposals and responses to proposals will be accompanied by supporting rationale.

Amendments to Ratified Contract

Any changes to the ratified contract will be done by mutual agreement of the parties and should then be formally documented and amended to the contract.

Laying "Cards on the Table"

Management and labor will bring "needs" and "wants" to the negotiations early on to identify all issues, prioritize, and plan for how best to address the issues.

Use of a Third-Party Neutral

If the negotiations are stalled, the team will consider delaying or deferring the discussions, and when necessary, a neutral third party, agreeable to both sides, may be called to assist.

The "Team"

The group will adopt language to communicate a spirit of collaboration by referring to the entire group as the Negotiating Team and the various groups as the Employee Group and the Management Group.

Sign-Off Procedures

The parties may use the Tentative Agreement sign-off procedure. The use of such procedures shall be strictly voluntary on the part of each party. Any initialed or tentatively agreed-to item or provision shall be subject to review, amendment, alteration, and/or deletion by either party at any time during the negotiation process until a complete and total agreement is ratified by both parties.

Duty to Bargain

Both parties will be required to negotiate over mandatory subjects for bargaining raised by the other party until either agreement or impasse has been reached.

Use of Caucus

Either party at any time during any negotiating session shall have the right to caucus at its own call.

Seating During Negotiations

Group members will sit non-aligned during meetings to support an atmosphere of collaboration.

Unresolved Matters of Meeting Process and Agreements

The group has not resolved how each of the following issues will be handled during the negotiations. These issues will be addressed at the next meeting.

- Agenda setting
- Meeting prep, logistics, communication
- Leadership during meetings
- Confidentiality
- Contact with the press
- Communication with constituencies
- Documentation of meetings

Appendix D
Bestdarned Community Group Tools for Reaching Higher Ground

Group Values (That Guide Our Approach to Our Work)

- Synergy: recognize that no one can do alone what we can do together.
- Positive thinking: practice a "can do" attitude.
- Democracy: practice full participation, self-determination, and shared responsibility.
- Community: nurture relationships and work to keep everyone "at the table."
- Honesty: help others to understand you, and work to understand others.
- Creativity: innovate, stimulate.
- Flexibility: don't be a slave to the schedule or the routines.
- Efficiency: people's time is precious; treat it with respect.
- Acceptance: trust that each will do their best and still mistakes may be made.

Group Guidelines (That Help Us to Live Out Our Group Values)

- Meet regularly and communicate routinely.
- Call in and communicate meeting agenda items in advance of meeting.
- Start meetings on time.

- Record and capture the group's work; use colorful recording.
- Use a facilitator who can respond to the needs in the group.
- Be relevant; stay on the subject.
- Invite everyone into the conversation; take turns talking.
- Express concerns. Be real and authentic, and say what needs to be said.
- Disagree with ideas, not with people.
- Build on others' ideas.
- Assume there are no fixed ideas or undiscussables.
- Invite laughter and creativity.
- Value lively debate. It can promote quality.
- Work for consensus. Decision rule: 85 percent support 4's and 5's, with *no* 1's.
    - 5 I wholeheartedly agree
    - 4 I agree; it's OK
    - 3 I'm neutral
    - 2 I disagree but will go along
    - 1 I *hate* this and will work to stop it!
- Use an arbitrator (project coordinator) if consensus has been tried and failed.
- Reach closure on each item and summarize conclusions at end of meetings.

References

Anderson, L., and Prawatt, R. "Responsibility in the Classroom: A Synthesis of Research on Teaching." *Educational Leadership*, 1983, *12*, 62–66.

Bergman, E. "'Enlibra Principles' Gain Following Among Western Politicians." *Chronicle of Community*, Winter 1999, pp. 27–29.

Blake, R., and Mouton, J. *The Managerial Grid.* Houston, Tex.: Gulf, 1964.

Bush, R.A.B., and Folger, J. *The Promise of Mediation: Responding to Conflict Through Empowerment and Recognition.* San Francisco: Jossey-Bass, 1994.

Common Ground Network for Life and Choice. *Common Ground on Teen Pregnancy: A Pro-Choice, Pro-Life Conversation.* Washington, D.C.: Common Ground Network for Life and Choice, 1996.

Common Ground Network for Life and Choice. *Common Ground on Clinic Activism.* Occasional Paper. Syracuse, N.Y.: Program on the Analysis and Resolution of Conflicts, Syracuse University, Dec. 1998.

Cormick, G., and others. *Building Consensus for a Sustainable Future: Putting Principles into Practice.* Ottawa, Canada: National Round Table on the Environment and the Economy, 1996.

Dukes, E. F. *Resolving Public Conflict: Transforming Community and Governance.* New York: St. Martin's Press, 1996.

Elgin, S. H. *How to Turn the Other Cheek and Still Survive in Today's World.* Nashville, Tenn.: Nelson, 1997.

Fisher, R., and Ury, W. L. *Getting to Yes.* New York: Penguin Books, 1991.

General Commission on Christian Unity and Interreligious Concerns, The United Methodist Church. *In Search of Unity: A Conversation with Recommendations for the Unity of The United Methodist Church.* New York: United Methodist Church, 1998.

General Conference of the Mennonite Church and Mennonite Church General Board. *Agreeing and Disagreeing in Love: Commitments for Mennonites in Times of Disagreement.* Akron, Pa.: General Conference of the Mennonite Church and Mennonite Church General Board, 1995.

Hubbard, E. *The Note Book.* New York: W. H. Wise, 1927.

Innes, J. E. "Evaluating Consensus Building." In L. Susskind, S. McKearnan, and J. Thomas-Larmer (eds.), *The Consensus Handbook.* San Anselmo, Calif.: Sage Press, 1999.

Jacksteit, M., and Kaufmann, A. *Finding Common Ground in the Abortion Conflict: A Manual.* Washington, D.C.: Common Ground Network for Life and Choice, 1996.

Kaner, S., and others. *Facilitator's Guide to Participatory Decision Making.* Philadelphia: New Society Publishers, 1996.

Kritek, P. *Negotiating at an Uneven Table.* San Francisco: Jossey-Bass, 1996.

Lemagie, S. "Agreeing to Disagree." *Newsweek,* July 6, 1998, p. 22.

Michaelson, L. "Core Values for the Practice of Public Participation." *Interact: Journal of Public Participation,* 1996, 2(1), 77–82.

Moore, C. M., and Montalvo, R. *A Facilitator's Manual.* Santa Fe, N.Mex.: Western Network, 1996.

Nā Kumu o Kamehameha. "Statement of Vision and Goals." Internal Document. 1998.

Podziba, S. L. *Social Capital Formation, Public-Building and Public Mediation: The Chelsea Charter Consensus Process.* Occasional Paper. Dayton, Ohio: Kettering Foundation, 1998.

Puzder, A. F., and Isaacson-Jones, B. J. *Adoption as Common Ground.* Washington, D.C.: Common Ground Network for Life and Choice, 1995.

Raspberry, W. "Time to Acquaint Students with Ethics." *Washington Post Syndicate,* Nov. 22, 1999, p. A23.

Roberts, C. "Reinventing Relationships." In P. Senge and others, *The Fifth Discipline Fieldbook: Strategies and Tools for Building a Learning Organization.* New York: Doubleday, 1994.

Schmuck, R., and Runkel, P. *The Handbook of Organization Development in Schools.* (3rd ed.) Palo Alto, Calif.: Mayfield, 1985.

Schwarz, R. M. *The Skilled Facilitator: Practical Wisdom for Developing Effective Groups.* San Francisco: Jossey-Bass, 1994.

Senge, P., and others. *The Fifth Discipline Fieldbook: Strategies and Tools for Building a Learning Organization.* New York: Doubleday, 1994.

Skinner, D. E. "Congregational Life: Writing a Congregational Covenant." *U-U World,* Jan.–Feb. 1999, pp. 12–13.

Smith, M. *The Catron County Citizens Group: A Case Study in Community Collaboration.* Albuquerque: New Mexico Center for Dispute Resolution, 1998.

Strickland, C. "A Personal Experience with Electronic Community." *CMC Magazine.* Available at [http://www.december.com/cmc/mag/1998/jun/strick.html]. June 1998.

Thomas, K. W. "Conflict and Negotiation Processes in Organizations." In M. D. Dunnette and L. M. Hough (eds.), *The Handbook of Industrial and Organizational Psychology* (2nd ed.). Palo Alto, Calif.: Consulting Psychologists Press, 1990.

Ury, W. L. *Getting to Peace.* New York: Viking Penguin, 1999.

Ury, W. L., Brett, J. M., and Goldberg, S. B. *Getting Disputes Resolved.* San Francisco: Jossey-Bass, 1988.

Index

A

Aborigines, 194–196
Acceptance, 247
Accountability: assessing process of, 153; in group covenants, 96–99; as key element in path to higher ground, 96–99; and revision, 99–102
Active listening, 105
Adler, P., 145
Adoption as Common Ground (Puzder and Isaacson-Jones), 199
Agreeing and Disagreeing in Love: Commitments for Mennonites in Times of Disagreement (General Conference of the Mennonite Church and Mennonite Church General Board), 91
Agreements, advantages of formalizing, 224
Albuquerque, New Mexico, 211
American West, 203–205
Anderson, L., 108
Anomie, 12
Arizona, 199
Aspen Institute, 200
Aspirations, level of: and book jacket blurb tool, 145; and determination of investment, 133; and individual metaphor metamorphosis, 144–145; for reaching higher ground, 226
Assessment, group: alignment for, 152; behavior summaries for, 153–154; elements of, 151; levels for, 151; of refinement, 153–154
Atmosphere, maintaining best, 103–104
Attention level: and commitment needed, 145–150; evaluation of, 153; to shared expectations, 146
Australia, 194–196

B

Bailey Alliance, 124
Bargaining, interest-based, 11, 243–244
Behavior: shared expectations of, 6–7; unproductive, 108–110
Bergman, E., 204, 205
Bernice, Princess of Hawaii. *See* Bishop, B. P.
Bishop, B. P., 205–207
Bishop, C. R., 206
Book jacket blurb tool, 145
Boundaries, moving beyond: and Catron County Citizens Group, 210–213; and Chelsea Charter Consensus Process, 213–215; and Common Ground Network for Life and Choice, 196–200; and Enlibra, 203–205; and International Association for Public Participation, 209–210; and Nā Kumu o Kamehameha, 205–209; and National Round Table on Economy and Environment (Canada), 201–203; and Native Title process agreement, 194–196
Brett, J. M., 11
Buffalo, New York, 197, 199
Buffalo Coalition for Common Ground, 198–199, 200
Building Consensus for a Sustainable Future: Putting Principles into Practice (Cormick and others), 201
Bureau of Land Management, 203
Bush, R.A.B., 11–12

C

California, 199
Canada, 201–203, 205
Carlson, C., 204
Catron County, New Mexico, 210–213

251

Catron County Citizens Group (CCCG), 211–213; ground rules for, 211
CCCG. *See* Catron County Citizens Group
Charters, and protocols, 221–222
Chelsea, Massachusetts, 213–215
Chelsea Charter Consensus Process, 213–215
Christians, 89
Civil, definition of, 12
Civility, guidelines for, 223–224
Cleveland, Ohio, 198
Collaboration, growing trend towards, 10–11
Commitment level: as group characteristic, 145–150; to shared expectations, 146
Commitments, community, 7. *See also* Behavior: shared expectations of
Common good, and common ground, 12
Common ground, higher ground *versus*, 7
"Common Ground/Faithful Ground" (Aspen Institute), 200
Common Ground Network for Life and Choice: approach to ground rules of, 199; and moving beyond boundaries, 196–200; statement of purpose of, 198; three main strategies of, 197–198
"Common Ground on Clinic Activism" (Common Ground Network for Life and Choice), 200
Common Ground on Teen Pregnancy (Common Ground Network for Life and Choice), 199
Common views, 134. *See also* Diversity, group
Communities at Work, 143
Community, as value, 247
Community commitments, 7. *See also* Behavior: shared expectations of
Conduct, agreement on, 223–224
Conflict: personal and structural reasons for avoiding, 18–19; reasons for not preparing for, 18–19
Conflict-handling modes, 26
Consensus: nested circles of, 138; seeking, on policy and regulatory matters, 221–222
Cook, J., 206
Core Principles Statement Between the Public Health Community and the Tobacco Producers Community, 14
Cormick, G., 201, 202

County Movement (Catron County, New Mexico), 210–213
Covenant: and delaying discussion of vulnerable topics, 230–231; and higher self-consciousness for performance and responsibility, 233–235; and living out promises, 228–229; shared expectations as, 81–82; and shared expectations of behavior, 7; and staying the course through challenging moments, 231–233; and value of covenant discussion, 229–230. *See also* Behavior: shared expectations of
Creativity, 247
Crowd control, 111–114
Culture, shared, 134. *See also* Diversity, group

D

Davenport, Iowa, 198
Democracy, 247
Desired outcomes: envisioning, 90–93; for pre-negotiation preparation, 243
Development, process of, 153
Difficulty, degree of, 133
Directives, *versus* elicitives, 42
Disputes, three ways of dealing with, 11
Diversity, group, 133, 134–135
Duck Soup (Marx Brothers), 180
Dukes, E. F., 11–12, 196, 204, 212
Duration, group: as characteristic determining appropriate investment, 133; and process prework, 135; and spiraled conversation, 136

E

Education, in group covenant, 87–90
Efficiency, 247
Elgin, S. H., 21
Elicitives, directives *versus*, 42
Enactment, level of, 153
Engagement, unspoken rules of: clashes between, 24–27; in community, 32–37; consequences of, 27–37; definition of, 17; in families, 28–30; in workplace, 30–32
Enlibra: eight principle of, 204–205; and environmental management, 203–205; and moving beyond boundaries, 193
Environmental Protection Act (Australia), 196
Environmental sustainability, 201

Error correction, 115–117. *See also* Feedback
Evaluation: in group covenant, 99–102; of group performance, 114–127; ongoing, of trust, 141
Expectations, shared. *See* Behavior, shared expectations of

F

Facilitator's Guide to Participatory Decision Making (Kaner and others), 105
Feedback: criteria for, 121; for error correction, 115–117; and feedback loops, 115; and feedback to promote intimacy, 117–118; and positive feedback, 107–108; to refine group's shared expectations, 127; skills for delivering, 119–126
Fish and Wildlife Service, 203
Fisher, R., 47
Fist to five technique, 138–139
Flexibility, 247
Folger, J., 11–12
Food & Drug Administration (FDA), 14
Forest Service, 203
Future, probable *versus* preferred, 140

G

General Commission of Christian Unity and Interreligious Concerns, 1998, 89, 224
General Conference of the Mennonite Church and Mennonite Church General Board, 91
Getting Disputes Resolved (Ury, Brett, and Goldberg), 11
Getting to Yes (Fisher and Ury), 47
Goldberg, S. B., 11
Grand Canyon Visibility Transport Commission, 205
Groan Zone, 105
Ground rules, common: absence of underlying principles of goals in, 56–57; application of, 49–55; comparison of, to RHG ground rules, 167; as culture bound, 55–56; directives *versus* elicitives in, 42; formal, limited, and prohibitive nature of, 42–43; inconsistency in, 49–50; lack of focus on outcomes in, 56; major problems with, 40–49; meaning of, 40; no recognition of tensions between, 51–53; opportunities for illustration, understanding, or revision of, 46–47; overlooking assets and opportunities in, 56; presented as preliminary to real work of team functioning, 45–46; problems with introduction of, 41–49; process for revision of, 53–55; scenarios for, 158–160, 169–172, 177–180; as shared expectations of behavior, 7; violations of, 50–51
Ground rules, proposed: for covenant meeting, 240–241; for reaching for higher ground, 237
Group covenant, creating: and accountability, 96–99; education and inspiration element of, 87–90; envisioning desired outcomes for, 90–93; establishment of need for, 83–86; evaluation and revision in, 99–102; and promotion of full participation, 93–95; six elements for, 82–102
Group management: and crowd control, 111–114; and evaluation of group performance, 114–127; first law of professionalism in, 106; and integration of new members into group, 128–129; and intervention in unproductive behavior, 108–110; and maintaining best atmosphere, 103–104; and preparing plan for trouble, 105–106; and recognizing good, 107–108; three different situations that need leader's direction in, 106–126
Group performance: evaluation of, 114–127; feedback for correction of, 115–117; and feedback to promote intimacy, 117–118; graphing of, 124; and learning as a group, 119; and refinement of group's shared experience, 127; and skills for delivering feedback, 114–127, 119–126
Group work, 10–11. *See also* Collaboration
Groups: and group values, 247–248; and growing trend of collaboration, 10–11; integrating new members into, 128–129; learning in, 119; trouble with, 8–10
Guidelines, principled: for living out group values, 247–248; for reaching for higher ground, 226–227; for reaching for higher ground covenant, 239–240
Guidelines for Civility (United Methodist Church), 89, 223

H

Hawaiian Islands, 206
Heterogeneous groups, tools for, 135
Higher ground, reaching for (RHG): as continuing challenge, 77–79; dimensions of, 59–79; ground rules for, 227–228; and new and enlarged perspective, 67–70; and new ground, 7–8, 63–67; overview of, 6–16; and principled ground, 7–8, 60–62; as refuge, 70–73; scenarios for, 155–190; as shared ground, 74–77
Holy Scripture, 89
Homogeneous groups, tools for, 134
Honesty, 247
Hubbard, E., 13

I

IAP2. *See* International Association for Public Participation
Innes, J. E., 21, 67
Inspiration, educational, 87–90
Interest-based bargaining, 11, 243–244
Internal Revenue Service, 207
International Association for Public Participation, 209–210
Intervention, 106–126; in unproductive behavior, 108–110
Intimacy, 117–118. *See also* Feedback
Isaacson-Jones, B. J., 199
Issues, significance of: as characteristic determining appropriate investment, 133; and personal impact, 139–140; and probable *versus* preferred future, 140

J

Jacksteit, M., 196–199

K

Kamehameha Schools Bishop Estate (Hawaii), 193, 205–209
Kamehamena I, King of Hawaii, 205
Kaner, S., 105, 121, 143
Kaufmann, A., 196–199
Kilmann, R. H., 25, 26
Kitzhaber, J., 203
Kritek, P., 25

L

Labor-management cooperation councils, partnering in, 221
Learning, group, 119
Leavitt, M., 203
Lemagie, S., 197
Life and Choice Network, 198, 199

M

Marx Brothers, 158, 180
Mediation: clauses in realty agreements, 222–223; training in, 105
Mennonite Church, 91
Metaphor metamorphosis, individual, 144–145, 226
Michaelson, L., 209, 210
Minjerribah (Australia), 195
Montalvo, R., 95
Moore, C. M., 95
Moreton Bay, Australia, 195

N

Nā Kumu o Kamehameha, 205–209; guiding principles of, 207–208
National Association for Community Mediation, 197
National Campaign to Prevent Teen Pregnancy, 199
National Council of Churches (United States), 200
National Environmental Justice Advisory Committee, 209
National Round Table on the Environment and the Economy (Canada), 201–203; ten principles agreed to by, 202
National Task Force on Consensus and Sustainability (Canada), 201
Native Title Act (1993), 194–196
Native Title process agreement, 194–196
Native Title Tribunal (Australia), 195
Necessity, 12
Neumann, R., 196
Neuse River, 221–222
New ground, 7–8
New Mexico Center for Dispute Resolution, 211
Newsweek magazine, 197
Nomination cards, of principles and behaviors, 141–142
Normal, relative definition of, 12
North Carolina, 221

O

Operation Rescue, 197, 200
Oregon, 203, 205

INDEX 255

P

Participation: full, promotion of, 93–95; public, 209–210
Partnering, in labor-management relations, 221
Pensacola, Florida, 198
Performance, higher self-consciousness for, 233–235
Performance contracting, 137
Perspective, new and enlarged, 67–70
Positive thinking, 247
Power, distribution of, 133, 142–143; and Get in Line game, 143
Praise, 107–108
Prawatt, R., 108
Pre-negotiation preparation, 224, 243–245
Principled ground, 7–8, 60–62
Prior, K. S., 198–199, 200
Problem, complexity of. *See* Task complexity
Professionalism, first law of, 106. *See also* Group management
Promises, and evaluation of results, 228–229
Protocols, 221–222
Public democracy, 8
Purpose, statement of, 239
Puzder, A. F., 199

Q

QLC. *See* Quandamooka Lands Council Aboriginal Corporation (Australia)
Quandamooka Lands Council Aboriginal Corporation (Australia), 193, 195
Quandamooka people, 195, 196

R

Raspberry, W., 13
Realty agreements, mediation clauses in, 222–223
Redland Shire Council (Australia), 193, 195, 196
Refinement, assessment of, 153–154
Refinement process, "three Cs," 138, 142
Refuge, higher ground as, 70–73
Relatedness, quest for, 11–12
Renewal, assessment of, 153–154
Responsibility, and higher self-consciousness, 233–235
Revision, 99–102
RHG. *See* Higher ground, reaching for
Roberts, C., 117
Runkel, P., 120, 121

S

Schmuck, R., 120, 121
Schwarz, R. M., 56
Search for Common Ground (SFCG), 197
Self-consciousness, 233–235
Self-critique, 114, 117
SFCG. *See* Search for Common Ground
Sigurdson, S. G., 202–203
Size, group: as characteristic determining appropriate investment, 133; and fist to five technique, 138–139; and nested circles of consensus, 138
Skinner, D. E., 91
Smith, M., 211, 212
Spiraled conversation, 136
Springfield, Massachusetts, 91
St. Louis, Missouri, 197
Stakeholder Advisory Committee for the Neuse River Buffer Rule, 221–222
Stakeholders, and group work, 11
Statement of Visions and Goals (Nā Kumu o Kamehameha, 1998), 207
Stephens, J. B., 199, 200
Stradbroke Island (Australia), 195
Strickland, C., 53
Sustainability, environmental, 201
Synergy, 247

T

Task complexity: articulation of work behaviors for, 137; and creation of explicit agendas, 136–137; and determination of appropriate investment, 133; and performance contracting, 137; and task analysis, 137
Thomas, K. W., 25, 26
Thomas-Kilmann Conflict Mode Instrument, 26
Tobacco farmers, and public health advocates, 13–16
Tolstoy, L., 27, 28
Trouble, preparation plan for, 105–106. *See also* Group management
Trust: and anonymous postmeeting feedback, 142; levels of, 133, 140–142; and ongoing evaluation, 141; and principle/behavior nomination cards in large groups, 141; and principle/behavior nomination cards in small groups, 142

U

UMC. *See* United Methodist Church
Unitarian-Universalist Church, 91
United Methodist Church (UMC), 61, 62, 69, 70, 89, 223–224
United States Environmental Protection Agency (EPA), 209
Unproductive behavior, 108–110
Ury, W. L., 11, 12, 47
Utah, 203

V

Vision, in covenants, 81
Vulnerability, 117

W

Washington National Cathedral, 200
Western Governor's Association, 205
Wik case (Australia), 194–196
Work style, questionnaire for, 150

About the Authors

E. Franklin Dukes, Ph.D., is Director of the Institute for Environmental Negotiation at the University of Virginia. He is the author of *Resolving Public Conflict*.

Marina A. Piscolish, Ph.D., is President of MAPping Change, LLC, a Hawaii-based practice serving the health, education and environmental sectors with holistic, culturally responsive and socially responsible mediation, facilitation and training services.

John B. Stephens, Ph.D., is associate professor and public dispute resolution program coordinator at the School of Government, University of North Carolina at Chapel Hill.

For more information or to contact the authors, you may email them collectively at info@reachingforhigherground.com or link to their individual email addresses through the Reaching for Higher Ground website, www.reachingforhigherground.com.

Made in the USA
Lexington, KY
24 February 2010